Faith and Reckoning after Trump

FAITH AND RECKONING AFTER TRUMP

Miguel A. De La Torre, editor

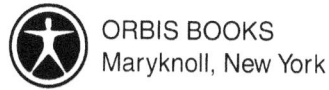

ORBIS BOOKS
Maryknoll, New York

Founded in 1970, Orbis Books endeavors to publish works that enlighten the mind, nourish the spirit, and challenge the conscience. The publishing arm of the Maryknoll Fathers and Brothers, Orbis seeks to explore the global dimensions of the Christian faith and mission, to invite dialogue with diverse cultures and religious traditions, and to serve the cause of reconciliation and peace. The books published reflect the views of their authors and do not represent the official position of the Maryknoll Society. To learn more about Maryknoll and Orbis Books, please visit our website at www.maryknollsociety.org.

Copyright © 2021 by Miguel A. De La Torre

Published by Orbis Books, Box 302, Maryknoll, NY 10545–0302.

All rights reserved.

The Scripture quotations contained herein are from the New Revised Standard Version: Catholic Edition, Copyright © 1989 and 1993, by the Division of Christian Education of the National Council of the Churches of Christ in the United States of America. Used by permission. All rights reserved.

No part of this publication may be reproduced or transmitted in any form or by any means, electronic or mechanical, including photocopying, recording, or any information storage or retrieval system, without prior permission in writing from the publisher.

Queries regarding rights and permissions should be addressed to: Orbis Books, P.O. Box 302, Maryknoll, NY 10545–0302.

Manufactured in the United States of America

Library of Congress Cataloging-in-Publication Data

Names: De La Torre, Miguel A., editor.
Title: Faith and reckoning after Trump / edited by Miguel De La Torre.
Description: Maryknoll, NY : Orbis Books, [2021] | Includes bibliographical references and index. | Summary: "Essays by religious scholars and activists assess the lessons of the Trump era, both for the nation and the religious community" — Provided by publisher.
Identifiers: LCCN 2021011918 (print) | LCCN 2021011919 (ebook) | ISBN 9781626984424 (print) | ISBN 9781608339051 (ebook)
Subjects: LCSH: Christianity and politics—United States—History—21st century. | Trump, Donald, 1946—Public opinion.
Classification: LCC BR516 .F279 2021 (print) | LCC BR516 (ebook) | DDC 261/.10973—dc23
LC record available at https://lccn.loc.gov/2021011918
LC ebook record available at https://lccn.loc.gov/2021011919

*We dedicate this book
to those among our friends and family who,
even after the storming of the Capitol,
continue to support Trump,
hoping beyond all hope
we can heal the division of this nation.*

Contents

Preface	xi
Introduction: The Biden Reprieve *Miguel A. De La Torre*	xvii
1. The GOP's Monkey's Paw: Storming the Capitol *Miguel A. De La Torre*	1
2. The Donald Went Down to Georgia: From God's Own Party to the Party of Trump *Juan M. Floyd-Thomas*	13
3. Dispatches from the Deep State: The Political Theology of QAnon *Rubén Rosario Rodríguez*	25
4. Fractured Truth in Post-Trump America *David P. Gushee*	36
5. Purple Rein, Purple Reign: Fashioning Womanist Witness, Work, and Worth of Black Women in the Making of Democracy *Stacey Floyd-Thomas*	47
6. Democracy or Whiteness? Trumpism, White Christianity, and the Queer Justice Agenda *Marvin M. Ellison*	61

7.	Environmental Violence and the Postmodern Condition *Aaron D. Conley*	75
8.	Environmental Racism in the "True" America: A Reflection on Race, the Earth, and Moral Action after Trump *Trad Nogueira-Godsey and Elaine Nogueira-Godsey*	85
9.	"Karen" and Liberation Theology *Susan Thistlethwaite*	98
10.	Racism Is a Religious Issue *Jim Wallis*	108
11.	¡WTF Miami!—Latinxs for Trump *Miguel A. De La Torre*	118
12.	Virus (of) Fear? Diagnosing the Trumpian Symptom within a Virulent History *Tat-siong Benny Liew*	130
13.	Black Lives *Still* Matter *Joshua Bartholomew*	146
14.	"I Can't Breathe:" Neocolonial Geotrauma and Violence in the Age of Trump *April M. Woodson*	155
15.	"Chickens Coming Home to Roost": American Muslims in the Aftermath *Amir Hussain*	165
16.	Rebuilding Jewish Orthodoxy after Trump through Interfaith Humanism *Joshua Shanes*	174

17. Much Ado about Nothing   184
    Tink Tinker

18. Option for Life: Remembering the Body of Christ,
    Re-membering Our Catholic Body   193
    Miguel H. Díaz

19. Reinstating Catholic Faith in the Public Square
    after Trump   204
    Simone Campbell

20. Seeking Healing in an Age of Partisan Division:
    Reckoning with Theological Education and
    Resounding the Evangel for the 2020s   214
    Aizaiah G. Yong and Amos Yong

21. Unite and Conquer: Cutting Taxes, Religion, and
    Relationships of Race and Class   228
    Joerg Rieger

22. Enough of Us Came Together to Carry
    All of Us Forward   238
    John Fife

23. Which God You Talkin'bout? Pastoring in a
    Divided Family, Church, Nation; Taking a Stand   247
    Jacqui Lewis

Conclusion: Is America Possible?   256
Miguel A. De La Torre

Contributors   262

Index   269

Preface

For many progressive religious leaders and scholars, the 2016 election of Donald Trump as the forty-fifth president of the United States came—to say the least—as a shock. He was the first person in US history who was elected president without any previous governmental or military experience. The country chose a mediocre businessman made rich through inheritance, known for bankruptcies, perpetuating scams, and starring on reality television. At that time the need was felt to speak up, to provide not just a pastoral word to many who were fearful of what that moment would unleash, but just as important, to sound the clarion for praxis, for action. Making room in an already busy and hectic schedule, several of us came together to write *Faith and Resistance in the Age of Trump*. This was probably the first book published from the perspective of faith communities providing a critical assessment of the coming Trump administration and offering guidance on how to remain authentic to our faith while resisting political policies detrimental to the most vulnerable within our society. Some of our trepidation proved to be well founded, as his four years in office unveiled an individual who lacked a moral compass. Governmental policies he championed proved to be diametrically opposed to the message of the Sermon on the Mount.

We took seriously the charge to stand in solidarity with the "least among us." While many within the community of white Christians aligned themselves with a figure whose actions repudiated the basic message of the gospel, others within diverse faith communities became the conscience of the nation. For the past four years, many of us raised our voices as the Trump administration, which claimed a mandate to "drain the swamp," instead saw six former campaign and White House aides criminally convicted.[1] A seventh, Steve Bannon, was indicted for defrauding Trump supporters, who sent him $25 million to build a wall on the southern border.[2] Trump profited off the presidency to the tune of at least $12 million as those entities seeking to curry favor with the government made reservations at his properties.[3] Additionally, federal agencies were forced to spend at least $2.5 million at his properties.[4] Meanwhile, having paid no income taxes for years, he bragged to his uber-wealthy clientele, "You all just got a lot richer," hours after signing the 2017 tax bill.[5]

A majority of US citizens voted against Trump in 2016, and when an even larger majority voted against him again in 2020, he refused to honor the will of the people. How easy, then, with the inauguration of Joseph Biden as the forty-sixth president, for religious leaders and scholars to simply shout "Hallelujah" and return to a more tranquil life, marked by less drama, chaos, and lawlessness. But if truth be known, we find ourselves still anxious for the future. We find ourselves on the other side of the Trump administration, residing in a nation—due to corruption—where trust in our democratic bonds has been frayed to the point of breaking. A nation, due to incompetence, is sicker, as the pandemic rages uncontrollably, and poorer, as we endure the worst economic crisis since the Great Depression. A nation, due to self-interest, is more divided by racist

---

1. Paul Manafort, Roger Stone, Michael Flynn, George Papadopoulos, Rick Gates, and Michael Cohen.

2. Kevin Johnson, "How Many Trump Advisers Have Been Criminally Charged?" *USA Today*, August 20, 2020.

3. Nicholas Confessore et al., "The Swamp That Trump Built," *New York Times*, October 10, 2020.

4. David A. Fahrenthold et al., "Ballrooms, Candles and Luxury Cottage: During Trump's Term, Millions of Government and GOP Dollars Have Flowed to His Properties," *Washington Post*, October 27, 2020.

5. Russ Buettner, Susanne Craig, and Mike McIntire, "The President's Taxes," *New York Times*, September 27, 2020; Kathryn Watson, "'You All Just Got a Lot Richer,' Trump Tells Friends, Referencing Tax Overhaul," *CBS News*, December 24, 2017.

dog whistles. If the transition period between the November election and the January inauguration was any indication of the future that awaits us, then this nation can expect a division not witnessed since the years prior to the Civil War.

During those long days in early November, glued to news programs before the election was called, the contributors to this book were asked to bring their analytical skills to this moment in time, the seventy-eight days between the election and the inauguration. While it was expected Trump would challenge the election results, we could never, in our wildest nightmares, have imagined what was in store. An attempt was made to disenfranchise voters from communities of color on the basis of false allegations of fraud. We witnessed (1) over sixty legal challenges to the election, all but one thrown out as frivolous, even by Trump-appointed justices; (2) a refusal by the Supreme Court, even though packed by Trump appointees, to hear Trump's case, even while the majority of Republican House members joined an *amicus curiae* brief; (3) pressure on Michigan state legislative Republican leaders not to certify the electoral votes of that state; (4) a request by the president of the United States to Georgia's secretary of state, a Republican official, to falsify the vote count; (5) an attempt by Republicans in Congress to challenge the certification of the Electoral College; (6) a call from the president of the United States to his followers to flock to the nation's capital, where he incited them to a riot, the storming of the Capitol where five lives were lost. And even after the insurrection was put down, six senators and 121 representatives opposed certifying the electoral votes from Arizona, while seven senators and 138 representatives—all Republicans—opposed Pennsylvania's certification.

By the time Biden was sworn in as president, a usually joyful event celebrating the peaceful transfer of power, Washington, DC, was fully militarized—an armed camp, facing a segment of the country's population, disproportionately represented by white nationalist Christians, who threatened the peaceful and democratic process. And not just at our nation's capital. Every state capital was also placed on high alert because of creditable threats picked up on chatter among domestic terrorist groups. The seventy-eight days between election and inauguration day were, by far, the longest days in US history. What a difference from previous transfers of power. When John Adam lost his reelection to his political archenemy, Thomas Jefferson, he handed off the keys to the government and returned to Quincy, Massachusetts, thus establishing the precedent of peaceful transitions. The few who lost reelections may have been disappointed, angry, or resentful; but none set out to employ *caudillo* tactics to deny the will of the voters.

For the first time, we have had a president who has refused to concede defeat, poisoning the well with conspiracy theories. Ironically, when Alexander Lukashenko—the autocrat of Belarus—declared victory in August 2020 after losing the election by employing the same tactics attempted by Trump (undermining the integrity of the election process, attacking the press, demonizing political opponents), the United States, along with other Western democracies, denounced the brazen defiance of the voters' will and imposed sanctions.[6] Four years of witnessing turbulent conduct that flirted with fascist sensibilities and authoritarian sentiments had left many of us dealing with a collective form of post-traumatic stress disorder. Or maybe, what was truly unnerving was the recognition that Trumpism was not decidedly repudiated by the 2020 electorate. We were obviously more divided on election night 2020 than we were in 2016. Though he received a winning majority, Biden did not inherit the political mandate to vanquish Trumpism, an ethos that will long survive the man.

Trump lost the election but won in capturing the soul of about half of the population. We who are religious leaders and scholars recognize the moral obligation to speak a word as the storms of racism, classism, homophobia, and sexism refuse to dissipate. With dire apprehension we wonder if some future Trump 2.0–type politician, one more politically savvy, could arise in 2024 or 2028, succeeding where Trump, due to his ineptness and incompetence, fell short. This responsibility to speak truth in solidarity with the powerless has found its expression in the book you hold in your hands. *Faith and Reckoning after Trump* continues that conversa-

---

6. Andrew Higgins, "Trump Borrows Election Tactics from Autocrats," *New York Times*, November 12, 2020.

tion begun four years ago. Recognizing that unless we continue to faithfully resist, the Biden years could easily be reduced to a temporary reprieve, as opposed to a sea change.

All contributors of this book were contacted within a week of Biden's election and asked to speak to this moment. They were asked not so much to give a commentary on what was occurring in real time but rather to use this moment as a springboard to explore (1) the damage of the past four years to our democracy; (2) what this moment reveals about the state of Christianity; (3) the role faith might play in reconciling a divided nation; and (4) possible signs that might point toward hope (or hopelessness). While our eyes were upon what was occurring in real time, our focus was on the future. How will this moment now shape the political theology of tomorrow? How might the lessons of the past several years be transformed into liberative praxis for a post-Trump United States?

Almost all of those I approached about this project responded positively. The book was completed less than two weeks after Biden's inauguration, some twelve weeks after his election. As you read this book months, if not years, into the Biden administration, you can better judge if the issues we raised and the concerns we voiced were warranted.

A special thanks goes out to all the contributors for their faithfulness to do their ministerial and/or academic work firmly planted in the reality faced by the disenfranchised, the dispossessed, and the disinherited. I am honored by how they rushed to the task at hand, despite their busy schedules. I am also grateful to Robert Ellsberg, the publisher at Orbis Books, who did not hesitate to give a green light to this project when I first proposed it, even *before* the election was called for Biden. But more importantly, I am thankful to the millions of faith leaders and lay people who refused to follow the MAGA bandwagon on the road to destruction but chose instead to tread the narrow, stony road that leads to life. So many of them demonstrated faith and resistance during the age of Trump. Trump may now be gone, but Trumpism remains, stronger than ever, entrenched in our national ethos. The political and spiritual battle is not over. Now is the time for faith and reckoning. We cannot afford to blink.

INTRODUCTION

The Biden Reprieve

MIGUEL A. DE LA TORRE

On September 4, 476 CE, the Roman Empire fell when the Germanic King Odoacer deposed Emperor Romulus Augustulus. But if truth be told, the end of the empire occurred some three hundred years earlier when Commodus ascended the throne after the death of his father, Marcus Aurelius, thereby bringing to a close the *pax Romana*. Unfortunately for them, many Romans at that time failed to read the signs of the times, which pointed to an eventual collapse. They instead went about their daily chores incorrectly reassured that the sun would not set upon their world.

Multiple factors played a role in the empire's ultimate collapse. These include (1) an unequal distribution of wealth, as illustrated by the heavy tax burden borne by the working population; (2) a change in climate, prompting the Late Antique Little Ice Age (global cooling of about 3.6° F) triggering a migration crisis from the Eurasian steppe, which the empire had failed to properly and justly administer; (3) the Antonine Plague (160–180 CE) followed by the Plague of Cyprian (249–262 CE), which decimated the population, weakening its institutions; (4) the rise of usurpers during chaotic times seeking to seize the throne; (5) a rise in abuse of power manifested as politically sanctioned cruelty and unchecked corruption; and, finally, (6) internal divisions leading to civil wars. It has been surmised that one other important factor contributed to the empire's eventual downfall. According to some historians, like Edward Gibbon, Christianity played a part in hastening the empire's demise.[1]

Will future historians, centuries from now, look to 2016 as the beginning of the end of the United States empire? This country and its political structures may very well endure for many more decades, if not longer. Still, we must wonder if what is transpiring before our very eyes will find its complete manifestation at some future date with the demise of what has come to be known as the most powerful and wealthiest empire the world has ever known. Like the previous Mediterranean empire, the United States also faces (1) an unequal distribution of wealth (plutocrats like Trump paying $750 in taxes); (2) a refusal to consider the implications of climate change; (3) a broken immigration system; (4) a colossal failure to effectively confront the Covid-19 plague, which has wreaked economic pain throughout the nation; (5) a rise in abuse of power (children in cages); (6) an attempt by President Trump, with support of some of the most powerful congressional leaders, to usurp his office by ignoring and challenging the 2020 election, even to the point of inciting mobs to storm the Capitol; and (7) the demonization of political opponents by domestic white supremacist terrorist groups salivating for a civil war. And most important for those of us contributing to this book, the role Christianity is playing to hasten the fall of this current empire.

After four years of ineptitude (almost 400,000 deaths from Covid at the end of Trump's term), four years of blatant racism ("very fine people on both sides"), four years of weakening democratic principles (storming the Capitol), four years of tacit support of white supremacist terrorist groups ("stand back and stand by"), and four years of lies, bullying, and self-enrichment, many progressives who hoped the national nightmare would be fully and unconditionally repudiated by means of an electoral landslide were sadly disappointed. Trump received eight million more votes than in 2016! CNN commentator Van Jones best captured this sentiment on election night when it became obvious the race was going

---

1. Edward Gibbon, *The Decline and Fall of the Roman Empire*, vol. 2 (London: Jones and Company, 1828), 482.

to be tighter than what pundits had predicted. "There's the moral victory and there's the political victory, and they're not the same thing," Van Jones told his television audience. "I think for people who saw babies being snatched away from their mothers at the border, for people who are sending their kids into schools where the N-word is now being used against them, for people who have seen this wave of intolerance, they wanted a moral victory tonight. We wanted to see a repudiation of this direction for the country, and the fact that it's this close, it hurts. It just hurts."[2]

Failure to repudiate has emboldened and invigorated a scorched-earth politics where power is maintained through gaslighting and the demonization of the other—and let democracy be damned. Politicians who did not face a down-ballot bloodbath for their complicity with four years of acrimonious presidential antics faced no consequences for their kowtowing. Fear of tweets from Trump and the threat of a primary challenge from their right flank in some future election was enough to keep them in line. Already, with the new year in 2021, Trump began calling for primary challengers in 2022 against "disloyal" Republican politicians like Georgia Governor Brian Kemp, Ohio Governor Mike DeWine, Arizona Governor Doug Ducey, or South Dakota Senator John Thune. And thanks to the cash-flush PAC he established by soliciting donations to "Stop the Steal," he has the muscle to make his threats more than simple bluster.

Yes, Joseph Biden did win the election with almost 81.3 million votes, the most ever cast for a presidential candidate in the history of the United States. And while Trump lost the popular count by some seven million votes, still, he garnered millions more votes than in 2016. Even after four years of Trumpishness, more people than in 2016, when Trump was still a relatively unknown quantity, made the conscious decision to vote for more of the same. There was no repudiation of the past four years; instead, election results indicated a more expanded and tighter embrace of Trump and his policies.

What does it mean that almost half of the population made a

---

2. Jessica Chasmar, "Van Jones Says 'A Lot of Democrats' Are Hurting Right Now," *Washington Times*, November 4, 2020.

preferential option for Trumpism? Yes, many may profess to be sick of his tweets, or put off by his boorishness. Still, at the end of the day, a major portion of the US population—for whatever reason—found his unapologetic racism, sexism, heterosexism, and classism acceptable enough. There is nothing he said or did that deterred them from supporting and voting for a morally corrupt and morally bankrupt individual. Trump truly proved he can stand in the middle of Fifth Avenue and shoot somebody without losing voters! This is not political gasconading, but reality, as we count the increased death of Black people at the hands of law enforcement, brown people on our nation's southern borderlands, and, of course, those whose Covid deaths can directly be traced to the failures of the government to provide an adequate response to the pandemic.

The Trump presidency will best be known for exposing extraordinary national fissures, culminating in the January 6 storming of the Capitol. Although Trump may be responsible for stoking the flames of division, capitalizing on centuries of racial hatred, we do well to remember he is not the cause of this nation's angst, but merely the symptom. When, during the campaign, Biden reflected on the impact of Trump's character upon the national ethos, he would often state: "It's not who we are, not what America is."[3] But contrary to Biden's cogent assertions, this is exactly who we are and what America is. Those who stormed the Capitol are not a fringe element of America—they *are* America. *We the people* are the problem. Trump is simply mirroring and reflecting who the United States truly is. Not only did he refuse to wear the mask, which could have spared him the coronavirus; he also refused to wear the mask of political correctness, which could have spared him the accusations of white supremacist tendencies, a mask worn by so many previous presidents. Trump signifies the unconscious desire of many to embrace a failed state. Many Americans, especially white Americans, are willing to vote against their best interest because they have bought into a racial zero-sum rule that believes that whatever advances and gains are made by communities of

---

3. Matt Flegenheimer, "Biden Says Trump Is 'Not Who We Are.' Do Voters Agree?" *New York Times*, November 3, 2020.

color must come at their own expense. What propelled Trump to the highest echelons of political power and what will prevent Biden from making major advances in expanding the concept of a more perfect union is what has plagued the development of this nation since its inception: white supremacy.

Comparing our country to other leading industrial nations, according to measures of human flourishing, the United States ranks among the worst. The wealthiest nation known to human history is nonetheless a failed state when it comes to the welfare of its citizens. A World Bank study ranked the United States twenty-seventh when it came to education and health care.[4] Specifically in education, the United States ranked twenty-eighth out of seventy-one countries in math scores and twenty-fourth in science.[5] The CIA reported that the Gini coefficient, which measures income inequality while ignoring other well-being qualifiers, positioned the United States as fortieth among 150 countries.[6] Not surprisingly, we are the only country in the Western hemisphere without a national paid parental leave benefit. We are also the only industrial country without universal health care, spending more on substandard care ($9,892 when the world's median is $4,033) than any other country.[7] Compared to other nations, whether developed or developing, the United States continues to place at or near the bottom when measuring mortality and life expectancy.[8] We work more hours for less pay and less leisure time.

---

4. Stephen S. Lim et al., "Measuring Human Capital: A Systematic Analysis of 195 Countries and Territories, 1990–2016," *The Lancet* 392, no. 10154 (October 6, 2018): 1217–34.

5. Drew Desilver, "US Students' Academic Achievement Still Lags That of Their Peers in Many Other Countries," Pew Research Center, February 15, 2017.

6. Mark Abadi, "Income Inequality Is Growing across the US—Here's How Bad It Is in Every State," *Business Insider*, March 15, 2018.

7. Gerard F. Anderson, Peter Hussey, and Varduhi Petrosyan, "It's Still the Price, Stupid: Why the US Spends So Much on Health Care, and a Tribute to Uwe Reinhardt," *Health Affairs* 38, no. 1 (January 2019): 87–95.

8. Jorge L. Ortiz, "'A Distinctly American Phenomenon': Our Workforce Is Dying Faster Than Any Other Wealthy Country, Study Shows," *USA Today*, November 26, 2019.

As the voting came to a close, the nation was entering a dark Covid winter. December proved to be the deadliest month for coronavirus deaths, as one American died of the infection every thirty-three seconds. As this book was nearing completion, an additional 100,000 had died since inauguration day, bringing the total count to half a million. The reality of a third-world health care system became apparent as citizens negotiated a deficiency of virus tests, protective masks, and ventilators, coupled with the utter failure of the initial vaccine rollout. Although twenty million were supposed to be vaccinated by New Year's Day, the actual number was only 2.1 million.[9] Complicating an effective response is the fact that, among industrial countries, we are among the few that lacks any federal law requiring paid sick days, thereby forcing the infected who live from paycheck to paycheck to show up for work and thus contribute to the spread of the virus. Because potential lost income trumps a required self-imposed quarantine, flattening the pandemic curve became an arduous task. The lack of paid sick leave, along with inadequate or no health insurance, helps explain why on the eve of the election, the United States, with just 4.25 percent of the world population, accounted for 19.5 percent of global Covid infections and 19.1 percent of Covid deaths, representing just shy of a fifth of the planet's total fatalities.[10]

The United States' dismal standing in the world did not start with Trump. And while it is true that he exacerbated the situation, the fact remains that the current failure of the state to safeguard the welfare of its citizens reflects a lack of political will constant during both liberal and conservative administrations, Democrats and Republicans alike. The question before us is whether Biden, who is seventy-seven years old and has been a moderate during his entire political life, is the best candidate to bring forth the chal-

---

9. Ellie Kaufman, Annie Grayer, Sara Murray, and Andrea Kane, "US Officials Promised 20 Million Vaccinated against Coronavirus by the End of the Year. It's Going Slower Than That," *CNN*, December 28, 2020.

10. "Coronavirus in the U.S.: Latest Map and Case Count," *New York Times*, November 3, 2020.

lenge of de-Trumpification. To his credit, Biden recognizes his limitations, seeing himself "as a bridge [to] . . . an entire generation of leaders . . . they are the future of this country"[11] (even though his cabinet tended to feature older political hands). While his humility is refreshing after four years of bluster, still, with a divided government and divided electorate, both undergirded by white supremacist tendencies, we are left wondering if the next four years will offer a temporary reprieve rather than a transformative moment.

If election reform is not enacted to allow the selection of presidents by means of the popular vote rather than the slavocracy-based Electoral College system, which privileges whites; if taxpayers of color in Washington, DC, and Puerto Rico are not given senatorial voice; if voter suppression tactics (i.e., voter purges, felony disenfranchisement, gerrymandering, and voter ID requirements) are not repealed; if tax laws are not passed which equitably spread the nation's debt obligations; if salaries are not legislatively raised to living wage standards; if universal health care and universal education are not implemented; if student-loan debts are not forgiven; if the institutionalized racism of law enforcement agencies are not dealt with; if a just and humane immigration policy is not enacted; and if the climate crisis humanity faces continues to be ignored—just to name a few of the most pressing issues—then all that was accomplished by the 2020 election will offer only a reprieve from Trumpism. Politicians historically lack the will to bring about such progressive policies. Most of the electorate, as demonstrated by many who split their votes between both parties, may rebuke Trump, but not the failed political state they inhabit.

On January 6, during the perfunctory receipt of the certified Electoral College votes, the Capitol was stormed by domestic terrorists, leading to the destruction of property, the death of rioters as well as members of law enforcement, and the bruising of our democracy. Such scenes of violence over election results, urged on

---

11. Eric Bradner and Sarah Mucha, "Biden Says He's a 'Bridge' to a New 'Generation of Leaders' While Campaigning with Harris, Booker, Whitmer," *CNN News*, March 9, 2020.

by the losing candidate who refused to concede defeat, are typical of failed states. How can this rupture be reconciled? Can it be? Or is the best we can hope for a domestic détente? If the moral obligation of people of faith (and those who profess no faith, which nevertheless has proven to be more faithful than the faith of white Christian nationalists) is to bring about healing through a transformative moment in solidarity with the least of these, then resistance to the status quo continues as *la lucha* for justice. Let this book that you hold in your hands launch a conversation truly seeking a more perfect union. Martin Luther King Jr. said that the "arc of the moral universe is long, but it bends toward justice." I argue the opposite. The moral universe could care less, and if left to itself will gravitate toward injustice. If we want the arc to instead bend toward justice, then it is up to us to do the bending.

CHAPTER 1

The GOP's Monkey's Paw: Storming the Capitol

MIGUEL A. DE LA TORRE

These are the gentry who are today wrapped up in the American flag, who shout their claim from the housetops that they are the only patriots, and who have their magnifying glasses in hand, scanning the country for evidence of disloyalty, eager to apply the brand of treason to the men who dare to even whisper their opposition to Junker rule in the United States. No wonder Sam Johnson declared that "patriotism is the last refuge of the scoundrel." He must have had this Wall Street gentry in mind, or at least their prototypes, for in every age it has been the tyrant, the oppressor and the exploiter who has wrapped himself in the cloak of patriotism, or religion, or both to deceive and overawe the people.
—Eugene V. Debs[1]

W. W. Jacobs's 1902 short story "The Monkey's Paw" revolves around the acquisition of a mummified paw by Mr. and Mrs. White. The paw has a spell placed upon it that grants its owner

---

1. Eugene V. Debs, "Canton (Ohio) Anti-War Speech of June 16, 1918," in *Reading the American Past, Volume 2: From 1865: Selected Historical Documents*, ed. Michael P. Johnson (5th ed.; Boston: St. Martin's, 2012), 127.

three wishes; though unbeknown to the owner, these wishes come at an enormous price. Skeptical of the paw's power and egged on by his son Herbert, Mr. White flippantly wishes for £200 to finish paying off their mortgage. That evening a coworker of Herbert visits the Whites with terrible news. Their beloved son died in a ghastly machine accident that mutilated his body. While the factory denied any responsibility, it nonetheless wanted to make a goodwill gesture of £200, the exact amount Mr. White had wished for earlier that day. A week after the funeral, racked with grief, a second wish is made, that their son returns to life. About an hour later, there is a terrifying knock at the door. The horrifying specter of the son's mutilated and decomposing body outside their abode grips Mr. White with fear. Realizing that whatever is at his doorstep is no longer his son, Mr. White makes his last wish before throwing the paw into the lit fireplace, at which time the knocking stops.

On January 6, 2021—another day that will live in infamy—the hellish consequences of the wish made upon the GOP monkey's paw did not knock but rather burst through the Capitol doors. Following the two terms of a Black president, Trump was the answer to the wish to win back the White House and cleanse the government of Obama's initiatives. Foundational in this wish was the desire to make the White House white again. But as it was for the appropriately named Mr. White, the deadly repercussions of the GOP wish were resurrected in the mutilated and decomposing body-politic of US nationalist Christianity. White Christianity's complicity with those leading the charge was evident in the Christian imagery visible alongside white supremacist symbols during the storming of the Capitol.[2] Among the mob there were numerous "Jesus Saves" and "In God We Trust" signs along with a banner reading "Jesus

---

2. Gina Ciliberto and Stephanie Russell-Kraft, "They Invaded the Capitol Saying 'Jesus Is My Savior. Trump Is My President,'" *Sojourners*, January 6, 2020; Jack Jenkins, "As Chaos Hits Capitol, Two Forms of Faith on Display," *Religion News Service*, January 6, 2021; Molly Olmstead, "'God Have Mercy on and Help Us All': How Prominent Evangelicals Reacted to the Storming of the U.S. Capitol," *Slate*, January 7, 2021.

2020."³ On the march to the Capitol, chants of "Christ is king" could be heard, while the white supremacist Proud Boys were being acclaimed by the mob as "God warriors."⁴ These are the same Proud Boys who wore shirts with "6MWE" insignia, meaning "6 million [Jews] wasn't enough."⁵ And when Enrique Tarrio was arrested prior to the riot (for burning a Black Lives Matter flag, stolen from a church), a Christian fundraising website, GiveSendGo.com, was used to raise $113,000 for his legal defense.⁶ The "Christian flags" were carried into the Capitol and even into the Senate chambers.⁷ This failed MAGA coup was made possible because of the spiritual cover provided by white nationalist Christianity, especially evangelicals, Trump's core supporters.

But the wish to whitewash Obama's contributions was not actually the first GOP wish upon the monkey's paw. I would argue that the original wish was made in 1940. Trumpism did not come into being *ex nihilo*. The roots of the storming of the Capitol can be traced back eighty years when the titans of capitalism associated with the Republican Party first rubbed that monkey's paw and wished to enlist white Christians in overturning Roosevelt's New Deal. The progressive political agenda known as the New Deal, enacted to combat the excesses of an unrestrained savage capitalism that plunged the nation into the Great Depression, was depressing the power, profits, and privileges of a small elite group of capitalists.

This first wish made on the monkey's paw, which eventually gave rise to Donald Trump, can be traced to a Christian minister named James W. Fifield, who gave the 1940 plenary address during the conference of the National Association of Manufacturers (NAM). The conference was attended by over five thousand heads

---

3. https://twitter.com/JordanUhl/status/1346924962938961924/photo/1.
4. https://twitter.com/i/status/1346864114208026626.
5. https://twitter.com/RoyaTheWriter/status/1347181249983614979/photo/1.
6. Amy Brittain and David Willman, "'A Place to Fund Hope': How Proud Boys and Other Fringe Groups Found Refuge on a Christian Fundraising Website," *Washington Post*, January 18, 2021.
7. https://twitter.com/i/status/1346910235399659532.

of corporations (e.g., General Electric, General Motors, Mutual Life, Sears, and Standard Oil). Dejected by their losses due to government regulations implemented during the New Deal era and the rise of powerful unions, their spirits were uplifted when Rev. Fifield preached salvation from the sins of Roosevelt's policies. Free enterprise and deregulation became the Christian response to liberalism. He suggested clergy could play a crucial role for the hearts and minds of the general public in the struggle against liberal legislation.[8] In this cooptation of Christianity, capitalism could become the eleventh commandment, God's ordained economic system, and Christians could serve as capitalism's lap dog.

J. Howard Pew, president of Sun Oil, and his brother Joseph started feeding this dog, becoming patrons of Fifield's ministry and outsourcing the task of persuading church congregants to embrace capitalist ideology. Pew's petroleum fortune drove out moderates such as presidential nominee Wendell Willkie from the Republican Party, replacing them with libertarian conservatives.[9] Through Fifield's organization, Spiritual Mobilization, capitalists like Pew provided the financial backing that shaped a religious message, merging a merit-based economic system (if you work hard you get rich) with a merit-based spiritual system (if you're good you go to heaven) while fear-mongering New Deal–type progressive policies which they defined as "pagan stateism."[10] Later, they would back an obscure, fiercely pro-capitalist, tent-revivalist preacher named Billy Graham. Graham, receiving his calling not from God but from Pew, preached against all progressive social programs: the New Deal, the Fair Deal, the New Frontier, and the Great Society. The illness of white supremacy can never be cured through legislation, Graham preached. Only Christ's second coming will remedy racism. Graham, along with Abraham Vereide and Doug Coe, merged Cold War anxieties over an anticapitalistic atheist Soviet

---

8. Kevin M. Kruse, *One Nation Under God: How Corporate America Invented Christian America* (New York: Basic Books, 2015), 6–8.

9. Darren Dochuk, "The Other Brother Duo That Brought Us the Modern GOP," *Politico*, September 2, 2019.

10. Kruse, *One Nation Under God*, 11, 17–18.

Union with crusades against progressive policies.[11] Aggressively seeking to take back America for Christ, they sought converts in the highest echelons of government. Thus, a nationalist Christianity took shape, merging a white supremacist political structure with the expanding influence of wealthy, white male capitalists.

Richard Nixon was probably the first president to harness the growing influence of white Christian nationalism by tying it to racism. With the exception of the war hero Dwight D. Eisenhower, a Republican had not served as president since 1933, some forty years prior to Nixon's election in 1968. Big business, the emerging Religious Right, and the rising anger among segregationists losing their power and privilege became key ingredients to ensuring Republican presidential wins. After Lyndon Johnson signed the Civil Rights Act in 1964, southern white Democrats—the party of Jim and Jane Crow—were disenfranchised and disillusioned. What proceeded was a political realignment. Blacks, originally faithful to the party of Lincoln, started switching to the Democratic Party, which was transforming itself to the party of desegregation. Nixon, along with former presidential candidate Barry Goldwater, developed a political strategy that could counter this trend and deliver electoral votes from southern states by appealing to racism—not overtly, as in the past, but through dog whistles recognized by their intended audience. The "southern strategy" secured the election of Nixon to the presidency with the support of segregationists who were switching political parties by becoming Republicans.

In the past, southern white politicians had been able to make direct white supremacist appeals without suffering any electoral consequences. But in the aftermath of the civil rights movement, that became difficult to get away with. Hence the deployment of coded language and dog whistles. Shortly after Reagan's presidential victory, Lee Atwater, political consultant and strategist for the Republican Party, advisor to Ronald Reagan, later campaign manager for George H. W. Bush, and chairman of the Republican National Committee said it best:

---

11. Kruse, *One Nation Under God*, 36.

You start out in 1954 by saying, "N*gger, n*gger, n*gger." By 1968 you can't say "n*gger"—that hurts you. Backfires. So you say stuff like forced busing, states' rights and all that stuff. You're getting so abstract now [that] you're talking about cutting taxes, and all these things you're talking about are totally economic things and a byproduct of them is [that] blacks get hurt worse than whites. And subconsciously maybe that is part of it. I'm not saying that. But I'm saying that if it is getting that abstract, and that coded, that we are doing away with the racial problem one way or the other. You follow me—because obviously sitting around saying, "We want to cut this," is much more abstract than even the busing thing, and a hell of a lot more abstract than "N*gger, n*gger." So, any way you look at it, race is coming on the back-burner.[12]

With the support of Billy Graham, a southerner, Nixon divided rather than united people by branding antagonists to his administration or his war in Vietnam as foes to Christian values.[13] The faithful (those committed to Nixon) were separated from those who were secular, ungodly, and unfaithful, giving rise to the culture wars. A ménage à trois among capitalism, racism, and white Christianity became a marriage of convenience that ensured power to whites. Capitalism got deregulation; Christians got to impose their definition of family values on everyone else, and white supremacy got to suppress the political power of the emerging majority of people of color. Reagan in 1980 masterfully satisfied all the participants of this threesome when he gave his first speech after securing the Republican nomination for the presidency at the Neshoba County Fair in Philadelphia, Mississippi. Philadelphia is where, in June 1964, three civil rights activists—James Chaney, Andrew Goodman, and Michael Schwerner—were brutally murdered. Skillfully blowing the dog whistle, he said: "I believe in states' rights. . . . I believe we have distorted the balance of our

---

12. Rick Perlstein, "Exclusive: Lee Atwater's Infamous 1981 Interview on Southern Strategy," *The Nation*, November 13, 2012.
13. Kruse, *One Nation Under God*, 256, 262.

government today by giving powers that were never intended to be given in the Constitution to that federal establishment."[14] The audience for this speech—every voter was alive during the murders committed sixteen years earlier—clearly understood that "states' rights" was coded language for granting states the right to ignore the federal Civil Rights Act.

Reagan's 1980 electoral victory was made possible because of the mobilization efforts of a minority of immoral white Christians calling themselves the Moral Majority. Paul Weyrich masterminded the creation of the Moral Majority, choosing a little-known anti-civil rights Baptist preacher named Jerry Falwell from Lynchburg, Virginia, to become the movement's public face.[15] Their goal was to expand Nixon's southern strategy by employing and exploiting racist, anti-abortion, pro-school prayer, and anti-LGBTQI views to facilitate the continuous abandonment of the Democratic Party by white southerners.[16] Falwell said it best: "Get them saved, get them baptized, and get them registered."[17] He called to "take back our children . . . take back our schools . . . take back our government . . . take back our Judeo-Christian culture." Believers weren't called to be on the defensive; rather they should be "charging the gates of Hell."[18] Through him and other culture warriors, the antigovernment, low-tax fringe wing of the Republican Party was finally merged with a Religious Right undergirded with southern Jim and Jane Crow white supremacist sentiments, thus creating a symbiotic

---

14. Ronald Reagan, "Transcript of Ronald Reagan's 1980 Neshoba County Fair Speech, *Neshoba Democrat*, November 11, 2007.

15. Deal W. Hudson, *Onward, Christian Soldiers: The Growing Political Power of Catholics and Evangelicals in the United States* (New York: Threshold Editions, 2008), 15.

16. Marc J. Ambinder, "Inside the Council for National Policy," *ABC News*, May 2, 2001; David Von Drehle, "Social Conservatives' Ties to GOP Fraying; Weyrich's Disillusion 'Touched a Chord,'" *Washington Post*, February 28, 1999.

17. Frank Lambert, *Religion in American Politics: A Short History* (Princeton, NJ: Princeton University Press, 2008), 224.

18. Jerry Falwell, "Massive Spiritual Aggression: A 21st Century Call to Action," sermon given at Thomas Road Baptist Church, Lynchburg, Virginia, May 1, 2005.

relationship. Meanwhile, the business community provided financial funding for Religious Right grassroots organizations that, in return, supported capitalist policies and ideals.

Even supposedly moderate Republicans, when finding themselves as the underdog in their presidential quest, would fall into the temptation of blowing the dog whistle. Think of George H. W. Bush's 1988 presidential bid when he found himself behind in the polls to Massachusetts Democratic Governor Michael Dukakis. William Horton, a Black man, at the time was serving a life sentence for murder, without parole, at a Massachusetts facility. Eligible for a weekend furlough, he raped and robbed a white Maryland woman. Because Dukakis was governor at the time of this crime, an opportunity for Bush arose. As Lee Atwater, Bush's campaign manager at the time promised: "By the time we're finished, they're going to wonder whether Willie Horton is Dukakis's running mate."[19]

This marriage of convenience among capitalists, Christians, and white supremacists would eventually face social and demographic challenges. The start of the new millennium revealed a steady decline of white births, dipping for the first time below 50 percent of all births. Unrestrained killings of persons of color at the hands of law enforcement began to be challenged through public demonstrations. Same-gender loving marriages became the law of the land; and white affirmative action, which, since the foundation of the republic, had privileged and supported white supremacy, began to be dismantled. To the dismay of these white Christian nationalist, the White House, which was supposed to be kept white, came to be occupied by a Black man.

Voices from marginalized communities grew louder and more demanding in their desire to share in the nation's bounty, holding white America accountable for its failure to live up to their rhetoric of "liberty and justice for all." Many white Christians grew resentful as they experienced a threat to their power, profit, and privilege. This was not the America in which they had grown up. They demanded to make America great again, returning to a sim-

---

19. Roger Simon, "How a Murderer and Rapist Became the Bush Campaign's Most Valuable Player," *Baltimore Sun*, November 11, 1990.

pler time before civil rights. Not surprisingly, many turned to a Trump presidency, regardless of what they thought of his personal character. Eight in ten white evangelicals cast their votes for Trump in 2020.[20] Even as he embodied the antithesis of Christian virtues, Trump was a modern savior of savage capitalism, bent on eradicating the last vestiges of the New Deal: the great white hope for reclaiming lost territory,

Abandoning the playbook of those Republican politicians who had mastered the art of the dog whistle, Trump immediately dismissed the whistle altogether and went straight for the jugular. Concerning Muslims, he called for a "total and complete shutdown" of their entrance to the United States.[21] To Jews he said, "I'm a negotiator, like you folks."[22] When it came to African Americans, they were "the" Blacks, and he spoke of "laziness [as] a trait in Blacks," all the while claiming, "I am the least racist person there is."[23] Asians had to deal with "the China virus," while Japanese were simply referred to as "Japs."[24] And of course Latinx, who "have lots of problems," brought "drugs and crimes," and many of them were "rapists."[25] Not all of Trump supporters are racist, understood in the sense of possessing feelings of superiority due to their skin pigmentation. Nevertheless, they are racist, understood as complicity with racist social and political structures in order to maintain and sustain their unearned power, profits, and privilege. Some are motivated to support an avowed racist president because of promised tax cuts, deregulation, and protectionism, an economic decision that nonetheless has race-based implications.

A day after the storming of the Capitol, 45 percent of Republicans—almost half of *all* Republicans—supported the insurrection,

---

20. Elana Schor and David Crary, "AP VoteCast: Trump Wins White Evangelicals, Catholics Split," *Associated Press*, November 6, 2020.
21. Nick Gass, "The 15 Most Offensive Things That Have Come Out of Trump's Mouth," *Politico*, December 8, 2020.
22. Gass, "The 15 Most Offensive Things."
23. Gass, "The 15 Most Offensive Things."
24. Gass, "The 15 Most Offensive Things."
25. Gass, "The 15 Most Offensive Things."

according to a YouGov survey,[26] with 52 percent blaming Biden for the violent rebellion.[27] Four in ten Republicans believe in the necessity of political violence.[28] The proselytization fostered by white Christians in defense of capitalism since the 1940s has nurtured an America that is not only life-denying for people of color but also damning for most whites. One has to wonder why so many whites embraced a president whose economic system was detrimental to their general welfare. White supremacy is so interwoven into the fabric of the American ethos that a normalized and legitimized repulsion exists for the idea that people of color might also benefit from governmental policies. Ronald Reagan's famous image of the "welfare queen"[29] remains so galling to many whites that they would rather vote against their own best economic interests than see governmental assistance given to nonwhites. The unexamined structural racism remains a powerful electoral motivator, more powerful than any desire to form a more perfect union in which whites' own standard of living could be improved. White America, and the nationalist Christianity responsible for providing spiritual cover to their own disadvantage, prefers a failed state than one where liberty and justice are indeed meant for all.

We find ourselves as a nation at a crossroads. We are either witnessing the last gasp of a Christian nation steeped in white supremacy or the resurgence of the Confederate "lost cause." After the storming of the Capitol, the political demise of the Republican Party is a possibility. Future electoral victories are probable only if we continue to employ the slavocracy safeguard of the Electoral College and voter suppression. No Republican has won the popular vote since 1988, with the exception of George W. Bush in his run for

---

26. James Walker, "45 Percent of Republican Voters Support Storming of Capitol Building," *Newsweek*, January 7, 2021.

27. Celine Castronuovo, "Poll: Majority of Republicans Blame Biden for Mob Storming the Capitol," *The Hill*, January 7, 2021.

28. Tom Gjelten, "A 'Scary' Survey Finding: 4 in 10 Republicans Say Political Violence May Be Necessary," *National Public Radio*, February 11, 2021.

29. Eduardo Porter, "Why America Will Never Get Medicare for All," *New York Times*, March 15, 2020.

a second term, and that second term was only possible because he won his first election to the presidency while losing the popular vote to Al Gore. A new generation, including whites who have chosen to be "traitors" to their race, want to see a more just and inclusive political system. With each passing year—as Georgia demonstrated in 2020 and states like Texas might demonstrate in 2024—presidential wins become ever more unattainable because the GOP continues to be the white man's party in an era of demographic changes. After Romney's 2012 defeat, a study was conducted by the Republican National Committee. They concluded that if the party fails to reach out to people of color, women, and youth, it would be destined for extinction, unable to win future elections.[30] Rather than begin to exorcise their racist, southern-strategy past in an effort to become more inclusive, they instead turned to Trump's nativist ideologies and voter suppression legislation.

The monkey's paw, thus far, has granted the GOP two wishes, both with hellish consequences. The first wish was for the demise of the New Deal, and the second was for the eradication of everything a Black president had implemented. One wish remains. Will the GOP throw the monkey's paw into the fire and begin the long difficult journey, for the good of the nation, to bind the wounds of the last eighty years? Or will it wish for ongoing political control by whites, an apartheid wish that can only be granted through undemocratic means, as witnessed on January 6. The manipulation of white Christianity has found its full manifestation in the Trump presidency, becoming so repulsive that even NAM—which originally sponsored and supported Fifield's 1940 call to use white Christians as a means of spreading capitalism—called for Trump's removal via the Twenty-fifth Amendment, days after the storming of the Capitol.[31] Additionally, a new generation of whites finds white Christianity so nauseating that churches are becom-

---

30. Sarah Wheaton and Michael D. Shear, "Blunt Report Says G.O.P. Needs to Regroup for '16," *New York Times*, March 18, 2013.

31. Jim Tankersley, Peter Eavis, and Lauren Hirsch, "Once a Prized Partner, A Lobbying Behemoth Wants Trump Removed," *New York Times*, January 10, 2021.

ing extinct. There can be no healing and reconciliation without the rejection and demise of the white supremacist tendencies of the Republican Party and nationalist Christianity undergirded by conspiracy theories. We can either begin to heal a divided nation or we will be witnesses to the fall of a divided house. The answer lies with the possessors of the monkey's paw.

CHAPTER 2

The Donald Went Down to Georgia: From God's Own Party to the Party of Trump

JUAN M. FLOYD-THOMAS

In advance of the US Senate runoff elections in Georgia on January 5, 2021, the twisted specter of the GOP's recent history reared its ugly head yet again. On the one hand, former Sen. Kelly Loeffler and the Republicans went into full attack mode against her Democratic opponent, Rev. Dr. Raphael Warnock. Prior to entering electoral politics, Warnock was best known for having earned a PhD in systematic theology from New York City's Union Theological Seminary under the tutelage of pioneering Black liberation theologian James Cone, serving as the senior pastor of the historic Ebenezer Baptist Church previously led by Dr. Martin Luther King Jr., and being spiritual minister to Rep. John Lewis. However, Loeffler hurled numerous attacks on Warnock's racial identity, progressive politics, and ultimately his Black Christian faith. She recycled age-old, threadbare attacks against Warnock and slammed his interpretations of the gospel and views on social justice as being far too dangerous for a notoriously conservative-leaning state such as Georgia. Notably, in light of the outrageous right-wing fearmongering Loeffler hurled against Warnock, she had not hesitated to speak from Ebenezer Church's pulpit—with Warnock's consent—while commemorating the King holiday on January 20, 2020.

On the other hand, Jon Ossoff's election to the US Senate in

2021 marks an equally important and interesting bookend event signaling the implosion of the GOP under Trump. As a young documentary filmmaker who used to work as a congressional staffer for Rep. Lewis (who had endorsed his protégé in both elections before he passed away), Ossoff was a progressive Democrat openly seeking a return to best-governing practices. It is important to remember that when Ossoff squared off against David Perdue in the 2020 Senate race, this was actually the young Democrat's second high-profile effort to garner national attention in a runoff election. In 2017, he sought a seat in Georgia's Sixth Congressional District against Karen Handel in arguably one of the most expensive and hotly contested congressional races in American politics. There were many people around the nation who viewed this special election as a proxy war for the Democratic Party's political prospects in the age of Trump. Although Ossoff lost that congressional race by a narrow margin, the Democrat remained both visible and viable in statewide politics.

For much of its recent history, Georgia's Sixth Congressional District had been a picture-perfect suburban Republican stronghold known for giving rise to notable figures in American conservative politics, such as former House Speaker and conservative firebrand Newt Gingrich, disgraced former Secretary of Health and Human Services Tom Price, and former US Senator Johnny Isakson. When Handel won the 2017 special election against Ossoff, it was assumed as an article of faith by many in the political establishment that Georgia's Sixth would remain safely ensconced in Republican hands for the foreseeable future. From 1992 to 2018, the persistence of GOP dominance in the district seemed almost certain until Handel lost to Democrat Lucy McBath. Spurred by the racist murder of her seventeen-year-old son, Jordan Davis, McBath went from being a former flight attendant to a gun-control activist, a journey that led to her eventual entry into elected office in 2018.

Quite frankly, no one ever argued that either Loeffler or Perdue had proven to be a powerhouse lawmaker, brilliant orator, or an original thinker by any stretch of the imagination. Yet, even by that incredibly low standard, this wretched pair simply campaigned the way any contemporary white Republican typically ran electoral campaigns in the South with the expectation that an extra dose of Trumpism would do the trick. They both strictly adhered to Lee Atwater's "southern strategy," based on the time-honored art of "dog-whistle politics," which had been successfully deployed by every GOP president from Nixon to Trump to win the White House.[1] Meanwhile, Loeffler and Perdue labeled the Democratic duo as rabidly "radical liberals" and told voters they were the last line of defense against this pair of reckless ideologues whom, they swore, would fundamentally undermine America's future. For instance, Perdue zeroed in on Ossoff by accusing the thirty-three-year-old Democrat of having questionable financial ties to the Chinese Communist Party, based on payments his company received from a Hong Kong-based telecom company. Aside from trying to sully Ossoff's moral integrity, patriotism, and business ethics, this attack maligns the Democrat as a "globalist," a term that has become a coded anti-Semitic slur in right-wing circles.

Throughout their respective campaigns, both Ossoff and Warnock focused on the most existential problem facing all Americans, namely, the coronavirus pandemic. The Democratic duo effectively criticized Perdue and Loeffler over making extremely lucrative, opportune stock market trades, possibly based on classified information received at the outset of the pandemic. Warnock and Ossoff hammered the incumbent GOP senators for having a personal monetary stake in negotiating a second coronavirus relief package. As a key flourish in his campaign stump speech, Ossoff poignantly branded the pair the "Bonnie and Clyde of political corruption in America."[2]

In order to truly understand the long, twisted history of the Religious Right's evolution within the Republican Party, all roads lead to Georgia. To paraphrase lyrics from Charlie Daniels's legendary country song, "The Donald went down to Georgia / He was

---

1. See Ian Haney López, *Dog Whistle Politics: How Coded Racial Appeals Have Reinvented Racism & Wrecked the Middle Class* (New York: Oxford University Press, 2015).

2. Quinn Scanian, "Georgia Runoff Campaigns Ending as Trump, GOP Continue to Contest November's Outcome," *ABC News*, January 5, 2021.

looking for an election to steal." For what it's worth, Trump filled a leadership vacuum in the GOP and, in turn, established a troubling template for future Republicans. Yet with the defeat of David Perdue and Kelly Loeffler, it needs to be asked whether the nation has ever witnessed any US Senate delegation that has ever undergone a more profound transformation in the last half century than Georgia? In one fell swoop, Warnock became the first Black senator from Georgia and only the second Black senator elected from the South since the Reconstruction era while Ossoff was elected as the state's first Jewish senator.

Even though a great deal of ballyhoo has been made of the 2018 Trump tax cuts and the GOP's court-packing bonanza (including three justices appointed to the US Supreme Court as well as countless judicial appointees to the federal bench), the paradigmatic shift of the GOP from "God's Own Party" to the party of Trump has largely been defined more by losses than victories. In the span of the past four years, the Republican Party has lost the following: the US Presidency; the US House of Representatives; the US Senate; a net loss of seven state governorships (with some trifectas—the loss of the governorship, legislature, and judiciary—in several of those states); the return of Michigan, Wisconsin, and Pennsylvania to the Democratic fold; and the loss of Arizona and Georgia as reliable GOP electoral bulwarks with each successive election cycle. Yet, as Wisconsin Democratic Party chairman Ben Wikler tweeted on January 20, 2021, it is important to remember that, despite receiving nearly eight million fewer votes than his Democratic rival, Joe Biden, if the Trump reelection campaign had flipped 10,342 votes in Wisconsin, 5,890 votes in Georgia, and 5,229 votes in Arizona in a few select counties, the entire nation would have had to endure Trump's second inaugural address.

Nevertheless, when looking at Georgia's GOP at the end of Trump's tenure in the White House, it was evident the Republican Party was slowly but surely tearing itself apart. After losing the 2020 election to Joseph R. Biden Jr., Trump unleashed an unrelenting onslaught on Georgia's Republican leaders—including Governor Brian Kemp and Secretary of State Brad Raffensperger—arguing they have not taken seriously enough his claims of voter fraud. He repeatedly called Mr. Kemp "a fool" and made incessant demands that the governor resign. On December 5, 2020, Trump urged Governor Brian Kemp to demand the state legislature simply reject Biden's victory in Georgia. Despite great pressure, Kemp refused and was subjected to a constant barrage of insults by Trump as a result.[3] A month later, the *Washington Post* obtained an hour-long recorded phone call of Donald Trump pressuring Georgia Secretary of State Brad Raffensperger to "find" enough votes to overturn his loss to Biden. "There's no way I lost Georgia," Trump insisted during the phone call. "We won hundreds of thousands of votes." During the infamous phone call, Trump offended, flattered, and implored Raffensperger to cooperate with him in reversing the election results. Despite Trump's best attempts at intimidation, Raffensperger calmly but forcefully rejected Trump's pleas, standing by his state's election results, constantly insisting that Trump and his allies had been given false information about voter fraud. Finally, Raffensperger stated, "Well, Mr. President, the challenge that you have is the data you have is wrong."[4] To be clear: Biden won the majority of votes in Georgia and rightfully earned the state's electoral votes. To appease Trump's delusional ranting about election irregularities, Georgia state officials tallied votes for the 2020 presidential election three times, including a taxpayer-financed audit required by state law and a recount demanded by Trump. All in all, each recount confirmed that Biden clearly won the state, making him the first Democratic candidate to do so since 1992.[5]

While the Senate runoff election reached a fever pitch and the GOP's stranglehold on federal politics hung in the balance, the party's entire fate hinged on Trump—a man Republican leaders and megadonors did not like, trust, or understand. Still, they were

---

3. Matthew Brown, "Trump Is Heard on Audiotape Pressuring Georgia Secretary of State to 'Find' Votes to Overturn Biden's Win," *USA Today*, January 3, 2021.

4. Michael D. Shear and Stephanie Saul, "Trump, in Taped Call, Pressured Georgia Official to 'Find' Votes to Overturn Election," *New York Times*, January 3, 2021.

5. Mabinty Quarshie, "OnPolitics: The Call Heard around the World," *USA Today*, January 4, 2021.

desperate enough to rely on him to whip his adoring voters into a frenzy at least one more time. During a Georgia GOP rally on January 4, 2021—the penultimate night before the final ballots for the closely contested runoff election would be cast—Trump repeated his litany of discredited and demented claims about election fraud. At an event purportedly intended to bolster Loeffler's and Perdue's political fortunes, Trump spent an overwhelming amount of time airing his own multitudinous grievances, while devoting little to no time supporting the two Republican candidates.[6] Additionally, Trump also used the Georgia rally to defame anyone who had refused to endorse the outlandish conspiracy theories about his imaginary election victory, from his own handpicked appointees for the US Supreme Court to Stacey Abrams, the undeniable mastermind behind the Democrats' unprecedented electoral triumph in the Peach State.

To make matters worse, Trump invited Marjorie Taylor Greene to join him onstage and speak to the MAGA crowd. "I love her," Trump said. "Come up here. Don't mess with her." Despite her well-documented record of dangerous and delusional comments, which epitomized her unabashed support of QAnon, Greene had recently won a primary runoff election for an open seat as a businesswoman and political novice in northwest Georgia's ruby-red Republican Fourteenth Congressional District. As the first QAnon conspiracy theorist elected to US Congress, her connection to the volatile fringe movement has gone from its shadowy online activity into electoral politics. However, QAnon is best understood as a baseless conspiracy theory rooted in racist, xenophobic, and anti-Semitic tropes whose followers believe Donald Trump to be a messianic figure combatting an evil cabal of Democratic politicians, liberal billionaires, and Hollywood celebrities engaged in pedophilia and other predatory, perverse acts. This group has been connected to repeated violent incidents and identified as a prominent domestic terrorist threat by federal law enforcement. Nevertheless, her campaign attracted support from opportunistic Republican

---

6. Richard Fausset, "Trump Calls Georgia Senate Races 'Illegal and Invalid,'" *New York Times*, January 1, 2021.

leaders and conservative media figures who consider her to be the vanguard of the GOP's future.

Despite several Republican officials denouncing her campaign after videos surfaced in which she expressed racist, anti-Semitic, and Islamophobic views during the election cycle, she amassed tens of thousands of followers on social media, and those videos helped propel her popularity with her burgeoning base, while also drawing strong condemnation from her current colleagues in Congress on both sides of the political divide.[7] As Travis View, co-host of the *QAnon Anonymous* podcast, asserts, QAnon followers tend to be "extremely politically active," both in terms of voting and promoting candidates online. This fact suggests one likely reason why there has been little to no condemnation of these candidates, or of QAnon itself, by senior Republicans.[8]

As alarming as the Republican Party's willingness to embrace and absorb QAnon supporters into its fold might be, this is not a rare or isolated situation. In fact, this move is actually reminiscent of the Religious Right's rise in GOP politics. Ever since so many of them embraced the Reagan revolution during the 1980 election, the political involvement of white evangelicals has garnered the attention of scholars and journalists.[9] For many of them, the story

---

7. "QAnon Supporter Denounced for Racism Wins Georgia Republican Primary," *The Guardian*, August 11, 2020.

8. Adam Gabbatt, "'They Need Voters': QAnon Is Finding a Home in the Republican Party," *The Guardian*, August 2, 2020.

9. D. G. Hart, *That Old-Time Religion in Modern America: Evangelical Protestantism in the Twentieth Century*, rept. ed. (Chicago: Ivan R. Dee, 2003); William Martin, *With God on Our Side: The Rise of the Religious Right in America* (New York: Broadway Books, 2005); Chris Hedges, *American Fascists: The Christian Right and the War on America* (New York: Free Press, 2008); Axel Schäfer, *Countercultural Conservatives: American Evangelicalism from the Postwar Revival to the New Christian Right* (Madison, WI: University of Wisconsin Press, 2011); Darren Dochuk, *From Bible Belt to Sun Belt: Plain-Folk Religion, Grassroot Politics, and the Rise of Evangelical Conservatism* (New York: W. W. Norton, 2012); Daniel K. Williams, *God's Own Party: The Making of the Christian Right* (New York: Oxford University Press, 2012); Matthew Sutton, ed., *Jerry Falwell and the Rise of the Religious Right: A Brief History with Documents* (Boston: Bedford/

of resurgent evangelical political involvement nationwide was presumably fueled by backlash. Reacting strenuously against progressive political gains and social protest movements emerging in the 1960s, white evangelicals embraced a conservative political agenda. In the late 1970s, the transformation of the GOP in the wake of both Nixon's ignominious ouster and Carter's political ascendency is crucial to the party's religious reinvention. When James Earl Carter Jr. became the thirty-ninth president of the United States in 1977, the country was still reeling from the Watergate scandal. Emerging from the obscurity of his distinguished naval career and later running the family's peanut farm in his native Georgia, Carter's platform had much popular appeal because of his public image as an honest, decent man. It is this folksy charm, plain-spoken integrity, and undaunted humility bordering on informality that defined his career as an elected office holder. Bar none, Carter embodied a mixture of born-again Christian spirit, a sense of independence, a liberal Democratic tradition, and steadfast opposition to racism. As president, he continued to teach Sunday School for children, and invited preachers to the White House, and always said grace before meals, even at state dinners with foreign dignitaries.[10]

Although initially enamored with Jimmy Carter for unapologet-

---

St. Martin's Press, 2012); Michael Sean Winter, *God's Right Hand: How Jerry Falwell Made God a Republican and Baptized the American Right* (New York: Harper One, 2012); Axel Schäfer, *American Evangelicals and the 1960s* (Madison, WI: University of Wisconsin Press, 2013); David Swartz, *Moral Minority: The Evangelical Left in an Age of Conservatism*, rept. ed. (Philadelphia: University of Pennsylvania Press, 2014); Lisa McGirr, *Suburban Warriors: The Origins of the New American Right*, rev. ed. (Princeton, NJ: Princeton University Press, 2015); Kevin M. Kruse, *One Nation Under God: How Corporate America Invented Christian America* (New York: Basic Books, 2016); Angela Denker, *Red State Christians: Understanding the Voters Who Elected Donald Trump* (Minneapolis: Fortress Press, 2019); Ben Howe, *The Immoral Majority: Why Evangelicals Chose Political Power over Christian Values* (New York: Broadside Books, 2019); Sarah Posner, *Unholy: Why White Evangelicals Worship at the Altar of Donald Trump* (New York: Random House, 2020).

10. "Jimmy Carter: Born-Again Statesman," *British Broadcasting Corporation*, December 6, 2015.

ically pronouncing himself to be "born again," many white evangelicals steadily soured and grew angry with his administration's increasingly progressive agenda in US foreign and domestic policies. Eventually, their seething frustration served as the foundation upon which Rev. Jerry Falwell Sr. established the Moral Majority in 1979. The same year, Beverly LaHaye launched the anti-feminist, anti-ERA, pro-life group Concerned Women for America. By 1980, white evangelical leaders openly expressed their uneasiness with certain developments at President Carter's White House Conference on Families. In turn, these dissenters subsequently led to the advent of the Family Research Council in 1983. A few years later, Pat Robertson and Ralph Reed launched the Christian Coalition in 1989 as a parallel organization to the Moral Majority. Emerging on the heels of Robertson's failed 1988 Republican presidential nomination bid, the Christian Coalition produced voter materials guiding many white evangelicals to cast ballots in national elections for pro-family candidates who tended to be Republicans. By the mid-1990s, the vast majority of white evangelicals had become reliably "values voters" aligned with the Republicans. This voting bloc was a crucial factor in the Gingrich revolution of 1994, which led to both the impeachment of President Bill Clinton in 1998 as well as the Electoral College victory of compassionate conservative George W. Bush in the 2000 presidential election.

The evolution of the Republican Party from the Religious Right to the relentlessly wrong has been a complicated and sordid affair, but it amounts to little more than a marriage of political convenience. On the heels of the tumultuous upheavals wrought by the 1960s, the emergence of the Christian Right certainly fit neatly into a backlash narrative akin to the rise of fundamentalism in the early half of the twentieth century. Many Americans today acknowledge the robust political force that is the Religious Right because this faith-based constituency has taken aim at government policies and practices they deem controversial with an onslaught of hundreds of DC lobbyists, millions of dollars of advertising spending, and a formidable grassroots response.

Whereas many interpreters of contemporary American Christianity attributed a reactionary motive either explicitly or implicitly to explain the raison d'être of the Religious Right, an alternate, equally compelling theory recently has emerged. Simply put, despite all its Bible-thumping dogma and holier-than-thou drama, the Religious Right simply wanted to galvanize itself into a cohesive, socially relevant voting bloc in order to wield their discrete political power as a white Christian nationalist party.[11] Toward this end, white evangelicals saw the GOP as the best available vessel for this task. White evangelical political engagement with conservative politics embraced a persistently antagonistic posture in the hopes of negating the insurgent wave of American liberalism. According to historian George Marsden (borrowed from the late Rev. Jerry Falwell Sr.), "a fundamentalist is an evangelical who is angry about something." Furthermore, according to Marsden, "'evangelical' is broadly defined to include those in traditions that emphasize the Bible as the highest religious authority, the necessity of being 'born again' or regenerated through the atoning work of Christ on the cross, pietistic devotions and morals, and the necessity of sharing the Gospel through evangelism and missions."[12] Arguably, this move by white evangelical power brokers toward the Republican Party since the 1970s had less to do with them being more pious and probably much more to do with them being morally pliable.

To be sure, both Trumpism and Trump himself have been described and depicted over the past five years in countless ways that indicate that the time is ripe for renewed theological and ethical reflection. While Trump's right-wing zealots have tried to suggest his faux grandeur and fictitious accomplishments as an iconic, albeit ersatz, paragon of latter-day conservatism, the vast majority of Americans have had to bear witness to the innumerable acts of gross criminality, governmental incompetence, and general catastrophe that culminated in his tumultuous tenure in the Oval Office. Despite this embarrassing avalanche of atrocities and offenses, the overwhelming majority of Republicans—from party leadership to

---

11. Elizabeth Dias, "Christianity Will Have Power," *New York Times*, August 9, 2020.

12. George Marsden, *Fundamentalism and American Culture* (New York: Oxford University Press, 2006), 235–36.

the rank and file—refused to address virtually any of the verifiable and self-evident wrongdoings of the Trump era.[13]

In one way or another, it is practically impossible to divorce the current crisis of legitimacy in American democracy from the hypocrisy of American (read white) "Christianity" in the aftermath of the 2016 presidential election. Reflecting on the role played by white evangelicals in the political rise of a racist, misogynist, xenophobic, transphobic, narcissistic, failed businessman and former reality television star to the White House, it would be wonderful to say that the so-called Religious Right actually rose up early on to properly and accurately attack the rambunctious sinfulness of Trump and his cronies. However, too many white conservative faith leaders—much like their political counterparts—have failed to explain why anyone should trust and welcome white evangelicals as fair and reasonable partners in the public square.

The GOP writ large seems either reluctant or negligent to acknowledge the deep trauma and apparent hypocrisy resulting from the fact that 81 percent of white evangelicals unwaveringly voted for Trump in 2016 with the outright endorsement of church leaders. Moreover, they have unrepentantly continued their support during his entire one term as US president despite his countless character flaws and immoral controversies. Confronted with this drastic sea change in presidential leadership from Obama to Trump to Biden, there are millions of people from all backgrounds yearning to actualize a radically honest and inclusive theology as well as a liberating vision of intersectional politics. When thinking about the impact of the Republican Party during the Trump era on BIPOCs (Blacks, indigenous, and people of color), millennials, refugees, immigrants, LGBTQIA folks, the poor, the physically challenged, non-Christian people, and other groups in this country, the existential threat to their very survival is woefully unconscionable.

Even more, it is almost inexplicable how the GOP's faith-driven political action as "God's Own Party" ignores the extent to which—in spite of its own worst actions—the countless vulnerable constit-

---

13. See Carlos Lozada, *What Were We Thinking: A Brief Intellectual History of the Trump Era* (New York: Simon & Schuster, 2020).

uencies named above must now make "plenty of good room" once again for white evangelicals to help fix a world-historical problem for which these particular Christians refuse to take any culpability. Moreover, the commonplace reference to "American" Christianity within the Republican self-described brand is as maladjusted and malformed by the harshly turbulent interplay of political polarization and theological reflection of the past half-decade of Trump's political ascendancy as any other realm of modern human activity.

Quite frankly, there have been far too many people who have been vilified and victimized during Trump's audacious and unabashed appeal to the worst beliefs and behaviors of his partisan base with the Republican elites standing in either silent complicity or steadfast conspiracy. Yet, given the nightmarish audacity of the US Capitol insurrection by Trump's rabid MAGA supporters on January 6, 2021, and the subsequent move by Republican senators to exonerate Trump during his second impeachment trial and ease the atrocity from popular memory, the highest echelons of the GOP's leadership have not offered a convincing case for why, based on the evidence of the most recent past, the increasingly diverse, disparate groups—who comprise the growing demographic majority of the American populace in the coming decades—should trust and find common cause with white American Christians ever again.

CHAPTER 3

Dispatches from the Deep State: The Political Theology of QAnon

RUBÉN ROSARIO RODRÍGUEZ

Any account of Donald J. Trump's presidency needs to account for the overwhelming popularity and influence of a fringe conspiracy theory that, thanks to certain media outlets, flirts with mainstream acceptance: QAnon. In 2020 nearly "two dozen Republicans across the country" embraced the QAnon conspiracy in their campaigning who "appear[ed] on the ballot this November in their congressional districts."[1] Of those, Lauren Boebert became the US representative for Colorado's Third Congressional District and Marjorie Taylor Greene became the US representative for Georgia's Fourteenth Congressional District.

Representative Boebert gained immediate notoriety when she vowed, in defiance of DC gun laws, to carry her semi-automatic weapon when "on the grounds of the U.S. Capitol and in the streets of Washington."[2] Now Boebert faces the possibility of a $5,000 fine for violating new security rules implemented by the US Congress in the aftermath of the Capitol riot of January 6, 2021.[3] Representative

---

1. Em Steck, Nathan McDermott and Christopher Hickey, "The Congressional Candidates Who Have Engaged with the QAnon Conspiracy Theory," *CNN*, October 30, 2020.

2. Meagan Flynn, "In Ad, Lawmaker Vows to Carry Her Glock around D.C. and on Hill," *Washington Post*, January 4, 2021.

3. Tom Batchelor, "Lauren Boebert Faces $5000 Fine after Setting off Capitol Metal Detector: Report," *Newsweek*, January 22, 2021.

25

Boebert's flirtations with QAnon include support and sympathy for the armed insurrection that attempted to overthrow the certified election of President Joe Biden. She is under investigation after "two Democratic lawmakers say they personally saw one Republican—Rep. Lauren Boebert of Colorado—with a 'large' group in a tunnel connected to the Capitol days before the attempted insurrection that left four rioters and one police officer dead," though Boebert vehemently denies the allegations and calls them "false" and "slanderous."[4]

QAnon is more than a fringe political movement. It has embraced the tradition of American exceptionalism, borrows language and imagery from the Bible, and its followers exhibit cult-like devotion. In effect, QAnon has unapologetically defined itself as a white Christian political theology whose ultimate goal—captured in Donald Trump's 2016 campaign slogan—is to make America great again *for white people*: "For white Christian nationalists, taking back the country is about more than just political power. They see themselves as faithful patriots fulfilling the American Founders' covenant with God."[5]

QAnon: What Is It?

Despite a constitutionally mandated separation of church and state that prohibits the establishment of a state religion, the myth that the United States of America is a *Christian* nation persists. Permeating our national narrative is a troubling theological counter-narrative interwoven and undermining the constitutional narrative: "American prophetic language not only draws its vocabulary and imagery from a particular scripture (the Old Testament), it is also deeply rooted in narratives of the founding of a particular nation (the American)."[6] Biblical prophetic imagery undergirded the Puritan mythos of a nation

---

4. Andrea Salcedo, "GOP Rep. Lauren Boebert Gave Capitol Tour to 'Large' Group before the Riots, Democratic Lawmaker Says," *Washington Post*, January 19, 2021.

5. Lauren R. Kerby, "White Christian Nationalists Want More Than Just Political Power," *The Atlantic*, January 15, 2021.

6. Talal Asad, *Formations of the Secular: Christianity, Islam, Modernity* (Stanford, CA: Stanford University Press, 2003), 144.

founded on religious freedom after fleeing Anglican persecution,[7] energized the nation building of the original thirteen colonies while resisting English despotism,[8] and fueled the westward expansion that gave rise to the ideology of Manifest Destiny.[9] In the collective imagination of US populism, this biblical language became conflated with the brand of American exceptionalism espoused by Ronald Reagan, when he borrowed Puritan preacher John Winthrop's "City on a Hill" sermon for his 1980 election eve address: "I have quoted John Winthrop's words more than once on the campaign trail this year—for I believe that Americans in 1980 are every bit as committed to that vision of a shining 'city on a hill,' as were those long ago settlers."[10] Recent scholarship has exposed the white racist ideology at the heart of "the American experiment" (Tocqueville), rejecting much of what passes for US Christianity as an ideology of white supremacy.[11] This

---

7. See John M. Barry, *Roger Williams and the Creation of the American Soul: Church, State, and the Birth of Liberty* (New York: Penguin, 2012); Robert Louis Wilken, *Liberty in the Things of God: The Christian Origins of Religious Freedom* (New Haven, CT: Yale University Press, 2019); Michael P. Winship and Mark C. Carnes, *The Trial of Anne Hutchinson: Liberty, Law, and Intolerance in Puritan New England* (New York: W. W. Norton, 2013).

8. See James P. Byrd, *Sacred Scripture, Sacred War: The Bible and the American Revolution* (New York: Oxford University Press, 2013); James Darsey, *The Prophetic Tradition and Radical Rhetoric in America* (New York: New York University Press, 1999); Nicholas Guyatt, *Providence and the Invention of the United States, 1607–1876* (Cambridge: Cambridge University Press, 2007).

9. See Anders Stephanson, *Manifest Destiny: American Expansion and the Empire of Right* (New York: Hill & Wang, 1995); Reginald Horsman, *Race and Manifest Destiny: The Origins of American Racial Anglo-Saxonism* (Cambridge, MA: Harvard University Press, 2009).

10. Ronald Reagan, "Election Eve Address 'A Vision for America,'" November 3, 1980, The American Presidency Project, UC Santa Barbara.

11. See J. Kameron Carter, *Race: A Theological Account* (Oxford: Oxford University Press, 2008); Jeannine Hill Fletcher, *The Sin of White Supremacy: Christianity, Racism, & Religious Diversity in America* (Maryknoll, NY: Orbis Books, 2017); Eric Weed, *The Religion of White Supremacy in the United States* (Lanham, MD: Lexington Books, 2017); Khyati Y. Joshi, *White Christian Privilege: The Illusion of Religious Equality in America* (New York: New York University Press, 2020); Robert P. Jones, *The End of White*

helps explain both the rise and rapid spread of QAnon's theological counternarrative.

Taken together, these examples confirm the role of explicitly theological beliefs on the formation and perpetuation of US political institutions. The paradigmatic example in the United States is the social critique of white Christianity by Martin Luther King:

> "Justice" for King is not primarily a secular legal concept, as it is for Malcolm X, but a religious one—the idea of redemption. To be redeemed and to redeem others was to restore an inheritance—the Judeo-Christian heritage in general and the American expression of it in particular. In this way the prophetic language of the Old Testament was fused with the Salvationist language of the New. To the extent that the civil rights movement presented itself as an instrument of redemption, its project became the moral restoration of the white majority.[12]

By no means is King's theo-political discourse being compared to QAnon. The argument is simply that the dominant Euro-American political discourses—however secularized—are shrouded in theological language. The spread of QAnon conspiracies within US Christianity—specifically white evangelicalism—reveals something deep-seated and unnerving about the dominant forms of Christianity and the role of religion in US politics.

According to the Rev. Dr. William J. Barber II, American evangelicalism is becoming culturally irrelevant as a result of its own idolatrous practices:

> I mean, Jesus is very clear. That's the problem for people like Graham and Falwell. They can't debate us publicly because there's no way they can say, "We're against guaranteed health care for all because Jesus was against guaranteed health care for all." Jesus never charged a leper a co-pay! How can you

---

Christian America (New York: Simon & Schuster, 2017); Robert P. Jones, *White Too Long: The Legacy of White Supremacy in American Christianity* (New York: Simon & Schuster, 2020).

12. Asad, *Formations of the Secular*, 146.

stand up and say God is for the oppression of the poor when Isaiah—in Isaiah 10—says, "Woe unto those who legislate evil and rob the poor of their right and make women and children their prey?"[13]

Barber is not alone in this assessment of US Christianity. As Christianity transitions from a predominately white European and North American religion to a religion of the Black and brown peoples of the global South, and as increased globalization brings American Christianity into contact with all the diversity that constitutes world Christianity, US Christians will have to confront much about their religion that is in fact "serving the purposes of another lord."[14] In the words of Miguel De La Torre, "The gospel is slowly dying in the hands of so-called Christians, with evangelicals supplying the morphine drip."[15] Lest we think this idolatrous perversion of the gospel of Jesus Christ is an isolated evangelical or Protestant phenomenon, Fr. Bryan Massingale concludes the following about US Catholicism:

> The only reason that racism continues to persist is because white people benefit from it. If we're always going to have conversations that are predicated upon preserving white comfort, then we will never get beyond the terrible impasse that we're in, and we will always doom ourselves to superficial words and to ineffective half-measures. That difficult truth is something that the Catholic Church in America has never summoned the courage or the will to directly address.[16]

---

13. David Marchese, "Rev. William Barber on Greed, Poverty and Evangelical Politics," *New York Times Magazine*, December 29, 2020.

14. David P. Gushee and Glen H. Stassen, *Kingdom Ethics: Following Jesus in Contemporary Context* (2nd ed.; Grand Rapids, MI: Eerdmans, 2016), xvi.

15. Miguel A. De La Torre, *Burying White Privilege: Resurrecting a Badass Christianity* (Grand Rapids, MI: Eerdmans, 2019), 4.

16. Regina Munch, "'Worship of a False God': An Interview with Bryan Massingale," *Commonweal*, December 27, 2020.

According to Massingale, the pervasive normative whiteness of Roman Catholicism is "a form of idolatry. It's the worship of a false god."[17]

On the surface, QAnon is a "baseless conspiracy theory, which imagines Trump in a battle with a cabal of deep-state saboteurs who worship Satan and traffic children for sex."[18] QAnon arose from another debunked conspiracy theory, the so-called "Pizzagate" scandal, which alleged that Democratic candidate Hillary Clinton was part of a pedophilia and human-trafficking ring headquartered in a pizza restaurant in Washington, DC.[19] White supremacist websites spread the story, claiming that the New York police department had raided Hillary Clinton's property and an anonymous FBI agent had confirmed the allegations. Pizzagate contributed to Clinton's electoral defeat but seemed to take on new life after the election. In 2017, "a writer on the anonymous message board 4chan, styling themselves as Q, wrote posts spinning a dark and cryptic fantasy—detailing how Trump was working tactically to dismantle the 'deep state' cabal that controls much of the world."[20] Throughout Trump's presidency—often encouraged by Trump or his operatives—the QAnon conspiracy wove an intricate tale employing "the militant language of good against evil, promising that Trump, a soldier messiah, would strike down a global cabal of pedophile politicians and Satanist media elites in a day of reckoning called the 'Storm.'"[21] QAnon began as speculation on a single fringe internet message board but became a national obsession that tripled in popularity during the Covid-19 pandemic. In 2020, QAnon conspiracies spread even to Canada and Europe,

---

17. Munch, "'Worship of a False God'"; also see Bryan Massingale, *Racial Justice and the Catholic Church* (Maryknoll, NY: Orbis Books, 2010).

18. Drew Harwell, Isaac Stanley-Becker, Razzan Nakhlawi, and Craig Timberg, "QAnon Reshaped Trump's Party and Radicalized Believers. The Capitol Siege May Just Be the Start," *Washington Post*, January 13, 2021.

19. Kate Samuelson, "What to Know about Pizzagate, the Fake News Story with Real Consequences," *Time*, December 5, 2016.

20. Harwell et al., "QAnon Reshaped Trump's Party."

21. Harwell et al., "QAnon Reshaped Trump's Party."

with German neo-Nazis hopeful that Trump would lead an army to restore the Reich.[22]

Christian Self-Deception and Passive Collaboration

Many thought the election of the nation's first African American president signaled a new postracial era in American politics. From the outset, President Obama remained a political realist: "At the inauguration, I think there was justifiable pride on the part of the country that we had taken a step to move beyond some of the searing legacies of racial discrimination in this country.... But that lasted about a day."[23] While Obama's political realism was undoubtedly tempered by a lifetime of growing up Black in a white supremacist culture, Obama still viewed his election as an opportunity to "continue the long march of those who came before us, a march for a more just, more equal, more free, more caring and more prosperous America."[24]

Eighty-one percent of white evangelicals and sixty percent of white Catholics voted for Donald Trump in 2016.[25] Progressive white Christians must deal more honestly with the realities of Donald Trump's presidency, a candidate whose path to the White House was made possible by the empowerment of fringe white nationalist groups with the tacit acceptance of white Christians. In Charlottesville, Virginia, the weekend of August 11–12, 2017, several hundred white nationalists from all over the nation descended on the small college town for a "Unite the Right" rally. Ostensibly a protest against the removal of a Confederate monument to Robert E. Lee, the rally was also a calculated move to draw national media attention to the various factions comprising the alt-right in an effort to

---

22. Katrin Bennhold, "QAnon Is Thriving in Germany. The Extreme Right Is Delighted," *New York Times*, October 11, 2020.
23. Justin Ewers, "Obama and Race Relations: Civil Rights Leaders Aren't Satisfied," *U.S. News & World Report*, April 30, 2009.
24. Barack Obama, "A More Perfect Union," published as "Barack Obama's Speech on Race," *New York Times*, March 18, 2008.
25. Jessica Martínez and Gregory A. Smith, "How the Faithful Voted: A Preliminary 2016 Analysis," Pew Research Center, November 9, 2016.

move from the internet fringes of US politics into the Trump-era mainstream. Protesters included white supremacists, white nationalists, neo-Confederates, Klansmen, neo-Nazis, and various heavily armed militia groups united by the alternative media's obsession with QAnon. Amidst the chants of "white lives matter," "Jews will not replace us," "Whose streets? Our streets!" (coopting a Black Lives Matter slogan used during the Ferguson protests), and the Nazi slogan, "Blood and soil," marchers carried signs with anti-Semitic slurs, brandished Nazi swastikas, and waved Confederate flags, while also carrying "Trump/Pence" signs. Instead of immediately repudiating the heinous acts of white nationalism, President Trump proclaimed there were "very fine people on both sides," and that the mob chanting hateful racist propaganda included "a lot of people in that group that were there to innocently protest and very legally protest."[26] On January 6, 2021, these same so-called "fringe" groups took part—in much greater numbers—in an armed assault on the US Capitol. QAnon believers documented their activities on social media, proud of the "starring role they had played in battling their hero's enemies," confident that Q would one day "be in every history book."[27]

On a day when Christians around the world celebrated the Feast of the Epiphany, armed subversives wearing camouflage, carrying Confederate flags, and brandishing the symbols and colors of white nationalism in all its forms—Neo-Nazis, Proud Boys, Ku Klux Klansmen—stormed the Capitol building. They were accompanied by the hymn "How Great Is Our God" were waving "JESUS 2020" placards, flags brandishing the Christian fish symbol, "In God We Trust" banners, and everywhere posters and flags with the motto "Jesus Is My Savior, Trump Is My President."[28] Lost amidst the day's many atrocities, which included the deaths of four rioters and one police officer, was the fact that the nation witnessed

---

26. Glenn Thrush and Maggie Haberman, "Giving White Nationalists an Unequivocal Boost," *New York Times*, August 16, 2017.

27. Harwell et al., "QAnon Reshaped Trump's Party."

28. See Robert P. Jones, "Taking the White Christian Nationalist Symbols at the Capitol Riot Seriously," *Religion News Service*, January 7, 2021.

the raising of a large cross on the Capitol steps: "The conflation of Trump and Jesus was a common theme at the rally."[29] The political theater centered around a "Jericho march," an imitation of the biblical account of the Israelites laying siege to the city of Jericho in the book of Joshua, complete with the blowing of shofars as they circled the Capitol building.[30] The walls of Jericho did not crumble, though for a minute it seemed the foundations of American democracy might crack.

Conclusion

In the aftermath of the Capitol riot, many evangelical Christians still support Trump, fueling "Trump's baseless allegations of widespread voter fraud."[31] For them, Trump is a savior, in the words of presidential counselor Kellyanne Conway, the "most pro-life president in history."[32] The Capitol insurrection was a coordinated attack weeks in the planning, and likely with support from the former president, who after all, ignored multiple pleas by the governors of Maryland and Virginia and the mayor of Washinton, DC, to send the National Guard to restore order. This was a temper tantrum writ large, the culmination of years of pent-up white male resentment during the Obama presidency and stoked by an opportunist president unable to face electoral defeat after running the most dysfunctional administration in the history of the United States. But like every production this president has ever been involved with, from bankrupt hotels and casinos, to the defunct Trump University, to his catastrophic plans to reopen the nation by

---

29. Jeffrey Goldberg, "Mass Delusion in America: What I Heard from Insurrectionists on Their March to the Capitol," *The Atlantic*, January 6, 2021.
30. Jack Jenkins, "As 'Jericho Marchers' Descend on Washington, Local Faith Leaders Brace for Attacks," *Religion News Service*, January 5, 2021.
31. Rick Jervis, Marc Ramirez, and Romina Ruiz-Goiriena, "'No Regrets': Evangelicals and Other Faith Leaders Still Support Trump after Deadly US Capitol Attack," *USA Today*, January 12, 2021.
32. Elizabeth Dias, Annie Karni, and Sabrina Tavernise, "Trump Tells Anti-Abortion Marchers, 'Unborn Children Have Never Had a Stronger Defender in the White House,'" *New York Times*, January 24, 2020.

Easter during the Covid-19 pandemic, this attempted insurrection also ended in failure. Thank God for mediocrity.

Unfortunately, the damage is done, and the effects will be long lasting. The revelations witnessed on January 6, 2021, confirm what many have worried about for years: there is a push by a large number of loosely connected popular organizations to impose Christian theocracy on the nation. Most alarming, these Christian groups are proclaiming a white racist nationalism in the name of Christ that seeks to dominate women, marginalize non-Christian perspectives, and, at its most rotten core, eliminate the racially other. The Capitol insurrection was perpetrated by a white Christianity in which wearing a "Camp Auschwitz" hoodie is tolerated even as outlandish comparisons are made between the Capitol rioters as a persecuted Christian minority and the European Jews exterminated by the Third Reich. We can thank Eric Metaxas for facilitating that twisted bit of logic with his self-serving evangelical biography of Dietrich Bonhoeffer.[33]

Scholars of religion have begun the arduous process of unraveling American Christianity to figure out what ethicists, theologians, and philosophers can do to diagnose, treat, and, if necessary, amputate the more cancerous parts of American religion. The "Silent Majority" that elected Donald Trump in 2016 became an emboldened white supremacist political movement with deep pockets and nationwide organization during the four years of a Trump presidency. This shift in US politics, elevating and celebrating "whiteness" as if white people are a repressed minority suffering under generations of oppression finally being delivered from captivity—an integral part of the QAnon mythos—ought to prompt bold theological responses from the church.

Two oft-quoted (and misunderstood) biblical texts frame US Christianity in 2021: the apostle Paul's defense of the state, "Let every person be subject to the governing authorities" (Rom 13:1, NRSV), and the apostle Peter's exhortation, "We must obey God rather than any human authority" (Acts 5:29, NRSV). No inci-

---

33. See Robert K. Vischer, "Eric Metaxas and the Losing of the Evangelical Mind," *Religion News Service*, December 1, 2020.

dent illustrates the inherent tension between compassion and the rule of law better than former attorney general Jeff Sessions's use of Romans 13 to defend US border enforcement policy separating undocumented immigrants from their children.[34] As Christians, will we err on the side of compassion? Do we take a prophetic stance with God against *any* authority that dehumanizes the other? All Christians—not just the Black church—ought to resist white supremacy in an America where Black lives still don't seem to matter. In this context, the cross transforms the lynching tree, inverting "the world's value system with the news that hope comes by way of defeat, that suffering and death do not have the last word, that the last shall be first and the first last."[35] Christian silence in the face of such cruelty is at best tacit approval of these policies, at worst complicity in the wave of nativist anti-immigrant violence and anti-Black racism plaguing our nation.

---

34. Lincoln Mullen, "The Fight to Define Romans 13," *The Atlantic*, June 15, 2018.

35. James H. Cone, *The Cross and the Lynching Tree* (Maryknoll, NY: Orbis Books, 2013), 2.

CHAPTER 4

Fractured Truth in Post-Trump America

David P. Gushee

I never thought that truth would become a major subject of inquiry for me as a Christian ethicist. Truth had been more a presupposition of my work and a minor ethical theme on its own. But after the events of the last four years in the United States, the social ethics of truth (and lies) strikes me as an essential subject. Truth has been fractured by Donald Trump and his enablers, while lies have been imbibed by Trump's most rabid followers—many of them self-proclaimed Christians. There is little hope for a better American future until this fracturing of truth is overcome. It will not be easy.

When the late Glen Stassen and I wrote the first edition of *Kingdom Ethics* from 1996–2002, we began with a study of existing introductory Christian ethics texts. In our research on what ended up being over fifty such textbooks, we saw that only six contained a section on truth, truthfulness, or truth telling. Discussions of the ethics of truth in those few books tended to devolve into technical arguments over whether it is ever morally permissible to lie. That familiar question in ethics *can* prove illuminating in terms of how one thinks about the nature of moral rules, principles, and obligations. Absolutists won't lie even to save life; others will lie in such extreme cases, but if so, they must then account for why lying is simultaneously wrong and yet permissible in some cases. This is all fun ethical noodling. Eggheads love it. The important point is that the classic discussion of the ethics of lying assumes a strict moral rule against it, only asking whether exceptions ever can be made. This older discussion of the ethics of truth in those nerdy textbooks could not imagine a social reality in which lying is routinized from the very top of society.

That was 2003. It feels like a million years ago. In *Kingdom Ethics*, when we briefly noted situations of systemic public lying, we focused on places like the Soviet Union. We really did not imagine that this line, from our last paragraph, would ever seem so relevant right here at home:

> The Scriptures remind us of occasions in which "truth has perished" (Jer 7:28) or truth has "stumbled in the public square" (Is 59:14). In such times justice, righteousness, and human life itself can become supremely threatened. Those who hold power are called especially to live in truth and to be aware of the many temptations they face to resort to duplicity, dishonesty and truth's suppression.[1]

I remember January 20, 2017. That was the day Donald Trump raised his right hand, put his left hand on a Bible, and swore his presidential oath of office. I did not have high confidence that a man with his track record could be trusted to keep his oath to "preserve, protect, and defend the Constitution of the United States." Little did I know how bad it would finally get. In swearing that oath, Trump was making a covenant with the American people, as all presidents before him had done. Covenants are freely given verbal declarations or oaths that articulate sacred commitments being made. Covenant declarations are speech-acts that verbally perform those commitments into existence.

In the Bible, and today, covenants can be between people only or between people and God. But even covenants between people often call upon or allude to God as witness, guarantor, or avenger if the

---

1. Glen H. Stassen and David P. Gushee, *Kingdom Ethics: Following Jesus in Contemporary Context* (1st ed.; Downers Grove, IL: InterVarsity Press, 2003), 388. This discussion contains occasional small extracts from that book, now available in a second edition (Grand Rapids: Eerdmans, 2016).

covenant is broken. Covenant promises bind the behavior of those making them. Having made sacred vows, the covenant partners are obligated to act accordingly. If God is invoked, sacred covenant promises ultimately are made to God and accountable before God. The theological imagination that lies behind covenant traditions like the presidential oath is profound—but today largely vestigial. This imagination includes the idea that the most important human relationships are covenantal, that God is the ultimate witness and judge of our covenant making, and that covenant promises preserve community and define the range of acceptable behavior within community.

Undergirding any public covenant oath is the largely implicit covenant to speak truthfully, including when making promises. Each statement we make, under normal circumstances, carries an implicit promise of truthfulness. Otherwise we would have to make vows of honesty before every statement, and our listeners would have to fact check every word we said. Sacred vows, like presidential oaths, mean nothing if words in general mean nothing and truth in general does not matter. *People who do not speak truthfully cannot make reliable covenant promises*, because none of their words can be trusted.

Every nation needs government leaders who contemplate deeply the nature of their covenant obligations. When nations pick leaders, they should carefully consider whether candidates have a covenantal understanding of the office—and whether they have a track record of truth telling and covenant keeping in earlier roles and relationships. This is one way in which private conduct and public responsibility are profoundly linked. Christians used to know this. So, in retrospect, here was the pivotal failure of the 46 percent of voters in the United States who elected Donald Trump in 2016. The United States elected a person with a long and well-established record of breaking his personal, financial, and professional covenants—as well as a demonstrably casual (if not pathological) relationship with the truth that is the prerequisite for all covenants. We had no reason to believe that such a person would prove seriously interested in the covenantal responsibilities of the presidency. And he did not. Anyone who had studied the history of twentieth-century politics could anticipate that a person with such a casual relationship with the truth, and such a track record of breaking his covenants, would not uphold his covenant with the American people (and God), would act in manifestly unjust ways, and would bathe his tenure in lies.

Václav Havel, the Czech dissident and finally president, who spent years in prison for speaking the truth under communism, documented with great profundity how truth is among the first casualties of political malfeasance and repression.[2] Dietrich Bonhoeffer, Alexander Solzhenitsyn, George Orwell, Elie Wiesel, and many other dissident luminaries of the twentieth century also focused attention on the relationship between tyranny, injustice, and the death of truth in public life. If their work (and subject) had been taken more seriously, perhaps fewer philosophers and regular people might have succumbed to the fashionable idea that truth is merely relative or a matter of perspective. Fewer might also vote for candidates with a record of habitual lying.

As Miroslav Volf has pointed out, under tyrannical regimes truth is concealed, redefined, controlled, and suppressed by the leader, party, or state. Fundamental to tyranny is the manipulation of truth, even the creation of an enforced empire of lies. *You will agree that $2 + 2 = 5$, because we say so, and we will enforce our redefinition of truth until we break you.* Yet no state has proven capable of destroying the human will to know the truth. No matter how intense the repression, there will always be stalwart souls who commit themselves to tell the truth about what is really going on. Such loyalty to the truth amid regimes built on lies may be the ultimate revolutionary act; it is certainly the condition for all other forms of resistance. That commitment to know and speak the truth can be costly. Many millions died in the twentieth century simply for telling the truth.

Reflecting on the dramatic scene of Jesus before Pilate, Croatian expat theologian Miroslav Volf sees a clash between "the truth of power" and "the power of truth."[3] One way to interpret Pilate's

---

2. Václav Havel, *Living in Truth* (New York: Faber & Faber, 1990).
3. Miroslav Volf, *Exclusion and Embrace* (Nashville, TN: Abingdon Press, 1996), 268.

famous "What is truth?" question is to view it as a taunt. *You speak to me of truth, Jesus of Nazareth. But I am the one who defines truth in this place and time. I will show you who defines truth by nailing you to one of our crosses.* Though Christ does end up hanging on the cross, his death ultimately marks the victory both of truth and of life. He could not be intimidated by Power into denying Truth.

In US public life over these last four years, we witnessed a reign of lies. Roughly one-third of the public believed the lies. Half never believed them. Most of the rest did not believe the lies—but they accommodated the liar out of fear and expedience. This was especially true in the Republican political class. The most interesting people to watch during this awful time were not those whose party affiliation and ideology made it easy for them (us) to know Trump was a liar and wannabe tyrant. Instead, it was the population of Republicans who had to decide whether they would submit to "the truth of power" or "the power of truth." The most impressive in this group are those who suffered real costs for choosing bedrock truth over Trumpian power. I think of the "Never Trumpers," and more recently, of Mitt Romney. But there were not enough of them. Not only has our democracy suffered great damage—quite literally, many people are dead today because of the predictable yet craven choices of those who chose power over truth.

Every fall semester at Mercer I teach a course on genocide—the intentional effort to destroy a national, ethnic, racial, or religious group. This past fall, perhaps because the presidential election of 2020 was under way, and with it the question of whether Donald Trump's depredations would be ratified by American voters, I noticed something in the readings that I had not focused on before: genocide is always correlated with lies. In every genocide studied by my class, a torrent of lies preceded, accompanied, and followed the evil events. In Nazi Germany, the former Yugoslavia, Rwanda, and colonized North and South America, genocide was bathed in lies. The same was true for other genocides that we touch on in the class, including the Turkish genocide against the Armenians. The relation between mass lies and mass murder also proves true when one considers the former Soviet Union and Communist China.

It appears to be an iron law that there is no genocide apart from massive, systematic governmental lying. First there are the lies told by regimes about the supposed dangers, threats, and evils of the targeted groups. Then there are the lies about the nature and consequences of the destructive policies that these regimes begin to implement against the groups. Next come the lies about what is happening to the group as its members begin to disappear. Afterward, there are the lying denials, dissembling, and finally (perhaps) snarling moral justifications of the atrocities once they are revealed. Almost always, after a genocide, a substantial contingent of genocidaires, perhaps even entire peoples and governments, denies that the genocides they perpetrated ever happened at all.

During the genocide in the former Yugoslavia, journalist Peter Maass was able to get an interview with Serbian/Yugoslavian president Slobodan Milošević, who (mis)ruled from 1989 until 2000 and was indicted by the International Criminal Tribunal-Yugoslavia for war crimes. Maass was struck by the comprehensive nature of Milošević's lying:

> Milošević existed in a different dimension, a twilight zone of lies, and I was mucking about in the dimension of facts. He had spent his entire life in the world of communism, and he had become a master, an absolute master, at fabrication. Of course my verbal punches went right through him. It was as though I pointed to a black wall and asked Milošević what color it was. White, he says. No, I reply, look at it, that wall there, it is black, it is five feet away from us. He looks at it, then at me, and says, The wall is white, my friend, maybe you should have your eyes checked. He does not shout in anger. He sounds concerned for my eyesight.[4]

Maass goes on to say that because he had spent so much time covering the war and genocide in the former Yugoslavia, he knew exactly what color the wall was.

Milošević's lies did not deceive this grizzled reporter. He went

---

4. Peter Maass, *Love Thy Neighbor: A Story of War* (New York: Alfred A. Knopf, 1996), 213.

right on reporting the truth. But they did at least confuse those who did not have as firm a grasp on the truth as Maass did, such as visiting reporters or US congressmen on a fly-by visit. Lies don't always have to persuade; all they need to do is confuse, to slow action, to weaken certainty, to create a plausible alternative narrative. Milošević's lies also proved convenient to Western diplomats serving governments that did not want to intervene in Yugoslavia's wars and genocide. These people knew the truth, but the lies helped them cover their inaction. This is a reminder that some people accept and even promote what they know are lies because they perceive it to be in their self-interest. We have seen plenty of that in the United States over the last four years. Milošević's lies proved perfectly convincing to large numbers of his own people, some of them actively perpetrating genocide and other war crimes, others of them needing a narrative of Serbian innocence in which to believe. This is a reminder of another truism: when criminals head governments, their lies not only intend to hide their crimes but also to distort reality for their own people—many of whom are readily willing to believe whatever lies might be available. The ability to persuade large numbers of people to believe outright lies is one of the greatest and most wicked powers of a skillfully evil leader.

Genocide is the worst form of organized, usually state-sponsored, evil. But the point applies down the line to less extreme forms of public or governmental wrongdoing. Systemic falsehood and systemic wrongdoing are inextricably related. Lying regimes distort reality in the perception of their people. They prepare their people to do evil against others while believing that they are doing what is right. Then they aid their people in not facing the truth of what they have done. When friends or spouses lie to each other, that is a problem. But when governments become lying regimes, the stakes are so much higher. Lies pave the way to injustice and even to mass murder.

I am thinking of a scene that took place in our country on January 6, 2021. On that awful day, a group of people who had been fed months of lies about our election by their beloved president and a right-wing media ecosystem stormed the US Capitol in an action that resulted in the deaths of five people. In public life, lies can kill. America's conservative white Christians were among the insurrectionists on January 6. In general, white Christians have not distinguished themselves as seekers of truth during the crisis of the Trump years. They bear primary responsibility for electing, supporting, and sustaining Donald Trump. White evangelical Christians have been his strongest base of support, but it should not be overlooked that white mainline Christians still voted for Trump in November at well over 50 percent.

There ought to have been many reasons why American Christians of all races should have had an immunity against finding Trump attractive or even barely acceptable as a president. I have outlined those reasons endlessly over the last five years. But one of the reasons—and the one I want to elevate here—is Trump's pathological, sinful, and socially cancerous mendacity. John 8:44 quotes Jesus saying this to his adversaries: "You are from your father the devil, and you choose to do your father's desires. He was a murderer from the beginning and does not stand in the truth, because there is no truth in him. When he lies, he speaks according to his own nature, for he is a liar and the father of lies."

I am not selecting this quote to identify Donald Trump with Satan, though we could have an interesting conversation about Trump and the demonic here. I want us to hear these cadences: "He does not stand in the truth, because there is no truth in him. When he lies, he speaks according to his own nature, for he is a liar." *There is no truth in him. Lying is his nature.* Long before he was elected president, disaffected former spouses, friends, family members, and employees told us this about Donald Trump, that there is no truth in him, that lying is his nature, that his relationship with truth is entirely broken, and that this makes him a very dangerous person.[5] *He is a liar and the father of lies.* Fathers spread their seed and produce offspring, sometimes in great abundance. You don't have to be Satan to father lies. You just have to be a highly

---

5. The most compelling account is Mary Trump, *Too Much and Never Enough: How My Family Created the World's Most Dangerous Man* (New York: Simon & Schuster, 2020).

influential and powerful person to whom people listen when you distort their understanding of reality. You just have to be a person whose lies connect in some profound way with the need of millions of people to believe in you and in them. Perhaps a president with a (now banned) Twitter account with 89 million followers.

Donald Trump has been a "father of lies" because he has produced an abundant offspring of sycophant liars and metastasizing lies through the body politic. Long after his presidency ends, his sycophantic liars and metastatic, cancerous lies will still course through the body of our people. The added tragedy is that white American Christians have shown no immunity to this liar and his lies. Instead, my people have been among the foremost sycophants and believers, cancer victims and super-spreaders. It must be that we had a susceptibility to this man and his lies that long preceded his emergence on the scene. Here is where in a deeper analysis one would have to link Trumpist lies with the long history of white supremacist Christianity in America—and its abundant lies. We have been believing massive lies for a long time. But over these four years, we have humiliated ourselves and the name of Christ in new ways. Among the leading conspiracy theorists, QAnon people, election-fraud claimers, and congressional votes for rejecting the electoral college results have been a disproportionate number of white, mainly evangelical, Christians.

Glen Stassen talked about "information integrity" as crucial for Christian ethics. The term makes an appearance in the first edition of *Kingdom Ethics*. I never asked him where he got this term, but a search reveals that it seems to have come out of the computer security world. Information integrity is "the dependability and trustworthiness of information. More specifically, it is the accuracy, consistency and reliability of the information content, processes and systems."[6] Stassen selected the term to help describe the significance of clear perception in Christian moral discernment. The basic idea is that we cannot think well in the realm of Christian ethics if

---

6. Quoted in ASQ Information Integrity Interest Group, Understanding Information Integrity (asq.org).

we do not have information integrity, defined by Glen as "truthfulness in facing reality and openness to evidence that calls people to change their perceptions."[7] If we process our moral choices based on undependable or untrustworthy information, our bad inputs will produce bad outputs. If where we go to get our information, and the way in which we process information, lacks integrity, we will consistently get bad results.

If, based on lies, we think the US presidential election was rigged/fraudulent/stolen, we might just storm the Capitol building and leave five people dead. If Christians are as urgently committed to seeking truth and doing justice as the Scriptures commend, then we will clean up our information processes, systems, and content. We will improve the "dependability and trustworthiness of information." We will not listen to inveterate liars, even if they tell us things that resonate deeply with us. We will value truth, seek truth, and love truth as a core aspect of being followers of Jesus Christ who is the Truth. The theme of truth needs to move off the backlot and onto the main stage of Christian moral reflection. Truth is not just a philosophical conundrum, theological claim, matter of personal character, or issue of moral quandaries about when it is okay to lie. Truth is also a fundamentally significant social ethical issue—indeed, a matter of life and death deeply connected to social justice and injustice.

But all these areas do go together. The fracturing of truth that we see in our country, in which our Christians are so deeply implicated, must be comprehensively considered. We need a fresh commitment to the idea that truth is real and is correspondence with reality. We need to stop toying with cynicism about truth's meaning. We need a recovery of the centrality of truth and truthfulness as aspects both of God's character and of the expected character of God's people. We need a reclaiming of that sturdy old-fashioned religious-ethical commitment to tell the truth in everyday life. We need to be able to expect people, including ourselves, to keep the covenants and promises they make. And yes, we need an expec-

---

7. Stassen and Gushee, *Kingdom Ethics*, 67.

tation that anyone who exercises leadership in major social institutions can be counted on to tell the truth except when they are forbidden to do so based on other fiduciary duties.

As of this writing, it appears that roughly 20 percent of the adult US population believes a poison cocktail of lies fomented by Donald Trump. This group will render the country ungovernable if they continue to resort to violence. Christians are disproportionately represented. All civilizing forces in American society, including Christians who remain tethered to reality, need to band together to drain this poison over the next few years. This fight will be costly. But it is the only way forward.

CHAPTER 5

Purple Rein, Purple Reign: Fashioning Womanist Witness, Work, and Worth of Black Women in the Making of Democracy

STACEY FLOYD-THOMAS

In 2016, the election of Donald Trump as the forty-fifth president of the United States on November 9 (11/9) ushered in a slow-burning tragedy of 9/11 proportions. On the one hand, many in the nation were "seeing red" on account of the vitriol and vengeance of the "Make America Great Again" rallying cry of the Republican Party and Trump loyalists—a thinly veiled exhortation to make America white again. Others in the nation were "crying the blues" because Democrats lost the election to a failed businessman, blowhard, and bigot, in spite of fielding a candidate, Hillary Clinton, who received the majority of the popular vote and possessed a professional profile that easily made her the meritorious candidate. Regardless of one's personal party affiliation, the divisive apocalypse that swirled about the forty-fifth presidency brought into stark relief what the musical artist Prince had to say regarding the imagery of his classic song "Purple Rain": "When there's blood in the sky—red and blue equals purple. 'Purple Rain' pertains to the end of the world and being with the one you love and letting your faith / God guide you."[1]

---

1. Matthew Wikening and Debra Ficman, "Prince Leaves Behind a World Bathed in 'Purple Rain'—365 Prince Songs in a Year," *Diffuser*, April 20, 2018.

In her novel *The Color Purple*, womanist novelist Alice Walker depicts in narrative fashion the irony of Prince's conviction of the divine purpose to be found within the purple shades of suffering. This hermeneutic of suspicion and discovery exists in the epistles of Walker's protagonist, Celie, the Black sharecropping, marital property of a cruel, unfaithful husband who allows her to speak of her suffering only to God. Celie discloses that she is a "confused Christian who was taught to worship [and follow the lead] of a god that's a big, white, old, bearded, barefooted man with bluish gray eyes." Due to this cognitive dissonance, she finds herself ultimately wanting more, so she ends up disavowing the god to whom she once submitted her will, bared her soul, and suffered abuse in silence and shame. In a letter to her sister, Nettie, she writes: "I don't write to God no more, I write you. . . . If he ever listened to poor colored women the world would be a different place. . . ."[2] Celie's recognition of a Eurocentric, anthropomorphic, sexist image of God is an expression of what has recently been referred to as "misogynoir"— what Black feminists have noted as a world wherein "all the women are white and all the blacks are men, but some of us are brave."[3] It is for this reason that the metalogue and meaning of the novel's title is captured by the statement "I think it pisses God off if you walk by the color purple in a field somewhere and don't notice it." For in so doing, God's handiwork becomes hidden in plain sight.

Beyond rhetoric or observation, the brave act of putting a false god in its place by linking divine justice to social justice has been the witness, worth, and work of womanist work. This deeper shade of purple has afforded Black women full rein to take democracy into their own hands. Rather than reeling from the 2016 presidential election or capitulating to the hostile personality who occupied the White House, a remnant of the American population defined this epoch not as an end-time, doom-filled event, but as a *kairos*

---

2. Alice Walker, *The Color Purple* (New York: Harcourt Brace Jovanovich, 2003), 193.

3. See Akasha Gloria Hull, Patricia Bell-Scott, and Barbara Smith, eds., *All the Women Are White, All the Blacks Are Men, but Some of Us Are Brave: Black Women's Studies* (Old Westbury, NY: Feminist Press, 1982).

moment. These are the actions of Black women who refused to clutch pearls, devote energy to fact-checking lies, or give bandwidth to the banality of political antics. Instead, they seized on the Trump era as a propitious opportunity to envision, organize, and initiate a movement that focuses on the bigger picture of justice. In this respect, purple became a color that marked good judgment and spiritual fulfillment.

To use Martin Luther King Jr.'s words, the "fierce urgency" of the catastrophic crisis that was the Trump presidency afforded Black women the opportunity, through womanist praxis, not only to thwart the reelection of Trump but also to begin building a better country in a way that exceeds the gravitas of political parties or personal power. The year 2020 became known as the "year of the Black woman" because Black women collectively and strategically set forth a multiphase "womanist metalogue" as an "exploratory process to discern mechanisms of exploitation and identity patterns that must be altered in order for justice to occur."[4] This essay explores the trifecta of contextual analysis, cultural disposition, and collective action of Black women as a prototype for womanist faith-moral praxis typified by Black women who worked to bend the moral arc of our universe toward justice by reining in every resource at their disposal for the deliverance of "a more perfect union."

Purple Rain: The Contextual Analysis That Black Lives Matter

The Trump era was a season of purple rain in which the Republican red rage and the brutal Blue Lives Matter police force trafficked in Black death. As James Cone reminds us, from slave ships to the Middle Passage to the lynching tree to our city streets today, "The blood of black people is crying out to God and to white people from the ground in the USA." Battered and bludgeoned Black lives and bodies cry out all over America today. "Purple rain" is a perennial

---

4. Stacey M. Floyd-Thomas, *Mining the Motherlode: Methods in Womanist Ethics* (Cleveland, OH: Pilgrim Press, 2006), 82.

refrain in various national great awakenings that reckon with the country's original sin of structural racism in the work to protect Black life that is constantly deemed invisible, irrelevant, and dispensable.

To be a Black woman in America is to take note and not lose sight of this reality. Freedom fighters such as Harriet Tubman, Sojourner Truth, Anna Julia Cooper, Ida B. Wells, Mary McLeod Bethune, Fannie Lou Hamer, Pauli Murray, Ella Baker, Barbara Jordan, and Shirley Chisholm have rejected ethical notions of "universality" that claim ideals that fail to take into consideration those who live on the underside of US history. Instead, the lived experience and practical wisdom of Black women, forged from the concrete realities of rabid racism, class discrimination, and sexual exploitation, have guided both their consciousness and ethical reflection. As womanist ethicist Valerie Dixon declares, to be conscious is to be aware of both "personal reality in the world and moral and ethical obligations in the world."[5] Operating from the conviction that fighting for and realizing the freedom of other women inherently frees others, Black women have been able to give sustained articulation to both the transcendent moments and usable truths from their everyday lives in such a way as to impact both the political arena and public square.

As a contemporary example, one sees contextual analysis in the actions of Patrisse Cullors, Alicia Garza, and Opal Tometi as they strive to create the #BlackLivesMatter movement,[6] which engages

---

5. Valerie Dixon, "Dance of Redemption and the Poetics of Obligation," Lecture for American Baptist Churches, June 28, 2007.

6. See Josiah U. Young III, "Do Black Lives Matter to 'God'?" *Black Theology* 13, no. 3 (2015): 210–18; Juan Floyd-Thomas, "'A Relatively New Discovery in the Modern West': #BlackLivesMatter and the Evolution of Black Humanism," *Kalfou: A Journal of Comparative and Relational Ethnic Studies* 4, no. 1 (2017): 30–39; George Lipsitz, "Making Black Lives Matter: Conjuring and Creative Place-Making in an Age of Austerity" *Kalfou: A Journal of Comparative and Relational Ethnic Studies* 4, no. 1 (2017): 40–58; Keeanga-Yamahtta Taylor, *From #BlackLivesMatter to Black Liberation* (Chicago: Haymarket Books, 2016).

and motivates people to take action through their own discomfort and dissonance with the historic reality in the United States that Black people have been regarded as bodies in service or submission to the state of white supremacy. Through the power of protest, these three Black women unapologetically and boldly address the issue that Black lives matter for the sake of Black livelihood. The grassroots conscientization of these women fomented sit-ins, die-ins, and a social media frenzy that has enabled them to amass social power through protest and rallies organized throughout the United States and worldwide. The contextual analysis of these women, their movement, and even "the Squad"[7] serves as another generation taking hold of the reins from past generations to work consistently for liberation in what Maya Angelou described as "these yet to be United States."[8] The #BlackLivesMatter movement holds up a mirror for some and a magnifying glass for others, reflecting and examining the racial realities of the United States. The movement also empowers individuals literally to become expert eyewitnesses and reporters, by video recording the countless acts and incidences of their own dissonance and disenfranchisement and posting it live on the World Wide Web, so they cannot be denied. Herein, Black women have tapped into the epistemological privilege of the oppressed in an effort to rein in political processes, discern mechanisms of exploitation, and confront the contestability of life, liberty, and the pursuit of justice.

---

7. "The Squad" is a popular moniker that signals to the initial female core of the Democratic members of the US House of Representatives elected to office in the 2018 United States House of Representatives elections: Alexandria Ocasio-Cortez of New York, Ilhan Omar of Minnesota, Ayanna Pressley of Massachusetts, and Rashida Tlaib of Michigan. They have since been joined by Jamaal Bowman of New York and Cori Bush of Missouri following the 2020 United States House of Representatives elections. They are all under fifty and are well known for being a generational force with which to be reckoned as they are among the most progressive members of the United States federal government.

8. "These Yet to Be United States" by Maya Angelou," https://genius.com/Maya-angelou-these-yet-to-be-united-states-annotated.

Purple Rein: Cultural Disposition as "Reclaiming My Time"

The cultural disposition of Black women's political prowess not only denies normative notions of dominant social structures but also guides how Black women are able to realize social change through their interactions with what does not resonate with who they are, what they do, and how they do it. In this respect, it is important to understand that the worldview and perspective of Black women is culturally disposed to be countercultural, given that their ways of living and thinking render a more robust critique of the historical narratives of power, privilege, and people. Leah Daughtry, former CEO of the Democratic National Convention Committee, calls this "freedom faith."[9] Springing from a bottom-up perspective, Black women in politics have not abandoned their freedom faith but rather have held fast to this homegrown epistemology for the insight needed to influence solidarity and demand social, political, and economic liberation as their divinely appointed inalienable right.

Key among them has been Representative Maxine Waters (D-CA). Currently serving her fifteenth term as congresswoman for the Forty-Third Congressional District of California, and affectionately known as "Aunt Maxine" on Black Twitter, Representative Waters has been lauded for her witty, pointed, and candid rhetoric, as she tells the truth to shame the devil (aka, speaks truth to power). Often caricatured during Trump years as his reigning meme queen, as well as vilified and marked as a dog-whistle target by his administration, Waters remained persistent in her procedural pushback.[10] She exemplified her strength during a meeting of the House Financial Services Committee, which became not only her most viral moment to date but also a mantra for those who felt silenced, stereotyped, and shunned by the mismanagement and mendacity of a trumped White House. During Treasury Secretary

---

9. Gwen McKinney "Leah Daughtry: Where Faith and Activism Meet." *Suffrage. Race. Power.* (blog), *Huffington Post*, October 2, 2020, https://srpunerased.com.

10. See Christine Emba, "'Reclaiming My Time' Is Bigger than Maxine Waters," *Washington Post*, August 1, 2017.

Steven Mnuchin's testimony before the committee about the state of the international finance system, Waters, at the time the committee's ranking Democrat, asked why his office had not responded to a letter from her regarding President Trump's financial ties to Russia. Mnuchin tried to sidestep the question with platitudes and compliments, apparently attempting to run out the clock on her questioning. Waters shut down his rambling by repeatedly redirecting him to her question with the expression "reclaiming my time"—a stone-faced invocation of House procedural rules.[11] But, even prior to her political outspokenness against the Trump administration, many knew Waters for her prolific expressions of womanish authority—one instance most legendarily enshrined in countless social media posts and internet memes was her defiant declaration she was "reclaiming my time." Faced with the Trump administration's efforts to obstruct and obfuscate while she endeavored to execute her sworn duty to inquire and ultimately investigate their malfeasance, she relentlessly endeavored to take her rightful power back in a political space too often dominated by white male voices and policing practices intended to keep women as political leaders squarely "in their place" as a silent, invisible, and ostensibly disempowered multitude within the nation's corridors of power.

Waters not only reclaimed her time but also took pride in her track record of "no more, no longer," indulging or overlooking the gross misuse and abuses of the Trump administration. This characteristic constituted part of a cultural disposition not born of her senior political post, progressive lawmaking collegium, or personal idiosyncrasies. Rather, Waters boldly affirmed that her efforts "to take on President Donald Trump and his allies" arose within her sense of divine calling. Standing in a pulpit at the First African Methodist Episcopal Church of Los Angeles, Waters stated:

> You've gotta know that I'm here to do the work that I was sent to do, and when God sends you to do something, you just

---

11. Jonathan Capehart, "Maxine Waters: Jeff Sessions Believes 'It's His Job to Keep Minorities in Their Place,'" *Washington Post* podcast, May 9, 2017, https://www.washingtonpost.com.

do it. . . . So I have. I'm going back to Washington. . . . I have no fear. I'm in this fight. I know that there are those who are talking about censuring me, talking about kicking me out of Congress, talking about shooting me, talking about hanging me. . . . All I have to say is this: If you shoot me, you better shoot straight. There's nothing like a wounded animal.[12]

Waters regularly evokes God's urging as motivation for her behavior. Her dogged tenacity and righteous indignation are both scathing to Republicans and at times regarded as politically incorrect by fellow Democrats. In fact, her allies, Senate Minority Leader Chuck Schumer (D-NY) and House Minority Leader Nancy Pelosi (D-Calif.), have urged her to tamp down her expectations and decrease her passion. Yet, Waters knew she needed "to do everything in her power to combat President Donald Trump." Congresswoman Waters's courage and idealism are tempered with realism and fueled by her freedom faith, with God on her side, the side of the oppressed.[13]

Purple Rein: Collective Action— "Leading from the Outside"

When democracy failed Georgia, Black women advanced the state, and their freedom faith and collective action made them affirm that failure was not an option. After her gubernatorial loss in 2018 because of the voter-suppression antics of Brian Kemp, former Georgia House Minority Leader Stacey Abrams took a ten-day political sabbatical. She came back renewed and ready to sacrifice her time, sleep, health, political resources, and energy to demonstrate democracy could still be revived in this country. Abrams created a political action committee named Fair Fight to promote fair elections as a means to mitigate voter suppression and increase political participation.

Additionally, Abrams reimagined campaign tactics from her governor's race to offer up a political blueprint to ensure democracy

---

12. "Maxine Waters Claims in Church Sermon That She Was Sent by God to Stop President Trump," https://www.beliefnet.com.

13. "Maxine Waters Claims . . . She Was Sent by God . . ."

didn't fail again. Where democracy rendered the marginal invisible, Abrams deemed them invaluable. One of Abrams's main strategies from her 2018 gubernatorial campaign involved refraining from expending her energy on unpersuadable voters while mobilizing the persuadable, the voters often overlooked or undermined, the irregular voters, and party-leaning voters.[14] Because predictability is favored in politics, this approach could have been interpreted as unconventional. However, unpredictability is never frightening to faith-filled Black women who have waded in the waters of poverty, systemic racism, and misogynoir disenfranchisement, all while having to find creative ways to produce and survive. As a candidate, Abrams raised money to fund a million-dollar campaign, which allowed her to tour across the Georgia countryside and send out to households 1.6 million postage-paid applications for mail-in ballots.[15] Abrams continued her campaign marketing efforts to the persuadable in 2020, leaving no stone unturned and finding no audience unworthy of marketing—from appealing to Verzuz battles on Instagram, to taking out Super Bowl ads, to leveraging her networks with political leaders such as the Obamas and Atlanta Mayor Keisha Lance Bottoms and entertainers such as Janelle Monae, to canvassing rural areas. She deemed no space or place off limits, which resulted in the registration of more than 800,000 new voters and the flipping of Georgia from red to blue.

Abrams affirms that her faith formed her for this fight, not her Yale law degree, successful career as a tax attorney, or her political status. She sees herself as fulfilling her family's long tradition and clarion call to "a sacred civil duty," stemming from her "passion for voting that began with her preacher parents," the Revs. Robert and Carol Abrams. Her call to collective voter activism has been long linked to her roots in the Black church, which historically has provided a safe haven to discuss politics, organize drives, and vet candidates and platforms. While speaking to the Brown Chapel AME

---

14. Dartunorro Clark, "Biden Says Four Black Women Are on His VP List but Won't Commit to Choosing One," *NBC News*, July 20, 2020.

15. Bill Barrow, "Inside Stacey Abrams' Strategy to Mobilize Georgia Voters," *Associated Press*, October 12, 2018.

Church in Selma, Alabama, on March 1, 2020, Abrams stated, "I hope my witness is always seen as one of perseverance. I may not have been the governor, but that didn't absolve me of the responsibility that my faith tells me I hold, which is to ensure that the marginalized, the voiceless, the disadvantaged, are able to be heard and to be served."[16]

Religious messages have been a part of Abrams's political campaigns, dating back to her "Boundless Belief" ad in her gubernatorial race that featured episodes of her faith in action and personal devotion.[17] Political scientist Andra Gillespie affirms how Abrams's Christian faith, moral witness, and church ties make her culturally disposed and trustworthy. "She's not going to go to the same places that everybody usually goes to because they only know a handful of Scripture," said Gillespie. "She's been around church her whole life, so, yeah, she's fluent in the Bible."[18] Abrams said she's going to keep up her message despite the disappointments along the way. "In this country, democracy is how we speak to those in power and how we determine who holds power," she said. "And that's my mission."[19]

The collective action of political actors like Stacey Abrams, LaTosha Brown, Atlanta Mayor Keisha Lance Bottoms, and the Black women of Alabama illustrates the forged-in-faith power of Black women, who often go unacknowledged as they lay the groundwork, carry the load, and keep the momentum going to its final destination. It was "women's work" of this nature that elected Doug Jones senator instead of Roy Moore, that flipped Georgia blue, that replaced incumbents Kelly Loeffler and David Perdue with Raphael Warnock and Jon Ossoff, that elected Nikema Williams as the first Black congresswoman from the Fifth District of Georgia, and that trumped the forty-fifth president's designs for a second term.

---

16. Adelle M. Banks, "Stacey Abrams' Passion for Voting Began with Her Preacher Parents," *Associated Press*, October 16, 2020.

17. Stacey Abrams, "Boundless Belief," YouTube, April 19, 2018, https://www.youtube.com.

18. Abrams, "Boundless Belief."

19. Abrams, "Boundless Belief."

Purple Reign: The Divinely Appointed Year of the Black Woman

The political victories hard fought and won by Black women's contextual analysis, cultural disposition, and collective action verify DNC Chairman Tom Perez's declaration that "Black women are the backbone of the Democratic Party," as he acknowledged the political victories of Black women in Virginia and Alabama.[20] But the catchy hashtag #BlackGirlMagic trending on social media and magazine cover stories fails to recognize Black women's perpetual labor to save democracy. Such trite slogans miss and render meaningless the actual point of such ongoing struggles. It is the social tenacity and political sagacity of Black women that may seem to be miraculous, but it's not magic at all. Seemingly, these so-called miracles only happened because Black women's activism, grounded in their freedom faith, reflects the sentiments found in Luke 4:18–19, a common refrain of liberationists: "The Spirit of the Lord is upon me, because [God] has anointed me to bring good news to the poor. [God] has sent me to proclaim release to the captives and recovery of sight to the blind, to let the oppressed go free, to proclaim the year of the Lord's favor."

Indeed, 2020 was the "year of the Black woman," but it should be noted that it was also marked by the freedom faith of Black women. To be sure, results in 2020 were built on the spiritual gumption and deliberate political work of not only the well-known historic women previously mentioned and their progenitors like Harriet Tubman, Sojourner Truth, Fannie Lou Hamer, Ida B. Wells, Ella Baker, Barbara Jordan, and Shirley Chisholm, but even more so on the efforts of unnamed and little-known faithful activists like Amelia Boynton Robinson, Selma marcher; Georgia Gilmore, chef and financier of Alabama bus boycotts; Claudette Colvin, teenage protester refusing her seat on a Montgomery, Alabama, bus before Rosa Parks did a retake of it; and the bloodshed of four little Black

---

20. Tom Perez (@TomPerez). 2021, "Let me be clear: "We won in Alabama and Virginia because #BlackWomen led us to victory. Black women are the backbone of the Democratic Party, and we can't take that for granted. Period," Twitter, December, 13, 2007, https://twitter.com.

girls in an Alabama Sunday school, professing their faith. Now, it is the contemporary Black women of Alabama who successfully mobilized and elected the first democratic candidate since 1992, the more than 98 percent of Black women who helped elect US former President Barack Obama (engineered by his wife, Michelle Obama, and billionaire Oprah Winfrey blazing the trail for his success). Additionally, in Alabama, 98 percent of Black women voted for Doug Jones.[21]

In all these instances, people fail to grasp the importance of religion in determining the moral motivation, worldviews, sense of civic duty, and how we draft laws. The role religion plays in US society remains enormous. No mode of religious witness or "work of the spirit"—either literally or figuratively—moves as profoundly or successfully as it does among Black women, and religion's impact on the US public scene reflects that reality. Black women have willingly and unwillingly sacrificed, slaved, and acted to help save democracy.

Nobody knew better than Joe Biden the odds he and the nation were up against in the 2020 presidential election. Biden was cognizant that his only chance of winning the campaign as well as the only hope of righting the multiple crises that had ransacked the country from the Covid-19 epidemic to Covid-45 depended on picking the best vice president to partner with him on his ticket. Having the hindsight of being in the vice-presidential seat himself, Biden understood how important the insight and integrity of a good vice president could be to a newly elected president. In turn, he knew a Black woman would not only be capable but was best suited for the role.[22]

His one-time rival for the 2021 presidential bid, Kamala Harris—this daughter of Jamaican and Indian immigrants—became central to accomplishing his presidential win. Harris became the first woman in American history to be elected to the executive. While she fully claims her biracial heritage and the love and nurture

---

21. Ben Jacobs, "The African American Voters at Heart of Doug Jones' Alabama Victory," *The Guardian,* December 13, 2017.

22. Clark, "Biden Says Four Black Women."

of her South Asian mother, Harris knew—just as her mother raised her to understand and embrace her identity—that her lot in life has always had ties to her manifestation as a Black woman. Harris knew that it was Shirley Chisholm's 1972 run for the US presidency that blazed the trail for her own success. She understood that it was the gift of Maxine Waters's repeated "reclaiming my time" that mirrored Harris's own bold proclamation "I'm speaking" in an effort to stop then Vice President Mike Pence from disrespecting her by talking over her comments during the one and only vice-presidential debate of the 2020 election. And she knew it was the work of women, unknown and known,[23] who were relentless in making sure that our country would be able to trump Trump by denying him a second term. Paying tribute to this fact, in the wake of the final election results declared on November 7, 2020, Harris said: "I want to speak directly to the Black women in our country. 'Thank you.' You are too often overlooked, and yet are asked time and again to step up and be the backbone of our democracy. We could not have done this without you."[24]

Without question, January 21, 2021, marked a turning page for America by the guiding hand of Black women. Madam Vice President Harris nodded to that fact by wearing purple to honor not only the color of the women's suffrage movement that led to the ratification of the Nineteenth Amendment in 1920, but also, as some have suggested, as a nod to Shirley Chisholm, the first Black woman elected to Congress, who also made a bid for the presidency in 1972 and wore suffragist purple, which stood for loyalty and hope.[25]

---

23. Like the more than 90 percent of Black women voters who were the single largest voting bloc for the Biden–Harris ticket, or Amelia Ward (owner of one of the nation's oldest Black press newspapers) who advanced, promoted and celebrated Harris when others doubted or derided her political ascension, or, of course, the Black female mayoral brigade and the soaring efforts and sky-high standards set by Michelle Obama and Stacey Abrams.
24. Suzette Hackney, "Black Voters Steer America Toward Moral Clarity in Presidential Race,"*USA Today*, November 12, 2020.
25. Sara M. Moniuszko, "Why Is Everyone Wearing Purple during Inauguration Week?" *USA Today*, January 21, 2021.

In the end, the action of Black women gave way to acknowledging the purple reign and collective power of the womanist witness, work, and worth of Black women who know where to place their faith. Purple is religiously symbolic, worn during Advent and Lent to symbolize sorrow and suffering in the Christian churches, and used to represent redemption in Judaism, mysticism in Buddhism, peace in Hinduism, and, for all religions and perhaps, most especially, Black women's spirituality, it has symbolized both faith and trust. January 21, 2021, celebrated a symbolic turning away from the damage and despair of the previous four years.

There are *kairos* moments that break into human history when people who were perennially forced to the margins of society are brought back into the center. Neither fear nor charity makes that change. Such change is always an uphill battle and a fight for one's rights. Defeating the divisive and apocalyptic activities of a Trump administration was not the first fight nor will it be the last for Black women. But their actions represent a divine moment in history. Indeed, purple has a special place for US women in politics, but Black women specifically have delved into its deepest shades and hues, taking up the mantle of what is just and doing so to move us out of the wilderness in the hopes of gaining all of us a parcel of the promised land.

CHAPTER 6

Democracy or Whiteness? Trumpism, White Christianity, and the Queer Justice Agenda

MARVIN M. ELLISON

> Queer rights are anything but distraction: they are a frontier, sometimes *the* frontier in the global turn toward autocracy.
> —Masha Geesen

In sharing her reaction to the outcome of the 2020 presidential election, a friend recently acknowledged that she finds herself struggling with contradictory feelings of relief and disappointment, feelings I share. While there's relief that Trump lost the election by a wide margin, making him a one-term president, there's also great disappointment—perhaps despair is more accurate—insofar as Trump received *even more* popular votes in 2020 than in 2016. Despite his mishandling of the Covid-19 pandemic, a steep rise in poverty and food insecurity, an imperiled global environment, and a wanton disregard for a national reckoning with the legacy of slavery and white supremacy's impact on politics, economics, and culture, more than 74 million people (46.9 percent of the electorate) voted to keep Trump in office. Far from a repudiation of Trumpism, this recent election highlights the deep divisions within the nation and underscores that the Trump movement will remain a force to be reckoned with for the foreseeable future. As journalist Katha Pollitt sums up the situation, "We may rid ourselves of Trump. But Trumpism? That will be with us for the rest of [my life] and maybe yours as well."[1]

Four years ago, while commenting on Trump's ascension to the White House, lifelong Republican Peter Wehner wagered that the problem with Trump would more likely be temperamental than ideological. "Donald Trump is a transgressive personality," Wehner observed. "He thrives on creating disorder, in violating rules, in provoking outrage.... For Mr. Trump, nothing is sacred." So, how would this bode for the country and world? Wehner surmised then, as many others have concluded since, that because "a man with illiberal tendencies, a volatile personality, and no internal checks [had become] president," it's likely that "this isn't going to end well."[2]

While I don't disagree about Trump's flawed character or minimize the probability of a bad ending, I believe we should focus less on Trump's disordered personality and more on the *Trump movement's disordered politics* of fear, its blatant hatred toward perceived enemies and the nonnormative Other, and its nostalgia for an imaginary past in which white political and cultural dominance were settled matters and people knew their places and kept them. As an autocratic movement, Trumpism stokes fantasies about the glorious past and the unassailable rule of a Strong Man to champion their cause, reassert white power, and restore their material and emotional security in a dangerous, increasingly alien world. Trump has eagerly positioned himself in this savior role, boasting that he alone can succeed where, by his estimate, "all others have failed."

As a self-aggrandizing bully, Trump has responded to, but also deftly cultivated, the pervasive fear, powerlessness, loneliness, and vulnerability among increasing numbers of people within a neoliberal social order that, for decades, has cast off more and more of

---

1. Katha Pollitt, "The Trump-Shaped Stain on American Life," *The Nation*, November 30/December 7 issue.
2. Peter Wehner, "Why I Cannot Fall in Line Behind Donald Trump," *New York Times Sunday Review*, January 22, 2017, 13.

its own as expendable "losers." Under the Trump regime, what has been called the "savagery of neoliberalism" has only intensified.[3] The wealth gap widens, prisons are overfilled, the environment suffers ever greater degradation, and the scale of social problems seems overwhelming. Those casually referred to as ordinary citizens have increasingly lost confidence in the capacity of democratic institutions to contain the super-rich or hold accountable those who abuse power.

From the start, the tone and worldview of the Trumpian "Make America Great Again" movement have been authoritarian, dividing the world between winners and losers and endangering democratic norms and institutions by undermining respect for the law, upending delicate systems of checks and balances, delegitimizing the media in its watchdog role, discrediting truth claims along with scientific and professional expertise, and, most disturbing of all, indulging in enemy making at every turn. Like other leaders with dictatorial ambitions, Trump has sought to dissuade his followers from investing in the common good by discrediting the cultural values necessary for sustaining cohesiveness amidst increasing cultural diversity, including a robust religious pluralism. By unashamedly promoting a white nationalist agenda, Trump and the Trumpian movement have, with mean spiritedness and cruelty, promoted a truncated vision of America, reducing "We the people" to those Trump loyalists who vote for, and financially support, the Trump agenda. Those not "in the count" are placed at heightened risk, especially Blacks in so-called inner-city wastelands, Mexicans and Central American refugees at the border, and immigrants from Muslim-majority countries. By insisting on putting "[white] America first," Trump and his base have signaled, loud and clear, that theirs is a restrictive preferential option: to protect and preserve all things white, male, heterosexual, and affluent within a white-supremacist social order.

This antidemocratic agenda is also a white *Christian* supremacist agenda. Ever since Lyndon Johnson signed the Civil Rights

---

3. Henry A. Giroux, "Militant Hope in the Age of Trump," *Tikkun*, January 8, 2017.

Act of 1964, socially conservative white Christians have flocked to the Republican Party, now even more explicitly the White Power party under Trump. A familiar national voting pattern has set in, in which white Christians vote almost exclusively for Republican candidates and policies while those whites affiliated with other religious traditions or identifying as religiously unaffiliated (the "nones") vote Democratic.[4] Taking the long view about these matters, this political alignment is nothing new for most white Christian churches. As Robert Jones analyzes in *White Too Long: The Legacy of White Supremacy in American Christianity*, it would be trouble enough if white, socially conservative Christians had been only complacent about, or merely complicit in, white supremacy. Far more problematic is the fact that, as the dominant cultural force throughout slavocracy, resistance to Reconstruction, Jim-and-Jane-Crow segregation, opposition to the civil rights movement, and more recently during the buildup of mass incarceration, white Christians "have been *responsible* for constructing and sustaining a project to protect white supremacy and resist black equality."[5] Because reactionary white politics and conservative white religion continue to operate so closely in tandem, it's not surprising that for many, "Christianity and a cultural norm of white supremacy now often feel indistinguishable, with an attack on the latter triggering a full defense of the former."[6]

In light of rapidly changing demographics and widespread predictions that by 2043 the United States will become a majority non-white nation, Trump has been able to exploit white fears about an increasingly diverse cultural landscape as anxieties have mounted about the loss of status and security in a hypercompetitive econ-

---

4. Robert P. Jones, *White Too Long: The Legacy of White Supremacy in American Christianity* (New York: Simon & Schuster, 2020), 15. In 2016, 81 percent of white evangelical Protestants voted for Donald Trump, but so did 57 percent of white mainline Protestants and 64 percent of white Catholics. In contrast, Hillary Clinton received 96 percent of votes cast by African American Protestants and 62 percent of white religiously unaffiliated voters.

5. Jones, *White Too Long*, 6.

6. Jones, *White Too Long*, 10.

omy. For white men this "fear of falling"⁷ is especially debilitating because they have been socialized to expect deferential treatment from others and regard their placement "on top" as God given. When they experience a humiliating decline in fortune and status or, even worse, observe that those "below them" are faring better than they, entitled men tend to become resentful and enraged, displaying what sociologist Michael Kimmel calls aggrieved entitlement. "The new American anger is more than defensive; it is reactionary," Kimmel explains. "It seeks to restore, to retrieve, to reclaim something that is perceived to have been lost. Angry White Men look to the past for their imagined and desired future. . . . Theirs is the anger of the entitled: we are entitled to those jobs, those positions of unchallenged dominance. And when we are told we are not going to get them, we get angry."

Under mounting threats of downward economic mobility and cultural displacement, white men also latch ever more firmly onto their racialized white identity because even though one may be at risk for losing everything else, at least the asset of whiteness remains. As Isabel Wilkerson analyzes in *Caste: The Origins of Our Discontents,* whiteness rescues one's endangered identity by granting "an inherited, unspoken superiority, a natural deservedness over subordinate castes." While radical democracy promises the security—and risk—of a shared humanity in a community of mutuality, in contrast, an unjust social order built on economic inequities and marked by hierarchies of superiority and inferiority operates with imperatives that make "equality feel like a demotion." In reflecting on the pervasive spiritual malaise that affects countless white Americans, Wilkerson asks poignantly, "Who are you if there is no one to be better than?"⁸

Contrary to Kimmel, I doubt that what Kimmel calls American anger or what W. E. B. DuBois called the wages of whiteness is all that new, given the scope of white racial resentments mani-

---

7. Barbara Ehrenreich, *Fear of Falling: The Inner Life of the Middle Class* (New York: Pantheon Books, 1989).
8. Isabel Wilkerson, *Caste: The Origins of Our Discontents* (New York: Random House, 2020), 180, 183.

fest throughout US history. However, with the rise of Trumpism, white male anger has intensified as downwardly mobile whites have watched the ascendance of Barack Obama as the first Black president, witnessed a vibrant LBGTQ movement obtain a wide range of civil rights, including the freedom to marry, and suffered through economic and cultural displacement at a more and more rapid pace. Thomas Edsall captures their plight this way:

> Less-educated white Americans feel that they have become "strangers in their own land." They see themselves as victims of affirmative action and betrayed by "line-cutters"—African-Americans, immigrants, refugees and women—who jump ahead of them in the queue for the American dream. They resent liberal intellectuals who tell them to feel sorry for the line-cutters and dismiss them as bigots when they don't.[9]

Tragically, such resentment can become blind fury, missing the mark by failing to critique the system of inequities that disempowers and penalizes all but the few and, instead, becoming wrongly fixated on a variety of scapegoats who can be blamed for hard times.

In promising to restore [white] America, Trump has, at the same time, pledged to reclaim the privileged status of white Christianity. While speaking at a conservative Christian college in Iowa during the 2016 campaign, Trump announced that he was totally prepared to defy conventions and violate social norms in pursuit of his restoration agenda, confident that he "could stand in the middle of Fifth Avenue and shoot somebody" and "wouldn't lose any voters." While it was that claim that made the newspaper headlines, it was another message from that same speech that more likely cemented the loyalty of his emerging base of white, evangelical Christian, noncollege educated, and rural Americans. It was to this "heartland" audience that Trump delivered his persuasive message about

---

9. Thomas B. Edsall, "The Peculiar Populism of Donald Trump," *New York Times*, February 2, 2017. Here Edsall is building on the work of sociologist Arlie Russell Hochschild in her 2016 study *Strangers in Their Own Land: Anger and Mourning on the American Right* (New York: New Press, 2016).

(white) Christian persecution and (white) Christian vindication: "I will tell you, Christianity is under tremendous siege. . . . And yet we don't exert the power that we should have." He promised that if white evangelicals elected him president, all that would change. "Christianity will have power. If I'm there, you're going to have plenty of power, you don't need anybody else. You're going to have somebody representing you very, very well. Remember that."[10]

Remember they did, and in 2016 and again in 2020, 81 percent of white evangelicals, along with strong majorities of both white mainline Protestants and white Catholics, voted to elect Trump to national office. Although evangelicals have long identified themselves as "values voters" who prize family, sexual morality, and biblical obedience above all else, in becoming captivated by Trump they have morphed into "nostalgia voters," energized by their shared determination to "redeem" the country as a "Christian nation" and reassert their social status—white and Christian—as politically and culturally normative. As Elizabeth Dias pointed out,

> Evangelicals did not support Mr. Trump in spite of who he is. They supported him *because* of who he is, and *because* of who they are. He is their protector, the bully who is on their side, the one who offered safety amid their fears that their country as they know it, and their place in it, is changing, and changing quickly. White straight married couples with children who go to church regularly are no longer the American mainstream. An entire way of life, one in which their values were dominant, could be headed for extinction. And Mr. Trump offered to restore them to power, as though they have not been in power all along.[11]

The disparaging of LBGTQ persons and rollback of gay rights are at the center of Trumpism's politics of restoration. The America to be made great again is white, Christian, and heteronormative, that is, decidedly not queer. Because transgenderism sharply dis-

---

10. Elizabeth Dias, "Christianity Will Have Power," *New York Times*, August 9, 2020. Emphasis in original.
11. Dias, "Christianity Will Have Power."

rupts the gender binary as natural, trans people, especially trans people of color, have been subjected to scorn, derision, and violence, all aimed to push them back into gender (and racial) conformity and thereby allow the cisgender cultural majority, pining for normalcy and certitude, to feel comfortable and at ease once again in a less complicated, less demanding cultural world.

Although it is probably accurate to say that Trump is not personally antigay, he has readily adopted an antigay stance as an essential weapon of his autocratic politics. Like other autocrats, Trump demands loyalty and tolerates no dissent. Like other autocrats, when confronted by an organized majority of voters who seek his ouster from office, he has refused to concede, refused to participate in the transition of power to the newly elected administration, and refused to acknowledge that his electoral defeat is anything but fraud and "fake news." But, make no mistake about it, like other autocrats, he has also intentionally stoked antigay sentiment. In promoting a nostalgic restoration politics, autocrats cater to their supporters' desire for simpler days, absent the kind of cultural upheavals that call into question conventional norms and practices. As Masha Geesen explains, "Nothing communicates Trump's commitment to the past as effectively as reversals of LGBT civil-rights progress—arguably the most rapid social change in American history."[12]

Following a pathway familiar to autocrats, Trump has curried the favor of white, socially conservative Christians by deliberately taking hold of something that exemplifies rapid change—in this instance the expansion of gay rights and rising support for transgender persons—and abruptly reversing its momentum. The Trump administration began this process of reversal on the first day he took office by removing from the White House website all references to LBGTQ persons or policies. Since then, Trump has sought to limit, if not eliminate entirely, the rights of trans military members, trans students, and queer adoptive and foster families, as well as to block access to health care and erect barriers for asylum

---

12. Masha Green, "How Trump Uses 'Religious Liberty' to Attack LGBT Rights," *New Yorker,* October 11, 2017.

seekers and others fleeing violence and persecution, an especially dangerous prospect for trans refugees. What is it like, then, to be queer in Trump's America? Hannah Murphy summarizes matters succinctly: "With remarkable efficiency, the [Trump] administration has embodied, emboldened, and enabled a vocal minority of Americans who believe that LGBTQ civil rights cannot coexist with their own." The result? "They've taken our seats at the national table and handed them to once-fringe hate groups; they've invited bigots out of the closet and tried to usher us back in."[13]

The diverse members of the queer community are only one among many other marginalized groups harmed by Trumpian policies and hateful rhetoric. Denied the respect and assurance of full civil and human rights owed to those who belong to "We the people," those on the margins share a common awareness, across our differences, that to be a robust democracy, this nation must include all persons and guarantee their full standing. As long as the United States embraces the skewed vision of itself as a white (Christian, heteronormative) nation, it cannot claim to be a democracy. An authentic democracy necessarily makes space for diverse peoples and shares—as a matter of justice, not charity—the goods, resources, and respect required by all to enjoy a dignified and safe life.

Justice-loving queers and other "misfits" recognize, quite soberly, that it is easier to vote one person out of office than it is to get rid of an authoritarian movement. Sadly, the Trumpian legacy most difficult to undo may be to recover from the soul corruption that has inhibited the everyday, ordinary exchange of "simple human decency." In pondering Katha Pollitt's claim that Trumpism has turned us into "a nation of braying bullies and conspiracy theorists and mean people proud of their indifference to the suffering of others,"[14] I think especially of those white, Christian, and predominately heterosexual people from whom the hatred and vitriol

---

13. Hannah Murphy, "What's It Like to Be Queer in Trump's America?" *Rolling Stone*, October 30, 2020. Murphy also documents how groups that vilify the LBGTQ community were identified in 2019 as the fastest-growing sector of hate groups.

14. Pollitt, "The Trump-Shaped Stain."

have largely emanated. When vast numbers of people in a divided nation refuse to recognize the humanity of those who do not look or love like them, but instead show contempt for the poor, the marginalized, and the less powerful, then our national crisis is as much moral and spiritual as it is political.

What kind of intervention might be sufficient to recover from this moral, spiritual, and political debacle? In the immediate aftermath of the November election, some quickly called upon Biden voters to reach out to Trump supporters in a gesture of reconciliation and unity and make an effort to "heal the nation." The presiding bishop of the Episcopal Church, Michael Curry, in an interview with *Religion News Service*, acknowledged that we're in a political mess, that we need "to figure out how to do the structural healing," and that it will be "hard work" to reach reconciliation, but he also insisted that "until you change hearts, you don't change" much of anything. For this reason, in encouraging the use of civil discourse programs such as "Better Angels" and "With Malice Toward None," Curry made a case for starting from the "common ground" of shared values, such as human decency and compassion. "You don't start from the differences," he advised. Further, the bishop suggested, as a practical first step, that folks from opposing sides "must go out and eat lunch together. When people eat together, over time, they actually get to know each other. And sometimes, a whole lot of stuff you assume about the other, you discover isn't true. At its best, you discover there's a story behind why that person thinks or feels the way they do. You may not agree with it, but you can kind of understand it."[15]

No doubt such efforts to locate common ground and build on shared values may make sense to those who have presumed all along that people backing Trump have been voting against their own interests and that, now that Trump has suffered defeat, they will "come around" and be open to switching loyalties or at least reconsidering options. Not so, counterargues Isabel Wilkerson,

---

15. Emily McFarlan Miller, "'You Can't Just Jump to Hope': Episcopal Presiding Bishop Michael Curry on Healing after the Election," *Religion News Service*, November 11, 2020.

who observes that the very large numbers of white people "voting this way were, in fact, *voting their interests*. Maintaining the [white racial] caste system as it had always been was in their interest," to such an extent that they were "willing to lose health insurance now, risk White House instability and government shutdowns, and external threats from faraway lands in order to preserve what their actions say they value most—the benefits they had grown accustomed to as members of the historically ruling caste in America."[16] Racial solidarity among whites was the decisive factor in determining how votes were cast. Moreover, as Chrissy Stroop observes, because many on the Christian Right view the world through the polarizing lens of spiritual warfare, they regard Democrats not as worthy opponents, but as demonic forces to be defeated. Enemy making in the Trump movement has reached such a fever pitch, Stroop writes, that "this much is clear: progress will not be made by pretending that unity and compromise are possible with people who regard you as literally evil."[17]

Religious studies scholar Eddie Glaude Jr. also warns against premature efforts to reach unity and reconciliation. In *Begin Again: James Baldwin's America and Its Urgent Lessons for Our Own*, Glaude candidly shares his perspective: "It seems to me," he writes, "that a large portion of white America today, especially white men, has lost its mind.... They are not going to listen; they don't want to know or hear the truths about the situation of black people. Theirs is a narrow concern: For them, this country must remain white."[18] This incapacity to enter into respectful, constructive dialogue and the inability to listen to and learn especially from those on the margins are, truth be told, characteristic of those inculcated over centuries into the habits and practices of white supremacy, a morally corrupting system that diminishes the humanity of the powerful as

---

16. Wilkerson, *Caste*, 326 and 324. Emphasis in original.
17. Chrissy Stroop, "Why Does Trump's Authoritarian Christian Base Ignore Never-Trump Evangelical Leaders?," *Religion Dispatches*, November 18, 2020.
18. Eddie S. Glaude, *Begin Again: James Baldwin's America and Its Urgent Lessons for Our Own* (New York: Crown, 2020), 144.

it aims to crush the life out of the powerless. The cumulative effect of prolonged exposure to supremacist thinking is to suffer a kind of willful ignorance, which blocks whites from paying attention to, or even really noticing, nonwhites and anyone else not at the center. As if that is not soul damaging enough, socially conservative Christianity's fixation on personal sin and moral purity has allowed its adherents to smother in "faux niceness" and a strained moral innocence, thereby giving themselves permission to ignore racial (and other kinds of) injustice and, more tellingly, discount their own hand in perpetuating systemic evil. White Christian theology's most powerful tool, Robert Jones explains, has been to constrict the scope of whites' moral vision, "render[ing] black claims to justice invisible while protecting white economic and social interests, all the while assuring [white people] of their own moral purity."[19]

In my judgment it would be a mistake to focus our energies on trying to "win over" or somehow "save" Trump supporters from themselves, who have shown no desire to give up their preferred comforts of whiteness or any interest in taking on the demands of living democratically. Restoring their moral character and making amends for their authoritarian bent is their work to do, not anyone else's. Instead, our moral energies should be directed at strengthening a genuinely multiracial, multicultural, and multifaith democracy by participating in grassroots social-justice advocacy and urgently pushing ourselves and our elected leaders to enact policies and practices to redress racial and other inequities and rebuild this nation. Along this score, it's worth mentioning three faith-based initiatives, among others, that offer resources for a progressive, multiracial justice agenda. The Poor People's Campaign, a national call for moral revival, is a model of grassroots mobilization that builds unlikely coalitions in order to advocate for social and economic justice. Auburn Seminary, in partnership with Columbia Law School's Law, Rights, and Religion Project, is promoting an expansive, justice-grounded moral vision of religious freedom in its project "All Faiths and None"; and the Baptist Joint Committee for

---

19. Jones, *White Too Long*, 75.

Religious Liberty (BJC) is gathering local and national support for its project, "Christians Against Christian Nationalism."

This is spiritual work. As queer religionists have come to appreciate, spirituality is about many things, including desire. Who do we desire to be, and with whom do we desire to live? Alas, these days, white Christianity invokes religious-liberty claims in order to discriminate "in good conscience," thereby refusing association with the nonnormative Other, for whom they do not wish to bake cakes, issue marriage licenses, share public restrooms, or serve alongside in the military. White repentance begins with repudiating such supremacist norms and practices. A queer social ethic, in contrast, is grounded in the belief that we are all common: we belong together, suffer together, and thrive together, or not. Queer moral wisdom also recognizes that there will be no healing or national reconciliation without substantial justice making, the kind that begins with truth telling about historical harms done, the parties responsible for the harm, and what must be done to repair the damage and set things right.

In order to engage wholeheartedly in movement building with diverse partners who are similarly energized by a radically inclusive moral vision, LBGTQ justice advocates have found it necessary—and liberating—to embrace the transformative power of coming out. The moral and spiritual discipline of coming out involves far more than publicly declaring one's identity or claiming self-respect, important as these are. To "come out" requires breaking with the tyranny of the status quo as inevitable and preferable ("It doesn't get any better than this"). Coming out is the ongoing pledge to identify with, and resist alongside, those suffering from injustice and refusing to give up. Casting our lot together requires, for whites, letting go of our "willful innocence" about white supremacy and, instead, making a steadfast commitment to use our power, personally and collectively, to help change social, economic, and cultural conditions so that all persons receive a fair share of goods, resources, and respect and can lay claim to the prospect of a good life. Therefore, Eddie Glaude names our moral, spiritual, and political life-work rightly: "Our task, then, is not to save Trump voters—it's not to convince them to give up their views that white people ought to matter more than others. Our task is to build a world where such a view has no place or quarter to breathe."[20]

At this moment of national division and personal uncertainty, our moral choice is clear: democracy or whiteness? Political consultant Cornell Belcher, in ruminating on this situation, predicts that "the future belongs to those who embrace a diverse America, not to those who reject it."[21] May this prediction be our prayer, and may we work to make it so.

---

20. Glaude, *Begin Again*, 112.
21. Cornell Belcher, "The Southern Strategy Is Dead; Here's to America's Future," *Washington Post*, November 27, 2020.

CHAPTER 7

Environmental Violence and the Postmodern Condition

AARON D. CONLEY

Any cursory inquiry into the Earth's changing climate will quickly encounter sensationalized and doomsday accounts of carbon dioxide levels, pollution, and fossil fuels, at least in the industrialized global North. Scientists have well-documented studies on rising greenhouse gases stemming back to the early days of the Industrial Revolution, and today have discovered microplastics in the snows atop Mt. Everest and in the waters at the bottom of the Mariana Trench. The frequency of tropical storms is increasing, now occurring in winter months, which have traditionally been their dormant season, bringing tons of waste to beaches in Indonesia, while washing away entire villages in Central America. It seems clear that the climate is changing faster than our willingness to curb our behavior as a countermeasure. From an ethical standpoint, what we are doing to our planet and correspondingly to our own neighborhoods has less and less potential for justification.

The problem of justification is one of the more pressing concerns of a post-Trump era. In the United States the concept of "truth" has stepped firmly into the liminal space carved out for it by postmodernity. Thrust forward in the labeling of "fake news," both knowledge itself and the authorities upon which it rests increasingly have become performance based and collected around the altars of alt-right attempts to "control the narrative." As a result, significant swaths of the US population find themselves huddling under the umbrellas of story telling that best confirm the world they want to see while demonizing all narratives that might call that myopic world into question. If the violent assault on the Capitol in Washington, DC, is any indication, the drum beats of denialism of counternarratives are getting louder.

This chapter provides an abbreviated account of the interplay between a worsening climate crisis and the thorough digestion of some of postmodernism's more problematic conditions brought about by the populous movement that culminated during the Trump years. Unfolding in three parts, we begin with a look into postmodernism's destabilization of truth claims with respect to social and economic dynamics observed between 2016 and 2020 in the United States. Then this essay turns more directly to what Rob Nixon calls "slow violence" against human and nonhuman groups that results from our climate crisis. Finally, we end with a specific call for self-reflexive thinking and action needed to work within our justification problems to rectify the imbalance of climate change and our seemingly insatiable capitalistic behavior.

Postmodernity, Truth, and Late Capitalism

Without a doubt, the concept of truth has been on the chopping block for quite a while now. One of the key markers of postmodernism, unsurprisingly, has been a destabilization of older normative authorities and power centers. Jean-François Lyotard outlined as much in his 1979 book, *The Postmodern Condition*, wherein he defines postmodernism simply as an "incredulity towards metanarratives."[1] If the Enlightenment in Europe culminated with modernism with its fortified gaze on the "new," and modernism was the attempt to fold all knowledge into tidy grand theories, such as Darwin's theory of evolution, then postmodernism is the shift to *petit l'écrit*, or small narratives that operate according to more

---

1. Jean-François Lyotard, *The Postmodern Condition: A Report on Knowledge*, trans. Geoff Bennington and Brian Massumi (Minneapolis: University of Minnesota Press, 1984 [1979]), xxiv.

decentralized locations of authority. These small narratives abide by their own "language games" and bubble up to rival one another for dominance in the cauldron that is the postmodern condition.[2]

Small narratives are exactly that: localized stories derived from local communities that carry meaning or truth for that community. According to Lyotard, language is the mode that carries meaning. If we no longer credulously accept the meanings supplied by the grand narratives, but meaning is still conveyed primarily through language, then those who can understand and control the rules of language (language games) are those whose knowledge, or truth, will garner wider acceptance. What is more, if language carries the burden of communicating truth, then scientific data does not stand on its own, or is not self-evident. Any data must undergo a successful performance to convince stakeholders of its veracity before it can be deemed true or correct: the better the performance, the more likely it will be accepted as true.

Throughout the Trump presidency, the world witnessed postmodern dynamics in full swing. "Fake news" became a negating concept in the struggle to delegitimize counterclaims to what Trump's administration wanted to promote. In turn and in the spirit of a true dualism, every positive claim of information the administration heralded was upheld as legitimate. For example, Trump repeatedly claimed at the beginning of his term in office that he would restore the coal industry and downplay investments in renewable energy sources. He repeated this narrative despite the counterevidence suggesting the decline in the coal industry had more to do with direct competition with lower-priced natural gas instead of renewables. "Coal" became a sign in his language game for blue-collar jobs and a version of traditionalism wrapped inside his larger claims to "make America great again.[3]

Playing this legitimation game over and over strengthened the social bonds of Trump's supporters across the nation, and indeed the world, because it clarified the parameters in which his narrative

---

2. Lyotard, *The Postmodern Condition*, 9–17.
3. Samantha Gross, "What Is the Trump Administration's Track Record on the Environment?" *Policy 2020 Brookings*, August 4, 2020.

operates. The decisions to pull the United States out of the Paris Climate Agreement, to largely defund and understaff the Environmental Protection Agency (EPA), and open up national monuments and wildlife zones to resource extraction did more than simply set a tone for his priorities; the decisions strengthened the language games that determine what is true and what the "liberal media" wants to deceive everyone else into thinking is true. The more often he and his administration cried foul on competing small narratives, the stronger his social bond grew.

While Lyotard's discussion of the postmodern condition gave a passing nod to the increasing place of governments and corporations, it does little to account for the role of narratives within capitalistic forces.[4] Fredric Jameson adds the additional comparisons needed to bridge the socio-political with the economic postmodern condition. He states that postmodernism is the "consumption of sheer commodification as a process."[5] Indeed, in 2017 the United States was consuming almost twenty million barrels of petroleum per day, which was responsible for 76 percent of its greenhouse gas (GHG) emissions.[6] Nearly two-thirds of global GHG emissions came from manufacturing and other industrial processes, not including transportation, used to supply the world's stores with consumable goods.[7] Given that growth in these consumption trends have only increased unabated until Covid-19 caused a shutdown of global activities underscores Jameson's pairing of postmodernism with late capitalism's drive for unabated consumption.

Jameson goes on to claim, "this whole global, yet American, postmodern culture is the internal and superstructural expression of a whole new wave of American military and economic domination throughout the world: in this sense, as throughout class his-

---

4. Lyotard, *The Postmodern Condition*, 8–9.
5. Fredric Jameson, *Postmodernism, or, the Cultural Logic of Late Capitalism* (Durham, NC: Duke University Press, 1991), x.
6. "Fossil Fuels," Environmental and Energy Study Institute, https://www.eesi.org.
7. "Global Greenhouse Gas Emission Data," United States Environmental Protection Agency, https://www.epa.gov.

tory, the underside of culture is blood, torture, death, and terror."[8] Lyotard's concern for new forms of the legitimation of knowledge finds its consequences here: knowledge and power are inextricably linked. The scientifically agreed-upon consensus that the climate crisis is directly linked with industrialization and the very industrialization that has given rise to global capital cut at the heart of capitalism as a grand narrative struggling to retain its dominance. When "jobs" and the "economy" become worth more than the lives of our global inhabitants, as in the example of shut-downs in the wake of Covid-19, the veil lifts enough to see the violence upon which we in the global North maintain our habits of life. It is to this violent underbelly of capital and climate that we next turn.

Slow Violence Speeding Up

The climate crisis deepens, irrespective of the postmodern language games in play, and the impacts are evident in more and more ways. The umbrella of "climate crisis" is much larger than melting ice caps and starving polar bears. It includes rapidly increasing extinction of species as their habitats unalterably change, the ever-burning gas plumes in the oil fields in the Niger Delta, and the poisoned water in Flint, Michigan. It also includes the mass consumers and producers of waste from material goods and energies that often find their way onto the shores of poorer nations. As difficult as direct causation might be to prove on such a massive scale, the climate crisis is human caused, which means those of us benefiting most from Jameson's "consumption of sheer commodification" are also responsible for the increased climate-related suffering inflicted on Earth's many biomes.

"Slow violence" is the germane term used by Rob Nixon for the host of causalities the amplifying climate crisis leaves in its wake. In direct contrast to the types of sensational and eruptive violence we are accustomed to by all our media outlets, slow violence is "a violence that is neither spectacular nor instantaneous but instead incremental, whose calamitous repercussions are postponed for

---

8. Jameson, *Postmodernism*, 5.

years or decades or centuries."⁹ It is slow because, for example, the widescale ramifications of a depleted or poisoned water supply are not immediately visible, nor does the civil unrest in regions rich with resources always point directly to climate in the line of causality.

Violence is present whether it happens in our backyard or not, and learning about the stories of slow violence can bring it into clearer view. Nixon claims, "if slow violence is typically underrepresented in the media, such underrepresentation is exacerbated whenever (as typically happens) it is the poor who become its frontline victims, above all the poor in the Southern Hemisphere."¹⁰ He goes on to say, "Impoverished societies located mainly in the global South often have lax or unenforced environmental regulations, allowing transnational corporations (often in partnership with autocratic regimes) the liberty to exploit resources without redress."¹¹ Ken Saro-Wiwa's story provides a fitting example. Fighting for the livelihood of his Ogoni people and land in the Niger Delta, he went up against Shell Oil Company in the early 1990s. Prior to this, Nigeria opened its doors to transnational corporations such as Shell around the same time their civil war ended in 1970. Within two decades, the slow violence of climate change among local Ogoni and the Delta region had become such a hotbed for corruption and exploitation that massive localized movements arose in opposition.

Saro-Wiwa was a key player in the funding and organization of these movements. He spoke about the environmental devastation of his region as a type of "lethal weapon in the war against the indigenous Ogoni people," which itself is an acknowledgment of the very real and violent consequences of the climate crisis.¹² The quest for oil led to spills, gas flairs lasting decades, infertile farmlands, and acid rain. In 1993, Shell and the local army arrested

---

9. Rob Nixon, "Slow Violence," *The Chronicle Review*, June 26, 2011, www.chronicle.com.
10. Nixon, "Slow Violence."
11. Nixon, "Slow Violence."
12. Quoted in Nixon, *Slow Violence and the Environmentalism of the Poor* (Cambridge, MA: Harvard University Press, 2011), 111.

Saro-Wiwa on trumped-up charges for the murder of some of his own Ogoni leaders. In prison he managed to garner attention from the international press who then put pressure on Shell, resulting in marginal "greenwashing" of Shell's image as they allotted a miniscule amount of funds for clean-up efforts and direct Ogoni reparations, but Shell did little to alter their extraction of oil.[13]

Saro-Wiwa was an intellectual and no stranger to tracing the lines of collusion between governments and corporations. Fully aware of the ways the British government aided the global efforts of Shell, he described how "these organizations find it easier to exploit Nigeria through the military dictatorships."[14] Saro-Wiwa knew that his efforts to challenge corporate destruction would likely end in his death. In the winter of 1995, Saro-Wiwa was executed by a military tribunal. Perhaps it was his steadfast commitment to the Ogoni cause that led to the continued pressure on Shell. In 2009 the oil company settled out of court for $15.5 million with the families of the Ogoni leaders whom Saro-Wiwa was falsely accused of killing.

The slow violence Ken Saro-Wiwa fought against culminated in conventional violence as he challenged the centrality of the utilitarian narrative of Shell and colluding governments. He saw himself as a member of a community comprised of both people and soil that was suffering under the weight of supply and demand chains. As such, "the condition of Africa is bound to that of the world," to borrow the words of Wangari Maathai, who worked for decades with the Green Belt Movement to resist governmental and corporate environmental destruction on the other side of the continent.[15] Her exhortation that we "all share one planet and are one humanity" is an inescapable reality as the slow violence inevitably makes its presence felt in all regions on the globe.[16]

---

13. Ken Saro-Wiwa, *Silence Would Be Treason: Last Writings of Ken Saro-Wiwa,"* ed. Ide Corley, Helen Fallon, and Laurence Cox (Dakar, Senegal: CODESRIA, 2013), 119.

14. Saro-Wiwa, *Silence Would Be Treason*, 73.

15. Wangari Maathai, *The Challenge for Africa* (New York: Anchor Books, 2009), 4.

16. Maathai, *The Challenge for Africa*, 4.

Ethical Thinking within a Postmodern Condition

The African continent with its examples of environmental destruction following corporate and governmental faults, deliberate or otherwise, is no outlier on the planet. Even a tertiary scratching of the surface will reveal slow violence at work, from deforestation in the Philippines to the oil sands in Canada. Trump performed denialist narratives over and over again and offered "MAGA" as justification. Centering a denialist human-caused climate change narrative shifts the focus away from slow violence and places emphasis instead on traditionally conservative talking points. It is doubtful that followers persuaded by these narratives actually want violence to result from their insistence on those talking points. Jeremy Brecher claims, "Climate destruction is not the result of actions by people whose aim is to destroy the climate. Rather, it results from people operating within institutional structures in which they pursue goals and practices the effect of which—whether they know it or not—is climate destruction."[17] Thus, we return to the problem of justification for measurable violence experienced in greater proportion by the global South.

Hannah Arendt proves helpful when navigating a seemingly well-meaning or duty-driven citizenry whose actions and policies prove destructive. Witness to the famous Otto Adolf Eichmann trial in Israel in the decades following World War II, Arendt marveled at his lack of self-reflexivity. Eichmann maintained his innocence even against the hard evidence of his role in orchestrating one of the most horrifying genocides in modern history. Had Germany won the war, the rules would not have changed, and he would have been praised for his actions, or, stated in postmodern terms, his team lost the language game and the winners enforced a new set of rules in which he was deemed guilty. Arendt describes such banality as "something quite factual, the phenomenon of evil deeds, committed on a gigantic scale, which could not be traced to any particularity of wickedness, pathology, or ideological conviction of

---

17. Jeremy Brecher, *Climate Insurgency: A Strategy for Survival* (Boulder, CO: Paradigm Publishers, 2015), 61.

the doer, whose only personal distinction was perhaps extraordinary shallowness."[18] Eichmann's refusal to compare his narrative to the measurable evidence of another narrative reveals his "authentic inability to think."[19] Even in the face of his own execution he parroted stock phrases and slogans consistent with his Nazi ideological commitments, and, in so doing, he shielded himself from the violent realities left in his wake.[20]

For Arendt, thinking is a "world building" process, whereby knowledge of the world joins in the self-reflexive process of identifying the limits of our own story.[21] This building is the very definition of "con-science."[22] Our capacity and need to think across competing narratives must become a new imperative while avoiding the trappings of both metanarratives and fetishizing small narratives. Trump has shown how myopic small narratives can be, and Lyotard and Jameson outline the dangers of universalizing metanarratives and their tendencies to repress ideologies into the "political unconsciousness."[23] If humans share in the capacity to think (broadly) and to know (specifically), it will be in this distinction that we ought to be able to derive ethical standards for addressing the climate crisis while also holding one another accountable within a postmodern condition. Arendt asserts, "If the ability to tell right from wrong should have anything to do with the ability to think, then we must be able to 'demand' its exercise in every sane person no matter how erudite or ignorant, how intelligent or stupid he may prove to be."[24]

Arendt's call for thinking as a world-building task might be better framed as a world-restoring task given the severity of the climate crisis. The social polarization around postmodern narratives solidified the rules of language games that mirror late capitalism's

---

18. Hannah Arendt, "On Thinking and Moral Considerations," *Social Research* 38, no. 3 (1971): 417.
19. Arendt, "On Thinking and Moral Considerations," 417.
20. Arendt, "On Thinking and Moral Considerations," 418.
21. Arendt, "On Thinking and Moral Considerations," 421.
22. Arendt, "On Thinking and Moral Considerations," 418.
23. Jameson, *Postmodernism*, 329.
24. Jameson, *Postmodernism*, 422.

abusive principles of scarcity and overconsumption. When abiding only by one's own convenient truths that reinforce denialist ideologies, the person or group divorces themselves from the responsibilities of wider contexts. Simply ignoring other narratives does not absolve the ethical duties contained therein. Instead of seeing narratives in active competition, is it possible to see the diversity of narratives as a source of enrichment rather than as divisive, to borrow the language of Emilie Townes out of context?[25]

Where do we go from here? Ockham's razor will not suffice; no single answer will rectify the damage already inflicted on our climate. There is no bringing back annihilated species or undoing the slow violence inflicted on fellow humans. Any response to this all-important crisis must be as multifarious as the problem reflects. Here governmental policy must pressure corporate interests for accountability while corporations must follow up with global suppliers to ensure they are receiving goods through earth-sustaining practices. On both large and small scales, the telling and retelling of stories like that of Ken Saro-Wiwa is a good place to start in the building of a new global solidarity. A self-reflexive awareness of the limits of our own narratives might better equip us to see how unchecked consumption comes at the expense of the Ogoni's loss of farmable land, Flint's access to potable water, and micro-plastics everywhere in between. If we fail to deal reflexively and in global solidarity, the slow violence will accelerate to match the rate of climate change itself, and we stand little hope of finding our collective way through it.

---

25. Emilie M. Townes, *Womanist Ethics and the Cultural Production of Evil* (New York: Palgrave Macmillan, 2006), 71, 157.

CHAPTER 8

Environmental Racism in the "True" America: A Reflection on Race, the Earth, and Moral Action after Trump

TRAD NOGUEIRA-GODSEY AND
ELAINE NOGUEIRA-GODSEY

In 2016, just ten days after the election of Donald J. Trump to the presidency of the United States, the authors and our two children boarded a plane and said farewell to South Africa one final time and looked forward to the next chapter of our lives in Ohio. Like so many others, we had only just begun to seriously consider what a Trump presidency might mean for us, because polling, pundits, and conventional wisdom had told us that Hillary Clinton had virtually no chance of losing to Trump's misogynistic, racist, climate-denying, xenophobic platform. Trad grew up in Alabama but had started a new family in Cape Town, South Africa, with Elaine, a Brazilian PhD student at the time, and her two children, Natalia and Lucas. The immigration process, as anyone who has immigrated to the United States can confirm, was arduous, stressful, expensive, and time consuming. We began the process seven months before we arrived, but with only ten days before our departure the news of Trump's victory cast a new shadow over the land of opportunity—a shadow cast by billboards suggesting America needed to be made great again, presumably by barring from it immigrant families like ours.

The Nogueira-Godsey family settled in middle Ohio, a state Trump carried in 2016 and 2020. On January 6, 2020, we watched in horror with many others as MAGA-hatted Trump supporters, many from our own state and possibly even our community, gathered in Washington, DC, believing the lie from Donald Trump that the election he lost two months prior was fraudulent and that a Trump victory was stolen by the opposition. Addressing the nation as the president-elect following a violent and deadly attack on the United States Capitol by a mob of Trump supporters, Joe Biden sought to restore calm and confidence in American democracy. "The scenes of chaos at the Capitol do not reflect the true America."[1] This sentiment was echoed in Twitter posts and interviews with declarations of "This is not who we are."[2] While the intent of such statements is meant, at least superficially, to condemn and shame the actions of the insurrectionists and promote "American values," it also signals a return to the myths that comfort white Christian patriots. This became clearer when President-elect Biden declared, "America is about honor, decency, respect, tolerance. That's who we are. That's who we've always been."

Suggesting that America in 2021 can be characterized with terms like "honor, decency, respect and tolerance" does not sound like the naïve optimism popularly associated with America. It sounds like a denial of reality. Many have pushed back on this sentiment, such as Democratic Representative Norma J. Torres of California, who demonstrated how to condemn the attack without retreating into myths of American exceptionalism by stating plainly: "It's horrible that this is America."[3] American denialism is often cloaked in an aspirational tone to make it appear virtuous, but that veil was torn

---

1. Biden's full remarks to the nation on January 6, 2021, can be viewed at https://www.c-span.org/video/?507742–1/president-elect-biden-at-hour-democracy-unprecedented-assault.

2. https://twitter.com/RepNancyMace/status/1346890373319299073.

3. "Mob Attack, Incited by Trump, Delays Election Certification," *New York Times*, January 6, 2021.

away when Americans elected Donald Trump in 2016 and 74.2 million Americans sought to elect him again in 2020. Moreover, the assault at the Capitol on January 6 was carried out by Americans who wanted the country and the world to see "who we are," as they took photos and videos, posted scenes and commentary to social media, and with zealous pageantry waved symbols of racism and hate. As this spectacle of hubristic white privilege unfolded, many Americans were grappling with death on a scale not seen in several generations. Data confirmed that Latinx and Black Americans were dying at over twice the rate of white Americans from the novel coronavirus (Covid-19) due to the systemic and environmental racism that has been steering vulnerabilities to Black and brown communities for generations.[4]

If there is hope for the post-Trump future, it does not lie in propping up the myths of "who we are" but in the reckoning of what "we" really means. Donald Trump speaks to white resentment, whereas Joe Biden speaks to white fragility; and therein both perpetuate the myth that America is a white nation, either explicitly and proudly as Trump does or implicitly by privileging the fragile identities of white Americans who cannot bear to accept that Trump's racism is only the most distasteful and unfashionable of the racisms America inflicts upon nonwhites. In this chapter, we explore how environmental racism differs from but is compounded by the "spectacular racism" of the Trump era to create a crisis that threatens American democracy and the lives of nonwhite people living in America.[5] As we will see, Donald Trump is only one archetype of racism, but one that has leveraged other, preexisting forms of racism to traumatize communities and individuals in a time when climate change is destabilizing weather systems and ecosystems. The

---

4. Harriet A. Washington, "How Environmental Racism Is Fueling the Coronavirus Pandemic," *Nature Research Journals*, May 19, 2020.

5. "Spectacular racism" is a term introduced by Laura Pulido, Tianna Bruno, Cristina Faiver-Serna, and Cassandra Galentine, "Environmental Deregulation, Spectacular Racism and White Nationalism in the Trump Era," *Annals of the American Association of Geographers* 109, no. 2 (2019): 520–32, with direct reference to the Trump administration, and it will be discussed later in the chapter.

world watches the proliferation of natural disasters, pandemics, sea-level rise, and dwindling biodiversity with the knowledge that the most and worst suffering will be borne by people of color. In the same way that Trump spews racist hate and Biden comforts with fairy tales of a nonracist America, religion has segregated around the same motifs, with Trump's most committed supporters being white evangelicals and many other Christians looking for shelter to weather this storm. If religion is to have a positive or generative role in the coming years, it must avoid settling into either of these modes of existence. Religions that already have settled are obstacles in the way of moral action required to sustain the Earth organism and the survival of humanity.

Spectacular Racism

Even before launching his 2016 presidential campaign, when Donald Trump promoted false claims that then-President Barack Obama was ineligible to be the commander-in-chief because of what became known as "birtherism,"[6] such claims were debunked and rightly identified as racist. It should not have been surprising that both of Trump's presidential campaigns and his presidency were steeped in racism—from the rhetoric, to the advisors and cabinet appointees, to executive actions. Even when challenged on his racism early in the campaign, Trump dismissed it by repeating, "I am the least racist person anyone has ever known."[7] The examples of racism from the Trump administration are too many to list and too sickening to contemplate for very long. The "least racist" president ended his term coining the racist phrase "kung flu"[8] and inciting a mob of Confederate flag-waving racists to riot their way into the Capitol while threatening politicians

---

6. Though Trump was not the first to accuse Obama of being born outside the United States, he arguably had the most influence in spreading the false accusation. For a more in-depth account of "birtherism," see Adam Serwer, "Birtherism of a Nation," *The Atlantic*, May 13, 2020.

7. Spoken on multiple occasions; see Donald Trump, *Tulsa Oklahoma Rally*, June 20, 2020, https://www.youtube.com/watch?v=fN2tgtcKGck.

8. Trump, *Tulsa Oklahoma Rally*, June 20, 2020.

with medieval executions. Donald Trump is not merely a racist. He is a spectacular racist.[9]

Laura Pulido et al. introduced the term "spectacular racism" in their analysis that shows a relationship between racism and environmental deregulation in Donald Trump's first year as president. This term draws on the work of Rob Nixon, who coined the term "slow violence" to refer to the violence that "occurs gradually and out of sight," as opposed to violence that is spectacular and explosive.[10] "Spectacular racism," in their analysis, refers to the overt racism associated with white supremacist movements and frequently employed by Donald Trump. Here, racism is "spectacular" because it is shamelessly transgressive and is intended to be a spectacle to keep media and public attention fixed while other misdeeds, such as unprecedented environmental deregulation, are overshadowed.[11]

Unsurprisingly, Donald Trump's spectacular racism was frequently the subject of news broadcasts throughout his single term. After the tragic events that occurred in Charlottesville, Virginia, in 2017, in which a young neo-Nazi murdered a young woman and injured more than twenty other protestors after purposefully driving his car into a crowd of counterprotestors who had gathered in response to the planned protest by various white supremacist groups, Donald Trump famously refused to condemn the attack and claimed that there were "fine people on both sides." The presidential debates of 2020 were consumed by Trump's teasing of support for white supremacists and shifting blame for the coronavirus pandemic he failed to address. Throughout the Trump presidency, spectacular racism became a motif in presidential statements, Tweets, and executive actions and served as a lightning rod for breaking news and late-night talk show comedic punditry.

Trump's spectacular racism is an anomaly produced by a sociopathic narcissist and is not "who we are." As relieved as many of us were that Trump and his racist rhetoric were denied a second

---

9. Pulido et al., "Environmental Deregulation," 520–32.
10. Rob Nixon, *Slow Violence and the Environmentalism of the Poor* (Cambridge, MA: Harvard University Press, 2011), 2.
11. Pulido et al., "Environmental Racism," 521.

term in office, the comfort is cold. In the lead up to the election, Democratic nominee for president, Joe Biden, frequently criticized Trump for his racist rhetoric. In July of 2020, in a virtual-town-hall meeting, Biden said, "The way [Trump] deals with people based on the color of their skin, their national origin, where they're from, is absolutely sickening." Biden followed his charge with a dangerously false assertion of his own, "No sitting president has ever done this. Never, never, never. No Republican president has done this. No Democratic president. We've had racists, and they've existed. They've tried to get elected president. He's the first one that has."[12] The media attention in Trump's 2016 campaign to the question "Is Trump a racist?" paved the way for a shocking denial of history. The farcical "debate" over whether or not Trump is a racist perpetuated the myth that racism is a relic from the past and exists only in fringe pockets in the United States. All of this works to redefine racism along narrow lines that miss the real impact of racism on individuals, on ethnic groups, on American society, and on the Earth.

Biden has a reputation for making gaffes, but to suggest that Trump is the "first" racist president is inexcusable for even a high school student in American history class. It also conceptualizes racism as if it were smallpox or a flock of dodo birds that "have existed." The cold comfort referred to above emerges from this kind of thinking—that rejecting Trumpism is to reject racism. In reality, it seems that it is the "spectacle" of Trump's spectacular racism that is being rejected, not the racism. Trump's spectacular racism is certainly sickening, but defining racism broadly by it is irresponsible and invites a return to a slower, more refined racism. In the analysis of Trump's spectacular racism and environmental deregulation, Pulido et al. found that "environmental issues were far more likely to be concrete actions, whereas racism was more likely to be rhetorical."[13] This finding demonstrates how important

---

12. Will Weissert, "Joe Biden Calls Trump the Country's 'First' Racist President," *Associated Press*, July 22, 2020.

13. Pulido et al., "Environmental Racism," 529.

it is that we understand and differentiate Donald Trump's "spectacular racism" from other forms of racism. Even more to the point, it reveals the insidious racism in environmental deregulation that is much more devastating, potentially to the point of genocide.

Environmental Racism

In contrast to spectacular racism, systemic racism is faceless and insidious. As quickly as spectacular racism began to dominate public discourse with presidential approval, it can recede to the whispers and "isolated incidents" where it lived prior to the rise of MAGA.[14] Systemic racism does not require whispers or words to inflict violence. As the novel coronavirus (Covid-19) reached global pandemic proportions, all the nations of the world were facing a common, indiscriminate threat. Yet, the impact of this pandemic is far from indiscriminate. American Public Media published "The Color of Coronavirus: 2020 Year in Review" in December of 2020 in which Andi Egbert and Kristine Liao presented research on Covid-19 mortality and race. They found that during the pandemic, "Indigenous, Black and Latino Americans [were] at least 2.7 times more likely to die than their White neighbors."[15]

Unlike spectacular racism, which traffics hate and fear, systemic racism traffics in vulnerabilities. More specifically, it funnels vulnerabilities to specific population groups. Environmental racism, a term coined by Benjamin Chavis,[16] refers to the manipulation of the consequences of human systems of consumption, such as polluted air and contaminated water, to affect some populations

---

14. MAGA stands for Make America Great Again, a Trump campaign slogan in both 2016 and 2020.

15. Andi Egbert and Kristine Liao, "The Color of Coronavirus: 2020 Year in Review," *APM Research Lab*, https://www.apmresearchlab.org/covid/deaths-2020-review.

16. Robert D. Bullard, "Toxic Waste and Race at Twenty 1987–2007: A Report Prepared for the United Church of Christ Justice & Witness Ministries" (Cleveland: United Church of Christ and Witness Ministries, 2007), viii.

more than others. In the 1987 groundbreaking study, "Toxic Waste and Race," it was found that racial identity was "the most potent variable in predicting where commercial hazardous waste facilities were located in the U.S."[17] More than two decades after this finding, Laura Pulido found that even "scholars of environmental racism have not seriously problematized racism, opting instead for a de facto conception based on malicious, individual acts."[18] It is no surprise, then, that racism is not well defined for the average person. It is often, as was the case with Trump, alleged only in reference to a specific utterance or act and then diluted with semantic equivocation and shrouded with ambiguous intent. In reality, racism is literally all around us. We imbue our institutions, our governance, our economic machinations, and even the natural world with our racism.

When detached from a human body, this form of racism is more destructive because it is both shielded from accountability and perpetuates racist attitudes and thinking as not only normative but even natural. Covid-19 has provided a clear example of how far our racism extends beyond us. Covid-19 is more fatal among Black and brown populations in the United States because the United States has shifted the vulnerabilities created by the harm racism inflicts upon the environment to Black and brown bodies. This fact has been empirically demonstrated in a number of studies, many of which were conducted before the discovery of the novel coronavirus. In 2018, a study by Christopher W. Tessum et al. quantified "pollution inequity" and found that air pollution (fine particulate matter, $PM_{2.5}$) is "disproportionately caused by consumption of goods and services mainly by the non-Hispanic white majority, but disproportionately inhaled by black and Hispanic minorities." They found that white people in America experience about 17 percent less air-pollution exposure than is caused by their own consumption, while Black and Hispanic people in America "on average

---

17. Bullard, "Toxic Waste and Race," x.
18. Laura Pulido, "Rethinking Environmental Racism: White Privilege and Urban Development in Southern California," *Annals of the Association of American Geographers* 90, no. 1 (2000): 12.

experience a "pollution burden" of 56 percent and 63 percent excess exposure, respectively, relative to the exposure caused by their consumption."[19]

The pollution inequity presented above allows researchers to explain the disparate mortality of Covid-19 along racial lines even when other relevant variables are present. In other words, we can see this vulnerability caused by pollution inequity even after accounting for differences in income, access to health care and education, professional hazards associated with employment, and other inequities that had already ensured that racial minorities would suffer more and die at a higher rate than white Americans. As more data are generated, greater disparity and inequity are coming to light. It was also discovered that the Navajo Nation is experiencing the highest *per capita* infection rate of Covid-19 of any ethnic or racial group, and links with environmental racism are already being found.[20] These are only the most recent examples of why we must think of climate change as, in the words of Christian ethicist Cynthia Moe-Lobeda, "a central moral issue of the early twenty-first century."[21]

There Is No "First"

Indeed, racism is a human invention, and nature, of course, is not inherently racist. Human domination over nature does, however, imprint it with our prejudices. Ghassan Hage, who explored the environmental threat posed by Islamophobia, notes that "[racism] reinforces and reproduces the dominance of the basic social structures that are behind the generation of the environmental crisis—

---

19. Christopher W. Tessum et al., "Inequity in Consumption of Goods and Services Adds to Racial-Ethnic Disparities in Air Pollution Exposure," *Proceedings of the National Academy of Sciences* 116, no. 13 (2019): 6001.

20. Nicholet Deschine Parkhurst, Kimberly Huyser, and Aggie Yellow Horse, "Historical Environmental Racism, Structural Inequalities, and Dik'os Ntsaaígíí-19 (COVID-19) on Navajo Nation," *Journal of Indigenous Social Development* 9, no. 3 (2020): 127–40.

21. Cynthia D. Moe-Lobeda, "Climate Change as Climate Debt: Forging a Just Future," *Journal of the Society of Christian Ethics* 36, no. 1 (2016): 27.

which are the structures of its own generation."[22] Not only does racism fuel and compound the environmental crisis, but it also reproduces our racism in the environmental crisis. Worse, it depersonalizes our racism when it boomerangs back from the natural world, which makes accountability and responsibility that much easier to evade.

This aspect of American racism is particularly troubling and relevant to Hage's discourse on Islamophobia, because twenty years after the terrorist attacks of September 11, 2001, Muslims and Arabic speakers around the world are still charged with the responsibility of domesticating their religion because the United States has used its power, influence, and military to hold them accountable. The United States has waged a twenty-year global campaign of violence and intimidation against Islam for the actions of a few extremists, yet it does not even occur to most white Christians that their whiteness or Christianity must give account for either the spectacularly racist rhetoric or the years of systemic and environmental racism that has placed people of color in positions of vulnerability, acting as human shields to bear the brunt of the consequences for anthropogenic climate change.

Humans and human systems imprint their racism onto natural systems in their violence toward nature, and that violence is passed on by the natural world onto Black, brown, and indigenous bodies first and mercilessly while the privileged, who contribute most to the initial violence, are able to shield themselves while lamenting the "misfortune" of those unable to evade the ricocheting violence. It is in this sense that the colonial structures are revealed and how power has not traded violence for mercy but traded conquistadors for pandemics, hurricanes, wildfires, and drought to continue the conquest.

There is no risk of overstating here the need for an alternative approach to Christian ethics that, as Willis Jenkins has written, "must help humanity imagine and construct new forms of respon-

---

22. Ghassan Hage, *Is Racism an Environmental Threat?* (Malden, MA: Polity Press, 2017), 15.

sibilities, or, in the failure to do so, face the portents of collapse."[23] Ecological collapse assumes a subsequent social collapse. The social and natural worlds cannot be extricated from one another—a fact ignored by aspirational lifestyles in the developed world. Although this point has been made by many academic ecotheologians it is still far too absent in the ethical priorities of most faith leaders. In his 2013 book, *The Future of Ethics*, Jenkins frames the difficult task humanity must take up to avoid the collapse we are quickly approaching: "Ethics must find a way to develop new and shared responsibilities among a pluralist and alienated human family. How to construct a global ethic from many moral worlds?"[24] In the time since the publication of Jenkins's book, we have seen the world's greatest concentration of power and influence, in the United States presidency, promote and exemplify a "me first" ethic.[25] It was arguably this ethic that motivated more white evangelicals to vote for Trump than any other candidate in history in 2016.[26] As timely as the question was in 2013, it seems as if the world, but especially the United States, has only regressed when it comes to constructing a global ethic that recognizes the connections among humans with the natural world as a starting point for moral action and saving humanity and the Earth from humans.

Conclusion

As we write this chapter, the Biden administration has pledged to address environmental and systemic racism, but past administrations have as well. As long as there is a significant group of privileged white people without commitment to understanding their

---

23. Willis Jenkins, *The Future of Ethics: Sustainability, Social Justice, and Religious Creativity* (Washington, DC: Georgetown University Press, 2013), 3.
24. Jenkins, *The Future of Ethics*, 4.
25. "America First" was another Trump campaign slogan.
26. According to Gallup, 80 percent of white evangelicals voted for Trump in 2016. In 2020 that number dropped only 4 percent to 76 percent. See Frank Newport, "Religion Group Voting and the 2020 Election," *Gallup*, November 13, 2020.

role in causing this disaster and in racializing it, there will be those ready to leverage shortsightedness and ignorance to wield power for their own hungry appetites. Racism must be eradicated in all its forms. White Christians have failed to lead the charge against racism, and we know from the events of January 6, 2021 that many white Christians are eager to lead the charge *for* racism.

The Christian right has long had a tendency to blame natural disasters and disease on social issues. Jerry Falwell, whose son was one of Trump's most staunch Christian defenders, referenced homosexuality as arousing God's wrath in the form of Hurricane Katrina. When churches began defying state-wide lockdown orders throughout the country, some claimed the virus was God's punishment for abortion. Such claims are easy to mock, but the irony lost on most Americans is that there is a causal link between the emergence of the novel coronavirus and human-induced climate change, and the higher rates of mortality among racial minorities are directly linked to the systemic, environmental racism that has compounded over generations.[27]

If Christianity is to play a role in reconciling this divided nation it can start by recognizing that the Covid-19 pandemic is not a punishment from God, as some evangelicals have claimed, but it is reflecting our own racism. The desire to dominate the Earth and gain advantage over other humans begets ideologies of domination that use distinctions to justify and further the domination (i.e., racism).[28] Just as the Covid-19 pandemic exposes the intergenera-

---

27. Robin G. Veldman, *The Gospel of Climate Skepticism: Why Evangelical Christians Oppose Action on Climate Change* (Oakland, CA: University of California Press, 2019), offers an in-depth study of evangelicals' complex and shifting attitudes toward climate change, the progress made toward a climate-conscious spirituality, and the infiltration of climate skepticism.

28. This is not limited to racial distinctions and is likely the same impulse that Elaine Nogueira-Godsey has called "the dominator-subordinated dynamic," which defined colonial modes of relationships and persists today along distinctions that are arbitrary or irrelevant. See Elaine Nogueira-Godsey, "A Decological Way to Dialogue: Rethinking Ecofeminism and Religion," in *Handbook on Religions, Gender and Society*, ed. Emma Tomalin and Caroline Starkey (London: Routledge Press, forthcoming).

tional avenues to shift vulnerabilities to the marginalized, the next climate-related disaster will follow the same avenues and devastate the most vulnerable. The virus, or any number of climate-change-induced threats to humanity, is not God's wrath. It is our own wrath that we inflicted on the Earth, and as it comes back to us it travels the paths humans have carved, however racist they may be. That is why we must take responsibility and include "racist" in any attempt to characterize "who is America."

CHAPTER 9

"Karen" and Liberation Theology

SUSAN THISTLETHWAITE

Years of reckoning will be needed to deal with the distortions of our democracy exacerbated by the Trump era. Long-standing hatreds have burrowed like parasites into the body politic,[1] finding receptive hosts in our national flesh kept alive by festering resentments. These parasitical hatreds must be probed for their dreadful destructiveness and exposed, even when this causes the wounds they have created to seem bigger. There is no other way to build a decent society.

Liberation theology is a way such distortions can be contextually analyzed, prophetically named, and effectively engaged.[2] To employ a liberation approach, I have chosen to examine the context of the white woman represented by the "Karen" meme,[3] a term now widely used to describe a white woman who calls the police

---

1. "This [analogy] is fitting for some protozoal parasites that progressively destroy cells of the body, until they become latent/dormant in the tissues. When the body's immunity diminishes, parasitic destruction resumes with full vigor, often debilitating or killing the host." From a veterinary educator friend who has taught parasitology for many years and who has read this paragraph; used by permission.

2. Susan Brooks Thistlethwaite and Mary Potter Engel, *Lift Every Voice: Constructing Christian Theologies from the Underside* (Maryknoll, NY: Orbis Books, 2000), Introduction.

3. Ashitha Nagesh, "What Exactly Is a 'Karen' and Where Did the Meme Come from?" *BBC News*, July 30, 2020.

98

on African Americans simply going about their lives. In a practical sense, given the police shootings of unarmed African Americans, this is a death threat. "Karens" represent the insidious, long-standing hatreds in the history of this country that have gained influence as they have been recently valorized in a cynical, political power grab. It will be no easy task to bring them to a just reckoning.

Wrong Directions

False naming of what has happened in recent years, and is still happening, as "differences that can be bridged" will impede national reckoning. It is dangerous, in fact, because it gives the appearance of change without engaging the deep, structural conflicts that feed the burrowing hatreds among us. In light of the right-wing, extremist attack on our nation's Capitol, which, polls show, was supported by 45 percent of Republicans,[4] it is clear the danger is real and growing. We dare not allow longing for imaginary unity to take hold of the national consciousness and suppress the drive to make deep structural changes at this liminal moment.

In the context I have chosen, I believe it is immoral to reconcile with the behavior of the "Karens" who are trying to police the boundaries of white supremacy. What is needed instead is the theology of struggle represented by liberation theology. A contextual analysis of the power dynamics at stake is a key part of liberation analysis and has to be applied in order for there to be any hope of change. Centrism will not make the changes we need. In fact, centrism risks feeding the parasites that grow exponentially if unchecked.

The Context of "Karen"

"Karens" gain power in white supremacist culture by using its norms to feel themselves derivatively in control over those whom, they want to think, are inferiors. African Americans, especially though not exclusively African American men, are a particular target. The

---

4. James Walker, "45 Percent of Republican Voters Support Storming of Capitol Building: Poll," *Newsweek*, January 7, 2021.

Latinix groundskeeper aggressively challenged for his presence in a white neighborhood or the African American woman threatened for just trying to park her car in a crowded parking lot are other examples, and there are many. The entitlement, privilege, and racism of these white women are a particular kind of racialized violence white women have instigated for centuries. White women have weaponized their social and religious "victimhood" as women for a long time in this country, and they have done irreparable harm in the process.

If I approach this attitude and behavior via liberation theology, however, then the systemic analysis of their weaponized victimhood has to go through patriarchy to get to the core of how and why they manipulate racism to such a dangerous degree. I know this may be controversial, but liberation theology demands that we take a sustained look at the structures of oppression to see how they interconnect and reinforce one another. "Karens" are the right-wing women about whom Andrea Dworkin, the brilliant feminist theorist, wrote. "Right-wing women have surveyed the world. They find it a dangerous place. . . . They know that they are valued for their sex— their sex organs and their reproductive capacity—and so they try to up their value: through cooperation, manipulation, conformity."[5] Cooperation, conformity, and above all, manipulation are at the core of the behavior of "Karens" as they try to work the racist, patriarchal system for their own survival.

The context out of which these white women arise is the abusive patriarchy that is part of the structure of white supremacy. Trump was and still is basically an abuser, as I have written many times.[6] It has been, and continues to be, his political philosophy, and it has shaped the Republican Party into adopting a startlingly submissive posture vis-à-vis even his most egregious acts.

The tearful, submissive tone of the "apologies" these "Karens" adopt when they are caught on social media is very telling. Amy

---

5. Andrea Dworkin, *Right-Wing Women* (New York: Perigee Trade, 1983), chap. 1.

6. Susan Brooks Thistlethwaite, "2017 Imperative: Counter Trump's Political Philosophy of Abuse," *Huffington Post*, December 29, 2016, updated December 30, 2017.

Cooper, the so-called Central Park Karen, called the police on Christian Cooper (no relation), an African American man who merely asked her to leash her dog in a part of Central Park that required it, invoking his race on the call. After the video went viral, she was fired from her job, and the Manhattan district attorney said she would face charges for filing a false police report. Then Cooper abjectly apologized. She said on CNN that she wanted to "publicly apologize to everyone" and claimed that she was "not a racist" and "did not mean to harm that man in any way." In an interview with ABC 7 News, Christian Cooper accepted her apology but urged viewers to focus on not just the viral clip, but the "underlying current of racism and racial perceptions."[7] Christian Cooper is, of course, correct.

Victim Mentality

The victim mentality is ubiquitous in the conservative movement out of which these "Karens" come. The movement as represented by its leaders and followers tirelessly holds that it is a victim of left-wing persecution and, despite having enormous power, that it is deprived of power at every turn by the "libs." It is getting worse. It used to be that abortion mostly carried the victim mentality of the right wing. In my experience talking to anti-abortion advocates, they identify with the fetus, and abortion is a perceived threat to them and, very often, their "faith."

Now the QAnon conspiracy about pedophilia has been added to this victim mentality.[8] Ashli Babbitt, the woman who was shot and killed breaking into the US Capitol building on January 6, 2021, began to tweet QAnon accounts in 2020. She had tweeted regularly about the conspiracy theory since February 2020.[9] The

---

7. Cady Lang, "How the 'Karen Meme' Confronts the Violent History of White Womanhood," *Time*, June 25, 2020 (updated July 6, 2020).
8. Moira Donegan, "QAnon Conspiracists Believe in a Vast Pedophile Ring. The Truth Is Sadder," *The Guardian*, September 20, 2020.
9. Lois Beckett and Vivian Ho, "'She Was Deep into It': Ashli Babbitt, Killed in Capitol Riot, Was Devoted Conspiracy Theorist," *The Guardian*, January 9, 2021.

QAnon conspiracies are a dangerous example of the parasitical power of long-standing corruptions in our history made current and given a horrific twist. Yes, there are real victims of child abuse, child sexual abuse, and child trafficking, but a vast conspiracy that includes the Queen and many Democrats is not the driver. Yet, many white women are drawn to QAnon, and it is spreading as they identify with these supposed victims. The irony, of course, is that some of these right-wing, white women are oppressed, but they are not oppressed *in these ways*. They are not aborted fetuses. They are not children being trafficked. Their real victimization, the systemic and/or physical violence of heteropatriarchal white supremacist culture is hardly ever allowed to come to consciousness because that would require them to question their conservative context. It seems safer to stay in that oppressive context, not challenge it directly and blame others.

Short-Term Strategies for Change

Short-term and long-term strategies are both needed going forward. Given our Electoral College system, small moves in the electorate can make a big difference if engaged with pinpoint accuracy. White Protestant evangelicals have become essential for Republican victories, as Robert P. Jones, head of the Public Religion Research Institute and author of *White Too Long* argues in his well-researched book.[10] Small moves in that electorate can make a huge difference. The best that can be done is to influence cultural Christianity with which these white evangelicals identify and move it slightly. One short-term strategy did have a small effect in 2020. "Vote Common Good" moved the needle slightly on this by faith-messaging targeted at white evangelicals.[11] This is a proven strategy for moving groups of people on issues. This approach makes it possible for them to stay within their known cultural contexts, but respected "insider" messaging and leaders can give them acceptable reasons

---

10. Robert Jones, *White Too Long: The Legacy of White Supremacy in American Christianity* (New York: Simon & Shuster, 2020).

11. "Vote Common Good: Critical Percentage of White Evangelical Voters Abandoned Trump," Wispolitics.com, https://www.wispolitics.com.

to choose an alternative candidate. This was the strategy used by the Vote Common Good organization, and it worked to a small extent.

Substantial change in this country, however, requires more than a few percentage points differences in voting patterns. Voting patterns, in fact, reveal the depth of the problem. White women vote Republican in greater numbers than women of any other racial/ethnic identification because, as Angelina Chapin, senior writer for *New York Magazine* has written, "The Republican Party is the party of keeping the white heteropatriarchy intact." It is confirming of their place in right-wing culture, and, at the same time, works for them to help them "to stay on top of the racial hierarchy." There is this big trade off, where "these women have agreed to accept second-class status with their gender, as long as the Republican Party puts them first with race and keeps them safe."[12] The way "Karens" quite literally police the borders of white supremacy shows how strenuously they cling to this racial hierarchy and the illusion that it "keeps them safe." Tragically, the source of their danger is not the racial/ethnic minority person whom they are harassing. It is within their white community, but it seems too dangerous to them to bring that to consciousness.

Because the "Karens" and conservative white women like them are so deeply beholden to white supremacist culture for their identity and sense of safety, I do not believe they can be moved as individuals in the short term. The community-influence approach does yield modest gains, but it is not a solution. In the case of their actual physical and psychological risk from domestic abuse, shelters and counseling centers can help them with the immediate violence, if they will seek help.

Longer-Term Strategies for Change

A liberation theology approach requires not only contextual analysis but also long-term, complex plans for strategic action. These

---

12. Angelina Chapin, "Of Course White Women Voted for Trump Again," *TheCut*, November 17, 2020.

actions must be informed by a changed praxis that recognizes the deep truth of what Taylor Crumpton, music, pop culture, and politics writer, wrote in her *Washington Post* piece immediately after the 2020 election: "You cannot vote white supremacy out."[13] Many progressive white Americans made the mistake of thinking that the election of Barack Obama as president of the United States had "fixed" racism in this country. Far from it. In many ways, it gave fleshly fodder to the always festering white supremacy in our past and present, and it grew, fed on a steady diet of lies.

It is also a mistake to assume that white women who do not identify as right-wing conservatives are aware of their racial privilege and are actively engaged in efforts to overturn white supremacy. Some are, but most engage racism as a problem that can be solved by better policy. And, underlying the policy approach is often unexamined whiteness, as Peggy McIntosh of the Wellesley Centers for Women has written. "Whites are taught to think of their lives as morally neutral, normative, and average, and also ideal, so that when we work to benefit others, this work is seen as work that will allow 'them' to be more like 'us.'"[14] In other words, for many progressive whites, racism is instrumentalized, that is, it is a problem to be solved through policy alone, policy crafted to reflect white normativity. It is not a problem of whiteness per se.

But white normativity is going away, at least demographically. The United States *already* has a nonwhite majority under eighteen years of age. In another decade, it will be those under thirty. And by 2045, the entire country is projected to be majority nonwhite.[15] Trump and his successor-wannabes will continue to use the tinder of these demographic changes to feed the already-existing racism. Heteropatriarchal white supremacists have a long-term strategy and

---

13. Taylor Crumpton, "Black Women Saved the Democrats. Don't Make Us Do It Again," *Washington Post*, November 7, 2020.

14. P. McIntosh, "White Privilege and Male Privilege," in *The Feminist Philosophy Reader*, ed. Alison Bailey and Chris Cuomo (New York: McGraw Hill, 2008).

15. Stef Kight, "America's Majority Minority Future," *Axios*, August 29, 2019.

it is clearly apartheid. A small and economically privileged group of white males will run the country by means of voter suppression and a highly militarized, racist police force. This is already underway.

What is the transformative alternative? The Biden/Harris win is instructive, but I would argue it is not the blueprint for the kind of substantial cultural change we need, or not entirely. It is true that Biden/Harris won with a highly motivated, widespread, and diverse coalition of activists who were strongly opposed to Trumpism and the catastrophic effects of the pandemic he and his administration enabled by their incompetence and cruelty. But an unspoken Biden/Harris motto, especially among centrist to progressive whites, could have been "Let's Return to Normalcy." Yet, a brilliant and effective multi-ethnic woman elected as vice president is not "normalcy," and that's the good news. It shows that a transformative politics is possible. Just barely possible.

Taking down heteropatriarchal white supremacy is incredibly complex, however, as this system has been built up over centuries with strong pillars that can hold it up despite even effective challenges to parts of the edifice. We must address slavery *and* capitalism, genocide *and* colonialism, and orientalism *and* war as Andrea Smith, Cherokee intellectual, feminist, and antiviolence activist, has argued about women of color organizing.[16] The Taylor Crumpton article quoted above points to the effectiveness of the organizing of African American women that was central to the 2020 election. Women in diverse racial coalitions were mightily effective. And certainly, no long-term strategies for reckoning and change that are not substantially designed and led by women of color activists will succeed. But this also means to me that there will surely be a struggle within our resistance movement as resisters themselves are not free of the many ways we have been formed by this racist, heteropatriarchal culture even as we reject it and try to bring about substantial long-term change. And that is acutely true for white activists.

---

16. Andrea Smith, "Heteropatriarchy and the Three Pillars of White Supremacy: Rethinking Women of Color Organizing," CPT.org, https://cpt.org.

Let me be very specific. As a white woman, I am not free of the kinds of forces that produce a "Karen." I can bring them to critical consciousness and reject them, but they are there, always lurking. Look at yourself. Can you really say, no matter who you are, that nothing of this culture, its temptations, its insidious corruption, has gotten to you? It is inevitable, and yet it does not have to be definitive. There is good news. The structural changes we need to overturn heteropatriarchal white supremacy are already emerging. You have only to look at the Black Lives Matter marches and demonstrations of the summer and early fall of 2020 to recognize this. One crucial thing that we have to recognize about the possibilities of long-term, systemic change is that power is not a thing that can be grasped and owned by authoritarians. This may come as a shock to the ownership class. Power is a relationship, and the power of noncooperation is immense. I highly recommend Gene Sharp's theories of power in nonviolent direct action and especially how authoritarian power does not exist if millions refuse to cooperate with it.[17] Look at what has happened in these last years as the violent faces of heteropatriarchal white supremacy were exposed again and again, and literally millions of people said, "No, I will not cooperate with that."

That is how we begin to craft a reckoning. It is a genuine start, but it is a risky start. Per Andrea Smith's list of the "pillars," the power of heteropatriarchal white supremacy is immense because we also have a relationship with many of its supports. For example, all my unearned privileges as a white person tempt me every day to cooperate, and I do cooperate, mostly unconsciously but sometimes consciously, as it seems the expedient thing to do. Per my analogy of parasites, they are in me, horrible to say. I always have inward and outward work to do. We need to realize that parasitical hatreds grow in the shadows, falsely naming themselves "patriotism" and "freedom" when threatened with exposure. But they also sneak in under the guise of uncritical "good intentions." Communities of faith must commit to a national reckoning with the parasitical

---

17. Brian Martin, "Gene Sharp's Theory of Power: Review Essay," *Journal of Peace Research* 26, no. 2 (1989): 213–22.

hatreds even now feeding on the flesh of our body politic. We have to drag them into view and make the divisions of our heteropatriarchal white supremacist society more visible, not less.

Faith Communities Need to Step Up

I looked for a disgusting analogy to describe our situation as I wanted to convey how deeply revolting it is. I think parasites come pretty close. I wanted us to have a visceral response. But it is also true that wallowing in how disgusting this is does not, by itself, bring change. We also need to feed the kind of right relationship that is the foundation of a just, diverse, and equitable society. Sacred texts tell us that "people without a vision perish" (Proverbs 29:18). But the vision is not imaginary. There are people and a planet, whole, well, and diverse right there in front of us. Yes, this present vision is fragmentary and under attack, but it exists and it is being brought into being even as I write this.

Over centuries, what seemed absolutely impossible in terms of human well-being has come into being. And immediately, it is true, the parasites tried to burrow into it and distort its gains. But some gains have endured. So this is what we do. We foster just, diverse, and equitable communities. We demand a functioning democracy and decent policy. We persist. We struggle on. As Ada María Isasi-Díaz of blessed memory often said, "La vida es la lucha."[18] Life is struggle.

---

18. Ada María Isasi-Díaz, *Mujerista Theology: A Theology for the Twenty-First Century* (Maryknoll, NY: Orbis Books, 1996).

CHAPTER 10

Racism Is a Religious Issue

JIM WALLIS

At a 2020 annual meeting, seminary presidents in the Southern Baptist Convention doubled down on the SBC's dismissal of "critical race theory," which examines the issues of embedded racism across institutions and culture in American society. Critical Race Theory (CRT) shows how white supremacy—the belief that some people are more valuable than other people because of their skin color—is not just a personal prejudice but a structural and societal practice in America. The seminary presidents' statement, declaring the "affirmation of Critical Race Theory, Intersectionality, and any version of Critical Theory [as] incompatible with the *Baptist Faith & Message*"[1] was not quite the prophetic witness we needed from our churches given the twin pandemics of Covid-19 and systemic racism we've experienced in the United States—a deadly combination that has disproportionally killed Black and brown people based on demonstrably inequitable life circumstances tied to both past and current injustices.

Apparently, Southern Baptist leaders see the problem as bad sociology, but what their statement truly reveals is the bad theology that still haunts the denomination founded in support of slavery. The Southern Baptist statement's failure is biblical, not just sociological. Racism, in its many forms, is *sin*; indeed, it is America's original sin based on the lie, the myth, the ideology, and the idol-

---

1. George Schroeder, "Seminary Presidents Reaffirm BFM, Declare CRT Incompatible," *Baptist Press*, November 30, 2020.

atry of white superiority, or the assumption of whiteness as normative, and white privilege practiced through domination. White supremacy assaults the image of God, throws away the *imago dei*, and undermines God's purpose for humanity clearly stated in Genesis 1:26, to make *all* humankind in the "image" and "likeness" of God and have stewardship *together* over all the rest of God's creation. Therefore, white supremacy—which condones some people exercising violent dominion over other people God created as equal—offends the Creator and is anti-God. To finally begin to understand how that sin of racism exercises itself both in human hearts and social systems—as we all saw last year in a white cop's knee pressed on a Black man's neck until he died, representative of all of those systems—is important. But seminary presidents wanted to attack the sociology instead of facing the theology at the core of the original sin of our country, in which God's children of color are at risk every day.

Imagine what these seminary presidents—entrusted with training their denomination's pastors and leaders—might have said if they'd chosen to confront this sin. The Southern Baptist seminary leaders could have called for their churches to begin preaching against white supremacy from their pulpits and confess that the segregation of their churches exacerbates the racial separation within the body of Christ. They could have acknowledged that any acceptance of racism in their political candidates is anti-Christ. They could have prophetically called for removing Confederate statues and monuments that Black people in all their communities are forced to walk by every day. They could have committed their communities to the safety of Black families, asking their churches and pastors to hold local police departments accountable to protect the rule of law for *all* people, and to commit to correcting the disproportionate incarceration of Black and brown people. They could have called for all their Baptist pastors and congregants to ensure all of our nation's families have health care, to promote the best education we have available for all of our children, and to encourage Christian employers to offer equal job opportunities for all. In particular, the Southern Baptist seminary presidents could have warned Southern Baptist pastors against the great and growing dangers of white Christian nationalism, including in their own congregations, which is now a chief national security threat to the peace of our country.

Now, that would have been a prophetic response to this once-in-a-generation time of racial inflection and reckoning. But we didn't get that from the Southern Baptist seminary presidents. We did not get *repentance*—meaning more than statements of confessions, but a "turning around" from both personal and societal racism, both individual and systemic, both overt and covert, both explicit and implicit. What we got instead was *distraction* from racism—an inarticulate attack on critical race theory and "intersectionalism." It's tantamount to them saying *racism is just something we should all get over personally as we are of course all doing. Right?* At issue here is the narrow and unbiblical individualism of private piety, with no concept of structural sin and what the New Testament calls "principalities and powers." This thinking is stuck in the privatization of both sin and the gospel. We need to teach our people better theology.

Here is what Jemar Tisby, a Black Christian leader who knows the white Southern Baptists well, said:

> In the year 2020—when a pandemic has ravaged Black and brown communities, when millions protested the murders of Ahmaud Arbery, Breonna Taylor, and George Floyd, when so many others have dedicated themselves to taking steps on the journey toward racial justice—Christians in the United States have a once-in-a-generation opportunity to take bold steps for racial justice. Instead, these Southern Baptist leaders have chosen to prop up whiteness. It is ironic that in their statement, these Southern Baptist seminary presidents claim they are "standing against the tide of theological compromise." There is no form of theological compromise that is more American than vigorously opposing those who advocate for racial justice while remaining silent about the racism and whiteness running rampant in the church.[2]

---

2. Jemar Tisby, "Southern Baptist Seminary Presidents Reaffirm Their Commitment to Whiteness," *The Witness*, December 1, 2020.

Rather, here is what seminary presidents all over the country and the pastors they turn out ought to now make their message: *It is time to call upon our seminaries and our churches to begin the long spiritual process of discipling white American Christians out of the idolatry of racism—both personal and systematic.*

This example of the lack of reckoning with and tacit support of white supremacy among white Christians generally and white evangelicals specifically is illustrative of the broader challenge facing all who would seek reconciliation with and among white evangelicals in the post-Trump era. Right-wing white evangelicals have been organized in pursuit of political power for the last half century and have done so largely by narrowing the scope of what should constitute so-called religious issues for Christian voters. In recent decades that set has been abortion, LGBTQ rights, and religious liberty. Candidates fall on one side or the other, and predictable controversies erupt. It's exhausting to see people of faith lumped into a media narrative that largely only follows white Christians.

I had hoped that this tired and oversimplified narrative would change in the 2020 election—partly as a result of the crises of 2020 giving renewed and increased visibility to the insidious presence of systemic racism in US society. Covid-19 changed American life and will continue to do so—not just in the sickness and death it has caused, but also by how it has laid bare the inequalities and injustices of our social system that makes the suffering so unequal. The Covid-19 pandemic has made plain the racial inequities in our society, as Black, Latinx, and indigenous Americans are hospitalized with the virus at roughly five times the rate of white Americans.[3] We've also seen far too-long-delayed awakening among many white people about our nation's systemic racism, sparked by the public killing of George Floyd. An excruciating nine minutes and twenty-nine seconds has led to a deeper conversation about the last 401 years of slavery and racism—partly because the whole nation

---

3. Samantha Artiga, Bradley Corallo, and Olivia Pham, "Racial Disparities in COVID-19: Key Findings from Available Data and Analysis," *Kaiser Family Foundation*, August 17, 2020.

was home and *watching*. These twin crises proclaim a message that must be centered in any reconciliation between and among white Christians who supported Donald Trump. That message: Racism is a religious issue.

It might seem like a bold idea that the word "Christian" could become more important than the word "white" when the opposite has been true for a long time. Especially since the rise of the Religious Right, white evangelicalism in particular has been successfully tied to right-wing politics indifferent or actively hostile to racial equity, which is a fundamentally religious issue. The Religious Right, in fact, was poisoned from its beginnings with white race, white identity, and white power being prominent among its organizing purposes.[4] We know the numbers: 81 percent of white evangelical voters supported Donald Trump in 2016, along with 60 percent of white Catholics and 57 percent of white mainline Protestants.[5] In spite of everything that happened in 2020 to bring systemic racism into the consciousness of white Christians, its effect on white Christian consciences appears to have been much more limited, given that similar numbers of white Christians supported Donald Trump's reelection as had supported him in 2016.

For decades, white political leaders in the United States have masked their racism, subtly stoking white voters' racial fears, grievances, and animosity; so that part wasn't new. But in the Trump era, racist rhetoric and policies moved from covert to overt in what I believe is a deliberate attempt to increase fear and animosity on all sides. Racial fear and division became a central campaign issue and strategy. In early 2020, I wrote this election would be a test of democracy and a test of faith. I wish those words hadn't proven true. I wish white Christians had performed better on that test.

When sorting our politics, I believe all Christians should go back to the Bible. In fact, the foundation for all our politics—as people of faith—is found in the first chapter of the first book of the

---

4. Randall Balmer, "The Real Origins of the Religious Right," *Political Magazine*, May 27, 2014.

5. Daniel Cox, "White Christians Side with Trump," *Public Religion Research Institute*, November 9, 2016.

Bible: In Genesis 1:26, our Holy Scriptures say that God created humankind in God's image and likeness. That is the foundation for every Christian decision: supporting what affirms the *imago dei,* the image of God, in others, and opposing what denies it. Appeals to racial fear, grievance, and hate are assaults on the image of God in others. Therefore, every act of racialized police violence, every family separated at the border, every wink or appeasement to white supremacists, and every attempted suppression of even one vote because of skin color is denying the image of God—*imago dei.* Until white Christians understand that loving their neighbors as themselves means fighting unrelentingly for justice for Black and brown people and dismantling the oppressive structures of white supremacy, white American Christian claims to understand the heart of the gospel ring exceedingly hollow. The call to recognize racism as the key religious issue our nation faces is invitational, not confrontational. It's about going deeper than our usual political ideologies and toward the moral politics of doing the right thing.

What we saw in the wake of the 2020 election was historic: continuous acts of *sedition* aimed at overturning the results of an American election by the then sitting president of the United States. There is obviously a very dangerous political lens to these actions. The future of democracy in America was put at grave risk. But I would argue that it also illustrated a profound theological problem—that the growing power of a distinctive American heresy was also at play. First, Donald Trump's whole presidency, and his dangerous behavior during the transition, represented a brazen assault on truth. Truth is supposed to be central to Christians. Jesus tells us, "You will know the truth, and the truth will set you free" (John 8:32). The converse is also true—lies can lead us to lose our freedom. Does the truth matter to Christians and Christian leaders who supported Donald Trump? As Desmond Tutu and Nelson Mandela knew all too well, truth is necessary to reconciliation.

Second, the biblical abomination of racism and its ideology of white nationalism stand at the core of the Trump base. It is telling that many of the president's claims originated in the dark corners of the web among QAnon conspiracy theorists and message boards often frequented by white supremacists.[6] Trump's clear attempts to disenfranchise people of color were rooted in the sins of racism and white supremacy. Accepting or ignoring that reality is fundamentally unacceptable for those who confess Christ as Lord. This goes far beyond politics; it is theological heresy, and one that needs to be exorcised from white Christianity in America.

Some conservative white evangelical leaders have publicly denounced white Christians' idolatrous embrace of Trump and his efforts to overturn a free and fair election. Southern Baptist author and speaker Beth Moore tweeted in mid-December: "I have never seen anything in these United States of America I found more astonishingly seductive & dangerous to the saints of God than Trumpism. This Christian nationalism is not of God. Move back from it."[7] Conservative author, lawyer, and evangelical David French wrote a piece after the previous Jericho March denouncing "The Dangerous Idolatry of Christian Trumpism," writing:

> A significant segment of the Christian public has fallen for conspiracy theories, has mixed nationalism with the Christian gospel, has substituted a bizarre mysticism for reason and evidence, and rages in fear and anger against their political opponents—all in the name of preserving Donald Trump's power. . . . When core biblical values are contingent, but support for Donald Trump is not, then idolatry is the result.[8]

More is at stake now than politics as our nation attempts to heal from this pandemic and this presidency. The future for white Christians in the United States is nothing less than a choice between theological integrity and the idolatry of white Christianity in America.

I have been reflecting on Jesus's instruction and invitation from

---

6. Ben Collins, "QAnon's Dominion Voter Fraud Conspiracy Theory Reaches the President," *NBC News*, November 13, 2020.

7. Roxanne Stone, "Evangelical Leader Beth Moore Trends on Twitter after Calling Trumpism 'Seductive and Dangerous,'" *Religious News Service*, December 13, 2020.

8. David French, "The Dangerous Idolatry of Christian Trumpism," *The Dispatch*, December 13, 2020.

John 8:32—"You will know the truth, and the truth will set you free"—more than ever after these last four years, thinking about what Jesus is saying and, perhaps just as importantly, isn't saying. He did not say to tell the truth in order to make us right and righteous and them wrong and unrighteous—or to show some of us to be good and others to be evil. Jesus didn't say to tell the truth by creating our own "facts" and weaponizing them against others. The issues around the truth, says Jesus, are deeper; they are about freedom and bondage—our own.

To lose the truth is to lose our freedom. As historian Timothy Snyder wrote recently in the *New York Times Magazine*, "Post-truth is pre-fascism, and Trump has been our post-truth president."[9] That is where we were headed, and that danger has not yet passed. When it comes to facts and the truth, we still live in a world of parallel universes, with allegations of "fake news" and affirmations of "alternative facts"—one nation with totally different experiences and realities. And the only thing that can help us become—for the first time in our nation's history—a genuinely multiracial democracy is the truth: to seek it, find it, and act upon it.

After the violent insurrection at the Capitol, the media narrative was about the "Big Lie" that motivated the seditious desecrators. It was the lie about the election being stolen, for which there was absolutely no evidence. But underneath the "Big Lie" is the "Bigger Lie" of white supremacy, which was a principal motivator of those who stormed the Capitol. As African American studies scholar Eddie S. Glaude Jr. has been trying to tell us, we have been in a cold civil war for a while now, and it got hot in the Capitol assault—with Confederate battle flags leading the way—just as in Charlottesville in 2017 and many other places before and since.

The Civil War against slavery and the brutal lie of white supremacy is not over, and the white terrorists who carried Confederate flags, Trump flags, and Christian symbols while attacking the Capitol were modern-day lynchers; they even brought nooses. The same cheering crowds who were always at lynchings were there too,

---

9. Timothy Snyder, "The American Abyss," *New York Times Magazine*, January 9, 2021.

on the steps and in the rotunda, with supporters all over the country and even enablers within Congress—all incited by the lies from the White House.

Over the past four years, Trump has radicalized many of his followers, calling them to violence in the name of racist white nationalism. Now, their objection to the rule of law and an increasingly multiracial democracy has placed our nation in mortal peril.

White supremacy has always been the "Big Lie" of the United States—that some of God's children are superior or inferior to other people, and that the former are therefore justified in dominating the latter by any means necessary. That lie is still an idol in the core of the white church. According to the Bible, idols separate people from God, and the idol of white Christianity has done just that; tragically, most white Christians believed the lies of Donald Trump—and many still do. This is a religious and theological crisis. Since January 6, I have spoken to top evangelical leaders who painfully wonder how many of their white evangelical constituents rampaged through the Capitol or sympathized with those who did.

We are at a turning point in which Christians and people of faith and conscience from all political persuasions must unite in prayer and action and commit ourselves to the hard but essential work of repair, healing, racial justice, and reconciliation. This will require a great deal of truth telling and shared determination to root out a politics fueled by fear, lies, and conspiracy theories that undermine God's truth. True reconciliation needs the truth; therefore, we can never reconcile with white supremacy. White supremacy is a lie and an idolatry that must be removed from all our churches. For white Christians, that must become our primary spiritual task.

In his inaugural address, President Joe Biden said, "each of us has a duty and a responsibility, as citizens, as Americans, and especially as leaders, leaders who have pledged to honor our Constitution and protect our nation, *to defend the truth and defeat the lies*" (emphasis added). Telling the truth is everyone's responsibility now, from presidents and political leaders of both parties to civil society leaders who must call all our secular institutions to moral accountability. Telling the truth will also require us to challenge the algorithms of social media companies that have amalgamated and amplified lies and undermined the truth—all for the sake of the business model of profit with no accountability.

For white faith leaders, it's long past time to call our own white churches and parishioners back to Jesus. Detoxifying our churches from racism will require discipling our churches out of sinful racism and back to Jesus Christ. That will take preaching from all our pulpits against America's original sin of racism; teaching the truth, not just about American history but also our racialized church histories; learning how racism is not just personal, but also systemic; and challenging the deep heresies of privatized religion in America—something we have often used to cover up our social and structural sins. And finally, it will mean reading and studying in our small groups and families to learn and listen to the stories of our brothers and sisters of color in the body of Christ—whose pain we have not suffered with or even acknowledged, in direct disobedience to 1 Corinthians 12:26, which says, "if one member suffers, all members suffer with it." The moral task before all white Americans is to become humble enough to learn the truth by listening and finally hearing the experiences of our fellow citizens of color. We need to really see how we have been in the same cities and towns and rural regions and nation but have lived in different countries. Perhaps if we can deeply understand how different it is to be Black and brown parents than to be white parents in America, that truth could unite us around the kind of nation we want for all our children, who are also all the children of God.

CHAPTER 11

¡WTF Miami! — Understanding Latinxs for Trump

MIGUEL A. DE LA TORRE

Trump may have been denied a second term partly thanks to the 70 percent of Latinxs who helped deliver key swing states; still, he can boast—based on exit polls—that he did better among Latinxs in 2020 than he did in 2016; 4 percent better among Latinos and 5 percent better among Latinas.[1] In other words, almost a third of the Latinx vote went to Trump, and more than four in ten voted to reelect him in the State of Florida. Surprisingly, 36 percent nationwide approved of his overall job performance. Those Latinxs more likely to approve of Trump were those with more pronounced evangelical religious affiliations. Fifty-seven percent of Latinxs who approved of the president's job performance and 58 percent of those who approved of his handling of the economy were Protestants. Forty-five percent of them even approved of how he dealt with racial-justice protests while 48 percent supported building a wall on the southern border to keep out immigrants![2]

Trump's improvement among Latinxs is important when we consider that 2020 marked the first time Latinxs overtook African

---

1. Trump also did 6 percent better among Black men, 5 percent better among Black women, and 7 percent better among Asians and other ethnic groups.

2. Natalie Jackson, "Religion Divides Hispanic Opinion in the U.S.," *Public Religion Research Institute*, November 17, 2020.

American's electoral participation, becoming the largest minoritized voting bloc.[3] It also exposed intra-Latinx fissures undergirded by colorism. The importance of the Latinx electorate in future contests has been cemented, and politicians who ignore the complexities of Latinx identity do so at their own peril. While Trump's numbers improved among all Latinx ethnic groups throughout the nation, the focus of this chapter is on those who reside in Miami's Dade County, whose votes placed Florida's electoral votes in Trump's column.

Over half of the residents of this county are foreign-born (second only to Los Angeles), 58 percent of them being Latinx of which 72 percent are registered as Republicans. There, Trump carried the Latinx vote by nearly 55 percent in 2020, securing his win of Florida's twenty-nine electoral votes. Trump's margin of victory was better than what any other Republican presidential candidate was able to obtain in the past sixteen years. He even won the county by 22 percent over what he obtained in 2016.[4] When we consider his draconian anti-Latinx policies and his zero-tolerance anti-immigrant rhetoric, even sealing off the United States from refugees and asylum seekers from Latin American countries (including Cuba and Venezuela), many who are not Latinx, mistakenly believing the Latinx vote belongs to the Democrats, ask: "WTF Miami?" Most Latinxs, however, were neither surprised nor shocked. Why then the disconnect?

Democrats in general, liberal specifically, continue failing to understand Latinxs and their ethos, instead gazing upon us as if we are some mindless monolithic voting bloc, rather than recognizing that we come from different cultures, regions, races, and religious perspectives. This ignorance concerning the Latinx community

---

3. Ed Morales, "What the 2020 Election Reveals about Latino Voters," *CNN*, November 16, 2020; Ashitha Nagesh, "US Election 2020: Why Trump Gained Support Among Minorities," *BBC*, November 22, 2020.

4. Lautaro Grinspan, "'Do They Just Not Care?' Miami Immigrants Troubled by Surge of Latino Support for Trump," *Miami Herald*, November 21, 2020; Patricia Mazzei, "How Miami's Politics Swung Right and Blindsided the Nation," *New York Times*, November 22, 2020.

was best expressed by former president Barack Obama, who during his presidency obtained from *la comunidad* the moniker of "Deporter-in-Chief." In an interview with the Breakfast Club podcast three weeks after the 2020 election, the former president excused Biden's poor showing among Latinxs, stating: "But there are a lot of evangelical Hispanics who, you know, the fact Trump says racist things about Mexicans, or puts detainees, undocumented workers in cages, they think that's less important than the fact that he supports their views on gay marriage or abortion."[5] He subscribes to the false paternalistic narrative held by so many liberals and Democrats. They simplistically believe that because Trump's incendiary comments and policies were anti-Hispanic and anti-immigrant, ergo, Latinxs would automatically vote against Trump. Hence, they need neither convincing nor persuasion, for their votes are taken for granted.

Forgetting for a moment that during Obama's first run for the presidency in 2008 he opposed gay marriage[6] or that his own immigration policies incarcerated some sixty thousand children during the summer of 2014, placing them in cages he funded and built,[7] we see that his condescending remarks explaining the increase of the Latinx vote for Trump trivializes the complexity of the issue. Yes, there are conservative Latinx evangelicals who voted for Trump for the same reason as conservative white evangelicals. But to stereotype all Latinxs who voted against Biden as evangelicals at best demonstrates lazy analysis based on unexamined ethnic stereotyping.

Republican analyses are not any better. During the CNN election coverage, former Senator Rick Santorum commented on Trump's increased share of the Latinx vote, stating that his upsurge in Latinx support should put to rest any future accusations con-

---

5. Eugene Scott, "Obama's Take on Evangelical Hispanics Could Reinforce Democrats' Challenges," *Washington Post*, November 26, 2020.

6. Patrick Healy, "If Elected . . . Hopefuls Differ as They Reject Gay Marriage," *New York Times*, October 31, 2008.

7. Ken Belson, "Child Migrants Strain Makeshift Arizona Shelter," *New York Times*, June 7, 2014.

cerning Republican or Trump being racist. Tokenizing those who voted against their own interest by ignoring the rampant ethnic discrimination sentiments and anti-Latinx policies (especially immigration policies) of the past four years provides insufficient cover for white politicians who supported racist policies. Just because light-skinned Cubans who possess a citizenship that they had little difficulty obtaining (thanks to the 1966 Cuban Adjustment Act[8]) voted for Trump does not excuse the Republican Party's fear-mongering through conjured-up images of threatening brown caravans invading white America.

This chapter focuses on the Cuban Miami community. The first item requiring exploration revolves around the concept of race (specifically colorism) and the economic privilege associated with whiteness. During the 2016 Republican primary elections, two candidates who ran against Trump were of Cuban descent, Senators Marco Rubio (R-Fla.) and Ted Cruz (R-Tex.). Commenting on this, Al Madrigal—comedian and former fake news correspondent of the popular cable television program *The Daily Show*—sought to explain to then-host Jon Stewart why he wasn't excited about two serious Hispanic candidates for the office of the presidency. The May 6, 2015 exchange between the two comedians went as follow:

> Madrigal: "I guess those guys are technically Latinos. I mean there's a lot more to 'being Latino' than being Latino."
> Stewart: "Because they're weak on immigration?"
> Madrigal: "Well, maybe—but mainly because they're Cuban; a small and—I gotta be honest—snooty subset; they're like the WASPs of the Latino world. You can't expect the bulk of us non-Cuban Latinos to go crazy for two Cuban guys who threw away a path to citizenship for a path to the White House."[9]

---

8. The Cuban Adjustment Act of 1966 was propaganda-based legislation during the Cold War that allowed Cuban refugees "escaping communism" (like this author who was "illegal" until then) to obtain permanent residency and an easy and speedy path to citizenship.

9. "The Legend of El Jebe," *The Daily Show with Jon Stewart*, May 6, 2015, http://www.cc.com.

While non-Latinxs who see no difference between a Dominican and a Puerto Rican scratch their heads asking WTF happened in Miami, Latinxs like Al Madrigal know all too well the answer to this question. Being Cuban born, I belong to this subset of Latinxs who possess what Pierre Bourdieu would recognize as a different historical habitus than someone like Al Madrigal, who is Mexican-American. Our Cuban immigration patterns fostered an ethos that privileged middle-class status and light skin pigmentation. The first wave (1959–1962), consisting of 215,000 Cuban refugees who saw themselves as "political exiles," were 94 percent white (by Latinx definitions), middle-aged (thirty-eight years old), educated (fourteen years of schooling), urban (mainly from La Habana) and literate in English. The second wave (1962–1973), numbering 414,000 migrants, consisted of those who before the revolution had economic links to the United States. On average they were semi-skilled, light-skinned, working-class people who capitalized on the emerging economic enclave being established in Miami by the first wave Cubans.

Demographically, these Cubans, upon whom the city of Miami was being rebuilt, were quite homogeneous: mainly white, educated, and middle class.[10] Yes, all strata of Cuban society were represented in these first two waves; nevertheless, the vast majority, unlike the three largest US Latinx groups—Mexicans, Puerto Ricans, and Dominicans—consisted of those from the upper echelons and the middle class who most benefitted from the pre-Castro regime.

Born into positions of privilege and power on the island, these refugees possessed the necessary habitus to recreate an elitist culture in exile. Their social constructs, manifested as customs, language, traditions, values, etc. existed before their birth on the island—social constructs that were whiter, possessed more formal education, and were more urban than any other migrant group

---

10. Max Azicri, *Cuba: Politics, Economics, and Society* (London: Printer Publishers, 1988), 67; Richard R. Fagan, Richard A. Brody, Thomas J. O'Leary, *Cubans in Exile: Disaffection and the Revolution* (Stanford, CA: Stanford University Press, 1968), 19–28.

from Latin American. From the moment of birth, these normalized social constructs were imposed, molding their childhood and guiding them toward an adulthood pregnant with possible privileges. Looking at the power, privilege, and profits obtained in Miami within one generation led many Cubans to erroneously conclude their superiority over other Latinx groups still stuck at lower economic levels. In reality, as Bourdieu would argue, they merely had to assert what they were in order to become what they are, an effort done with the unselfconsciousness that marks their so-called nature.[11] Such a habitus, which normalized and legitimized privileging whiteness and capitalist paradigms, simply continued on the northern side of the Florida Straits.

Paulo Freire's concept of "submerged consciousness" also helps explain why these first two waves of Cubans desired at all cost to resemble their oppressor, yearning for equality with the "eminent" men of the United States.[12] The ethnic identity forged by these first two waves attempted to imitate the dominant white North American culture, the same culture whose neocolonialist ventures in their homeland during the first half of the twentieth century contributed to the rise of a 1959 rebellion forcing many (myself included) into exile. The nation that took us in is responsible for our displacement in the first place! Emasculated by neo-imperialism on our own homeland, these two first waves now looked to the procurers of their disenfranchisement as the means by which to define themselves. In order to assimilate, a genealogy was created portraying Cubans as white people coming from a white nation, fleeing tyranny with only the clothes on their backs, a narrative that all too often ignores our African and Chinese roots.

Although beyond the scope of this chapter, a word should at least be spoken concerning the toxic masculinity prevalent within the Cuban overall community, on both sides of the Florida Straits.

---

11. Pierre Bourdieu, *A Social Critique of the Judgement of Taste*, trans. Richard Nice (Cambridge, MA: Harvard University Press, 1984 [1979]), 169–72, 258.

12. Paulo Freire, *Pedagogy of the Oppressed*, trans. Myra Bergman Ramos (New York: Bloomsbury, 2000 [1970]), 62, 95.

What is it about a people who have a proclivity for authoritarian figures, whether it be a fascist Batista, a communist Castro, or a populist Trump? Why do the descendants of those who "escaped communism" still embrace personality cults? The children of those who placed signs in their yards in la Habana that read *"si Fidel es comunista ponme en la lista"* today wear hats proclaiming "Make America Great Again." When Trump informed the public that "I alone can fix it,"[13] he demonstrated he had more in common with what those Miami Cubans fled from than the democratic ideas to which they fled.

Assimilation by embracing whiteness assumes belief in its superiority. Surrendering to a submerged consciousness has its benefits, as ontologically white Cubans are placed on pedestals to serve as unsolicited spokespersons for white supremacy and at times are rewarded with occupying positions in the highest echelons of business and government (e.g., Enrique Tarrio, chairman of the Proud Boys). Building on Zora Neale Hurston's well-known quote, my colleague Stacey Floyd-Thomas constantly reminds us: "Not all skinfolk are kinfolk, *and not all kin are kind.*" There are always those from marginalized communities willing to step up and wear white masks or MAGA hats, either as a means of survival or for making a profit. They volunteer to become the apologists for white supremacy within their communities.

In spite of the biracial Cubans who immigrated during the 1980 Mariel boatlift (who more resembled the Cuban population), the construct of the earlier two waves persisted as the self-defining norm for the community. As painful as it is to admit, Al Madrigal is correct in asserting that Cubans are the WASPs of the Latinx world. Republicans in 2016 who arrived at the simple conclusion that Rubio and Cruz were the Republican answer to the Latinx dilemma were sorely disappointment when Latinxs failed to support them in spite of their claims to shared ethnicity. Likewise, in 2020, Democrats were foolish to think Latinxs would simply line

---

13. Michael Tackett, "Trump's 'I Alone Can Fix It' View and State Powers Collide," *AP News*, April 14, 2020.

up behind Biden just because Trump continued to voice and tweet racist and anti-immigrant rhetoric.

Reducing Latinxs to Spanish-speaking, brown immigrant caricatures assures future Democrat electoral losses. The assumption exists that Latinxs would vote for Democrats with the same consistency as Black voters, as if all people of color vote the same way. The Miami vote, as opposed to other Latinx votes elsewhere that were influenced by either evangelism-based beliefs or purely economic concerns (same concerns influencing white voters), can never be understood until we realize that Dade County, unlike any other county in the United States, has domestic policies driven by foreign politics. Rather than nuancing the economic collapse brought about by a failed leadership in responding to the unchecked spread of the coronavirus, the debate was oversimplified between those who are "good Americans" and those who are "evil socialists." Missing from the debate were discussions concerning minimum wages, stimulus bills, income gap, or the unraveling safety net. Labeling Democrats in general, Biden specifically, as socialists was, and continues to be, sufficient.

The Trump campaign's relentless attempt to define Biden as a socialist, and the Democrats' continuing strategy of ignoring the Latinx community on the assumption that they could count on their votes, provided big dividends for Trump, and not just in Miami. Democrats have a history of ignoring Latinx voters. Simply saying "I'm not Trump" was not, nor should it ever be, enough. The Biden camp spent little time and resources outreaching to Latinx voters. Written off as infrequent voters not worth the investment, we are blamed when Democrats do poorly at the polls. But the problem is not with Latinxs; rather, it is with Democrats who continue to assume we will fall into line. Electoral loyalty should not be expected if we continue to be ignored and essentialized. There is no Latinx vote, for we, like the rest of the nation, are deeply divided. And there is no one Latinx issue for we, like the rest of the nation, have different concerns based on our race, nation of origin, years in this country, geographical location, and economic class.

Latinos helped Biden win in Arizona, Colorado, Nevada, and New Mexico. And in cities like Philadelphia, Milwaukee, and Gwinnett, Georgia, the Latinx vote built on the Black vote margin of victory. But when it came to Miami, Latinxs helped Trump carry Florida. One major difference that exists between Cubans (as well as Venezuelans) that is not necessarily shared with other Latinx groups is a knee-jerk hatred for anything resembling socialism; and this, more than anything else, explains why it will continue to be difficult for Democrats to ever win over Miami Latinxs. A deep-down personal hatred for Fidel Castro (or Hugo Chávez), and the dysfunctional country he (they) represented, is ingrained in the soul of the Miami community (as well as in the soul of this author, ever since childhood). Before I even understood spiritual concepts, I was taught to view Castro as the earthly personification of Satan. My earliest memories of life are of extreme poverty, a poverty for which my parents personally blamed Castro. He was the reason why my parents lost their middle-class privilege in Cuba. He was the reason why I was separated from my grandmothers and never got to meet them. He is the reason why friends and family were lined up against a wall and executed. I recall a friend telling me about an *abuelita* who every morning walked throughout her house appearing to recite the rosary, when in reality, with each bead she touched, she whispered, "God damn you to hell, Fidel." For the majority of exilic Cubans, everything that is good, holy, pure, true, and sacred is the antithesis of Castro and his regime. Liberals demonstrate great insensitivity when they fail to recognize this PTSD and grief. When presidential primary candidates like Bernie Sanders say it is "unfair" to say "everything is bad" with communist Cuba during a *60 Minutes* interview, it only reinforces the perception among exilic Cubans that the Democrats are all socialist.[14] Even though my original support was for Sanders, his comments—although I understood the context in which he made them—caused me pause. This explains why Cubans recoil, me included, when uninformed liberals decide to wear their Che Guevara T-shirts in our presence.

---

14. Patricia Mazzel, "Sanders's Comments on Fidel Castro Provoke Anger in Florida," *New York Times*, February 24, 2020.

One need not look to the distance past to note examples of political oppression. Regardless of romanticized notions of socialist paradises held by some among the US liberal left, human rights abuses remain a reality in both Venezuela and Cuba. People are willing to die for a different form of government, a fact ignored by US liberals. So, when the word *socialism* is uttered, white people may conjure up images of Nordic countries' successes in furthering human flourishing—as they should. But when socialism is mentioned to Cubans and Venezuelans, what comes to mind is left-wing despotic regimes, dictatorships that have stripped them of everything and are responsible for the tragedy and grief they have been forced to endure. Liberals' and Democrats' insensitivity to our historic pain, generationally passed on to our descendants (what Asian theologians call *han*) is the reason they will continue to lose votes in Miami. Those who ignore this pain, this *han*, or are overly critical of neoliberalism run the risk of being labeled a socialist and thus ostracized from the community. A simplistic dichotomy is established where any support for the Castro regime (like my own position to end the embargo) or attempts to create a more just US economic structure are defined as socialist.

Ironically, both the Trump regime and the political structures of Cuba have much in common. The governments representing both sides of my identity as a Cuban American may differ politically, but the people under those regimes share much. When their citizens protest, they are first demonized so that their abuse at the hands of the government can be justified. But we who are citizens—in Cuba and in the United States—protest when our governments do not listen. We protest when our voices in the form of votes become a charade that can be overturned. We protest when the economic system is rigged to benefit the few. We protest when racism has been institutionalized. Here is what I learned by studying the political structures of the Right and of the Left: (1) The United States has lost (as if they ever had) the moral authority to dictate what is justice to another sovereign nation. (2) People-to-people dialogue (not government-to-government dialogue) is what unites us against the abuses of governments on the left and on the right, hence the need to end the embargo. (3) Arts and the humanities are the foundation upon which liberation is built. (4) Both sides of the political spectrum abuse their people; and when they do, ideologies must be set aside to stand in solidarity with those being oppressed—regardless if one agrees with their political views. (5) Failure to be able to criticize the political views or political ideas one holds dear is akin to cult worship—the lowest intellectual level any human can obtain. Yes, Cubans and Americans have much in common.

Eurocentric politicians (whites and Blacks) are not the only ones who mistakenly attempted to construct Latinxs as monolithic. Scholars, specifically religion scholars, are just as guilty. The Cuban-American habitus had originally made it difficult to be accepted among other Latinx ethnic groups. What do other Latinx ethnic groups have in common with mainly white, middle-class, politically conservative Cubans? When some of us work as scholar-activists for Latinx social justice, should we be surprised to be viewed with suspicion by non-Cuban Latinxs? Unfortunately, some of the early Cuban religion scholars attempted to mask these differences by advocating for some essentialized pan-Hispanicness. During the early development of what came to be known as Latinx theological thought (during the 1980s and 1990s) many of the original architects of the discourse were of Cuban descent. Hence an emphasis was placed on minimizing their Cuban background by constructing a pan-Hispanic identity. Many of these early Cuban religious scholars engaged in a strategy not duplicated in other academic disciplines. Most wrote on pan-Hispanic themes, at times appropriating the religious symbols of other non-Cuban Latinx groups—like *la Virgen de Guadalupe*. Today many scholars recognize the importance of differences; still, essentializing terms like "*latinamente,*" as in "doing theology *latinamente,*" continue. The danger of insisting on one Hispanic religious trajectory is that those who get to define what *latinamente* is, submerge, if not silence, other religious perspectives that may not be the norm but are no less crucial to constructing Latinx identity.

In the final analysis, Democrats must recognize that the Latinx vote is not a given. If they wish to prevail in future elections, then they must fight for every single Latinx voter, not with rhetoric but with policies that uplift our communities by providing a level playing field. And, of course, it goes without saying that they need to learn how to speak to a Cuban differently than to a Mexican, differently than to a Puerto Rican, differently than to a Dominican, differently than to a Salvadorian, and so on. We may all speak Spanish, but we speak different languages.

As for Cubans and Venezuelans, we must choose to be Latinx, a process that requires making a preferential option for the marginalized among those who are genetically connected to one of the many Latin American countries. For us Cubans, this can occur by crucifying any race or economic privilege we hold (or just claim to have) and making a conscious choice to stand in solidarity with the vast majority of Latinxs who are disenfranchised and dispossessed by white Eurocentric supremacy. For Cubans to be Latinxs, they must move away from aliening themselves from those who benefit from the way society is constructed, hoping to capitalize on the tokenism of organizations seeking brown faces, assuming that Cubans are brown with white voices. Yes, there is more to "being Latino" then being Latino. For us Cubans, we cannot claim to be Latinx while supporting policies and legislation that continue to harm the overall Latinx community. If a Latinx tree is known by its fruit, then what are the fruits produced by the Rubio and Cruz red maple trees? Or by my own Cuban palm tree? Whatever identity we claim remains irrelevant. What we do among and in solidarity with the Latinx community is what ultimately defines if a Cuban can ever be a Latinx.

CHAPTER 12

Virus (of) Fear? Diagnosing the Trumpian Symptom within a Virulent History

Tat-siong Benny Liew

"We fight like hell and if you don't fight like hell, you're not going to have a country anymore." These are the words of Donald J. Trump during a rally in Washington, DC, on January 6, 2021, before his supporters stormed the Capitol in a violent attempt to overturn the presidential election. In his speech that day to "save America," Trump also attributed the "fraudulent" election to Democrats, "using the pretext of the China virus and the scam of mail-in ballots." With his repeated references to the virus as "kung flu," the "China virus," or the "Chinese virus," the negative impact of Trump's divisive words has been palpable for not only Chinese/Americans in particular but also Asian/Americans in general. In this chapter, I will look at the present pandemic, including its current impact on Asian/Americans, in light of rather than losing sight of past history. After that, I will argue that the scapegoating of Asian/Americans during public health crises is connected with many of the -isms to which Trump is committed, and show in the process that the Trumpian regime, if and when considered with a longer view of context and history, is different more in degree than in kind. I say this not to minimize the harm that Trump has brought about, but to maintain that the end of Trump's presidency will not necessarily mean real change without our persistent resistance.

Sickness and Scapegoats:
A Long and Continuous History

According to the Stop AAPI Hate website, over 2,500 anti-Asian incidents—including verbal harassments, "shunning," physical assaults, "potential civil rights violations," and vandalism—were reported within four-and-a-half months of the website's launch in March 2020 to register and address the xenophobia and bigotry that have been unleashed against Asian Americans and Pacific Islanders because of the coronavirus pandemic.[1] Significantly, many of these reported incidents entailed the use of racial slurs and racist rhetoric that betrayed an "anti-immigrant nativism."[2] Hannah Tessler, Meera Choi, and Grace Kao have also gathered information on vandalism and physical confrontations at various locations, including an attack on a Burmese American family in Texas because the attacker "thought the family was Chinese, and infecting people with coronavirus." Many of these encounters also involved direct linkages being made to the coronavirus, with aggressors calling their Asian American victims "coronavirus," "Chinese virus," or "diseased," and telling them that they should "be quarantined," or "go back to China." Perhaps less dramatic but no less harmful would be the loss suffered by Chinese business owners. For instance, restaurants in New York City's Chinatown experienced an 85 percent drop in profits from mid-January to mid-March—that is, before any mandate to close down indoor dining. Besides losing business, "phrases such as 'take the corona back you ch*nk' . . . and 'watch out for corona' . . . have been documented on Asian-owned restaurants."[3]

Given Trump's incendiary words during this pandemic period and his refusal to address or even acknowledge the ensuing "bonfires" of harassment and harm, there are certainly good reasons

---

1. https://stopaapihate.org/reports.
2. https://stopaapihate.org/reports.
3. Hannah Tessler, Meera Choi, and Grace Kao, "The Anxiety of Being Asian American: Hate Crimes and Negative Biases during the COVID-19 Pandemic," *American Journal of Criminal Justice* 45 (2000): 639–40.

to call him "the biggest 'superspreader'" of anti-Asian racism.[4] Trump is, however, not alone in this. News media were not at all shy in churning out reports about "the hygiene of the seafood market in Wuhan and wild animal consumption as a possible cause of coronavirus," and many posted "memes and jokes about bats and China."[5] Having said that, it is important to note that neither the rhetoric nor the results of anti-Asian racism are new in the history of the United States of America. Trump's personality aside, the connection that he and many people make between people of Asian ancestry and infectious virus that endanger the nation—just like Trump's policies on the economy, on the military, and on race in general—are in many ways continuations of past practices and symptomatic of a deep-rooted white supremacy. Asian-raced bodies as foreign, undesirable, diseased, and harmful is just another trope to reinforce and intensify the imagined threat of the "yellow peril." Sadly, even a prestigious university listed xenophobia as one of many "common reactions" to the Covid crisis.[6]

Cholera

Given the prevailing assumption of the time that diseases were caused and spread by miasma or "bad air" or "bad vapor," the link was immediately made during the cholera epidemic of the 1850s between cholera and what the West viewed as the "unsanitary" living conditions and "filthy" habits of the Chinese people, who after 1849 began to arrive in larger numbers in Hawaii and the West Coast. Because whites did not feel at ease with their different looks, smells, and cuisines, they conveniently collapsed what they saw in Chinatown, including the sickness and poverty, with the moral

---

4. https://www.huffpost.com/entry/trump-anti-asian-racism-covid-19_n_5f905c0fc5b62333b24133f5.

5. Tessler, Choi, and Kao, "Anxiety of Being Asian Americans," 637, 639.

6. Allyson Chiu, "'Stop Normalizing Racism': Amid Backlash, UC-Berkeley Apologizes for Listing Xenophobia under 'Common Reactions' to Coronavirus," *Washington Post*, January 31, 2020.

corruption of the entire Chinese population.[7] Instead of considering if and how racism and economic inequality might have led to the living conditions and infection rate of the Chinese, those of the dominant culture quickly categorized Chinese bodies as diseased. It made sense, therefore, that (1) the location of San Francisco's first pesthouse, which was built for cholera, ended up being the area of the city's Chinatown; and (2) the new pesthouse that the city built in 1861 was nicknamed "China House."[8]

Smallpox

With the smallpox epidemic of the late 1860s and the 1870s, San Francisco's Chinatown was once again portrayed as the "plague spot," a "cesspool," or a "moral purgatory," although the virus could have been brought there by rail travelers from the East Coast.[9] Again, Chinese were seen to be lacking the strength of those of European stock, and particularly susceptible to smallpox because of their "racial inferiority."[10] Separating a "true" and "healthy" San Francisco from the "'hell' of Chinatown underground," city officials justified and carried out "sanitary" raids of Chinatown and aggressive segregations of the Chinese population, but no other crowded space (such as the city dockyards) or social group was identified as a health threat.[11] As Nayan Shah explains, three words may summarize the negative connotations that Chinatown communicated to the dominant population at that time: "dens, density, labyrinth."[12] To stoke fear, Thomas Logan, who became president

---

7. Nayan Shah, *Contagious Divides: Epidemics and Race in San Francisco's Chinatown* (Berkeley: University of California Press, 2001), 21–22.

8. Guenter B. Risse, *Driven by Fear: Epidemics and Isolation in San Francisco's House of Pestilence* (Urbana: University of Illinois Press, 2016), 18, 79, 81.

9. Joan B. Trauner, "The Chinese as Medical Scapegoats in San Francisco, 1870–1905," *California History* 57, no. 1 (Spring 1978): 75; Shah, *Contagious Divides*, 1, 11, 58.

10. Risse, *Driven by Fear*, 25.

11. Shah, *Contagious Divides*, 6, 43, 53–54; Risse, *Driven by Fear*, 119.

12. Shah, *Contagious Divides*, 18–19.

of the American Medical Association during this epidemic, "popularized the eye-witness journey into Chinatown's dens" to show (off) how "'hereditary vices' or 'engrafted peculiarities' preordained the Chinese to chronic and unusual illness."[13] It's little wonder that the first and only race-based law passed in the history of the United States thus far was the Chinese Exclusion Act in 1882.

Syphilis and Leprosy

Like smallpox, contagious diseases such as syphilis and leprosy were viewed in the late nineteenth century as "essentially Chinese," with the former being labeled "Guandong boils" or "Chinese ulcer," and the latter "Mongolian leprosy" or "disease of the semi-civilization" that afflicted the entire China.[14] In fact, these two sicknesses were often linked, with many seeing "leprosy among the Chinese [as] 'simply the result of generations of syphilis.'"[15] Clergy and missionaries referred to the Bible to talk about leprosy and provoke panic among whites and to emphasize the need for "heathen Chinese" to convert to Christianity; medical doctors blamed Chinese prostitutes for spreading syphilis—even though prostitution was not a monopoly of the Chinese and syphilis could be spread to Chinese prostitutes from their solicitors.[16] Chinese spreaders of these poisonous viruses were not limited to prostitutes, however. Chinese service providers, including domestic, laundry, or food services, were also blamed, because they shared pipes to smoke opium, or because they supposedly used a "dangerous mouth spray" to soak their customers' clothing or dampen the clothing before ironing it.[17] Dr. Mary Sawtelle made Chinese not only the source but also the embodiment of syphilis and leprosy when she wrote in a medical journal: "every ship from China brings hundreds of these syphilitic and leprous heathens. They sit in the streetcar beside our wives and daughters. They are a stench. Their mean stature, their ugly faces

---

13. Shah, *Contagious Divides*, 28–29.
14. Shah, *Contagious Divides*, 99; Risse, *Driven by Fear*, 68, 49, 129, 149.
15. Trauner, "Chinese as Medical Scapegoats," 75.
16. Shah, *Contagious Divides*, 80–81; Risse, *Driven by Fear*, 51–53.
17. Shah, *Contagious Divides*, 68–69, 95; Risse, *Driven by Fear*, 27.

and their imbecile nastiness mirrors to us what syphilis will do for a nation."[18]

Bubonic Plague (Black Fever)

Fearing the spread of the bubonic plague, steamship companies in the summer of 1899 openly refused Chinese passengers who could only afford to buy the cheapest tickets.[19] When the black fever finally broke out in Hawaii and California in 1900, it was once again labeled as an "oriental disease" for "rice eaters" (including this time those of Japanese and Indian ancestry), so non-Asians enjoyed greater freedom to travel, for instance.[20] A broader category of so-called Asian foodstuffs was considered to contain and carry the virus, with newspapers in Honolulu reporting that the first white person who died of the plague in Honolulu "had been eating Chinese candy she bought at an Asian market shortly before she came down with plague."[21] In Honolulu, attempts to disinfect Chinatown ended infamously with a fire on January 20, 1900, that ended up, whether wittingly or unwittingly, burning down the entire Chinatown. Worse, an armed city police force, joined by civilians picking up anything that could be used as a weapon, formed a blockade "to prevent the dispersal of a potentially plague-carrying population throughout the city." As if that was not enough, arsonists burned another block near a Chinese theater in the city exactly a week later.[22] When the plague erupted again in San Francisco in May 1907, it became more difficult to make Chinatown the culprit because (1) the outbreak was citywide; (2) more whites died from the plague than Chinese; and (3) medical understanding had changed with the advent of bacteriology and the plague was under-

---

18. Shah, *Contagious Divides*, 88.
19. Shah, *Contagious Divides*, 127.
20. Trauner, "Chinese as Medical Scapegoats," 78–79; Shah, *Contagious Divides*, 155; Risse, *Driven by Fear*, 56.
21. James C. Mohr, *Plague and Fire: Battling Black Death and the 1900 Burning of Honolulu's Chinatown* (New York: Oxford University Press, 2005), 118; see also 175.
22. Mohr, *Plague and Fire*, 133, 159.

stood to be carried by rats.²³ Some, however, began to suggest that the broken sewage from the 1906 earthquake made it possible for "infected rats" or "refugee rats" from Chinatown to infect the city with the plague.²⁴

Trachoma and Other Contagions

The dominant culture in the twentieth century continued to connect other less lethal but equally contagious diseases with Asia. When trachoma, an eye disease that can lead to blindness, became a threat in the early decades of the twentieth century, it was either seen as endemic only among Asians because of the "poor physical state of the average Oriental"²⁵ or it was considered to be no longer threatening exclusively to Asians because Asians had been exposed to it for generations. Similarly, the fish diet of Asians, especially Chinese and Japanese, supposedly made them more liable to host parasites, but they could, again, be "healthy carriers" who endangered whites without the built-in resistance that Asians had built up over generations. Clonorchis sinensis, which causes clonorchiasis, for example, was (and still is in some circles) also called the Chinese liver fluke.²⁶

Asians of different ethnicities quickly became suspected carriers of contagious diseases as they began to come into the United States in larger numbers and when debates flared about Asian immigration during these early decades of the last century. Complaining against the dangers of "Manila cigars," a William Backner wrote in 1909:

> Now every soldier knows the uncleanliness of the average Philippino, and if you ask him he will tell you that many a poor fellow came home in a box by too close association

---

23. Trauner, "Chinese as Medical Scapegoats," 80; Mohr, *Plague and Fire*, 12; Risse, *Driven by Fear*, 57.
24. Shah, *Contagious Divides*, 153; Risse, *Driven by Fear*, 28–29.
25. Shah, *Contagious Divides*, 188.
26. Shah, *Contagious Divides*, 190, 198–99.

with them, as they are poison to the white man. They are all affected with a skin disease and a large majority are covered with open sores and scars. Leprosy, beri-beri, cholera, bubonic plague and other infectious disease, are, as everyone knows, prevalent there.[27]

Five years later, Charles T. Nesbitt testified before the House of Representatives claiming that "Asia was the 'fountain' of the 'most destructive pestilence' in recorded history and that Asians have consequently 'acquired such a high state of immunity to [its] effects that they have been unconscious carriers.'"[28]

Severe Acute Respiratory Syndrome (SARS)

Despite the repeal of the Chinese Exclusion Act in 1943 and the removal of the quota system by national origin with the implementation of the Immigration Act in 1965, Asian Americans have often continued to be targeted immediately whenever there is an outbreak of a contagious virus. During the SARS scare of 2003, the Centers for Disease Control (CDC) felt the need to state that SARS "is not in any way related to being Asian," and a health official in California tellingly referred to the bubonic plague in 1900 and said, "We are back where we were a century ago in dealing with an emerging infectious disease."[29] After all, while the nature of the virus is different, the same race of people was profiled and stigmatized. A study that sampled over half of the calls made to the CDC's Public Response Service in May 2003 that had to do with SARS-related concerns shows that the major concerns have to do with "fear of buying Asian merchandise," "working with Asians," "living near Asians," "going to school with Asians."[30] Fourteen percent of people in the United States reported avoiding "Asian businesses."[31]

---

27. Shah, *Contagious Divides*, 175.
28. Shah, *Contagious Divides*, 196.
29. Cited in Risse, *Driven by Fear*, 195, 196.
30. Bobbie Person et al., "Fear and Stigma: The Epidemic within the SARS Outbreak," *Emerging Infectious Diseases* 10, no. 2 (February 2004): 360.
31. Tessler, Choi, and Kao, "Anxiety of Being Asian Americans," 640.

Between SARS and Covid, we had the Hollywood movie *Contagion* in 2011. In ways that are perfectly understandable but perhaps less forgivable, the movie about a worldwide pandemic not only locates the origin of the virus in China but also attributes its spread to a white family in the United States to the female lead's business trip to Asia. As if that is not enough, the movie portrays China as corrupt in managing the outbreak. Not only do we see Chinese men kidnapping a white female epidemiologist who works for the World Health Organization to ensure by extortion that the vaccine for the virus would be available to them, but we also see Chinese officials being agitated and impatient with the investigative work done by this foreign epidemiologist in Hong Kong. This latter scenario brings to mind the accusation made against the Chinese during outbreaks of various viruses in the nineteenth century: Chinese had secret diseases, but they would try to hide the sickness and keep it from being known.[32] Finally, depicting a blogger and conspiracy theorist who takes advantage of the pandemic to make money by promoting a plant used in traditional Chinese medicine (Forsythia) as an effective cure but ends up causing a mass infection with people rushing to pharmacies to purchase the plant, the movie brings back memories of the conflicts between Western and traditional Chinese medical practices in earlier outbreaks of cholera, smallpox, and the bubonic plague.[33]

Trump as Symptom: A Web of Traditional National Values

In the last 150 years, people of Asian ancestry in general and of Chinese ancestry in particular have repeatedly been the scapegoats when there is a public health threat involving contagious diseases, and individual infections among them were turned into a generic or genetic condition of the entire race. While whites who contracted these contagious diseases are seen as victims and unwitting spread-

---

32. Risse, *Driven by Fear*, 24, 28.
33. Mohr, *Plague and Fire*, 9, 31–37, 76, 103; Shah, *Contagious Divides*, 55–56, 213.

ers of the diseases, Asian Americans who don't even have the virus are often seen as culprits and deceitful predators who bring about the virus to harm whites and endanger the nation. Trump's reference to the coronavirus as the "China virus" is, therefore, merely running a play that has been repeatedly run out of the United States' political playbook.

Characterizing a contagious disease as foreign is partly expressing a fear of foreign invasion. Similarly, many were anxious that if the 1900 bubonic plague would kill hundreds daily, as it was doing in Hong Kong, Honolulu would face "the prospect of appearing to be, or perhaps even becoming, 'Asian.'"[34] Trump is, of course, known for his promise to build a wall against "illegal" immigration. Besides his problematic insistence on giving the coronavirus names that associate the virus with China and the Chinese, Trump has signed and implemented various policies and executive orders between January and October 2020 that "explicitly target China or disproportionately impact Asian Americans" by, for example, limiting (immigrants and refugees from Asian nations) and barring (researchers and students from China) entry into the United States of America.[35]

Trump's "China virus" rhetoric and anti-immigration emphasis are both blame-game politics in times of trouble. Besides virus outbreaks, blaming the other as the threatening cause is often employed in face of economic uncertainties. China is widely expected to overtake the United States as the largest world economy, and, according to Trump, "illegal" immigrants exploit the benefits and drain the resources of the United States without contributing anything. Conceptualized a year after the 2008 recession, *Contagion*'s plot revolves around China's growth as an economic power. The female lead was in Asia for the opening of a factory of her transnational corporation. While this may seem like a celebration of trans-Pacific cooperation, the subplot of Chinese holding a white female epidemiologist as (a willing) hostage to get the vaccine shows the under-

---

34. Mohr, *Plague and Fire*, 56.
35. https://stopaapihate.org/

lying tension and competition between China and the West.[36] The movie's closing scene, which reveals the origin of the virus to be the deforestation in China that destroys an infected bat's natural habitat, further puts China's economic development in a negative light.

Racism, xenophobia, and white supremacy cannot be separated from capitalism and imperialism, since the United States is always reaching overseas to extract cheaper resources (including labor) and to expand the market. Economic concerns that kept Trump from ordering any kind of nationwide lockdown were also at play in these other contagious outbreaks in the history of the United States. Politicians and businesspeople worried that news of any epidemic or pandemic would cripple commerce and devastate the economy. Just as Trump waited to inform the nation about the severity of the coronavirus and occasionally disputes the statistics about its infection and mortality rates, California's Governor Henry T. Gage during the 1900 bubonic plague also, out of fear that San Francisco's commerce and tourism would be negatively affected, refused to acknowledge at first that the plague was present in the city, and later the findings of a national commission about the plague.[37] In other words, both Trump and Gage were doing exactly what they accused the Chinese of doing by not being forthcoming about a contagious virus. One should not forget that the Marine Hospital Service's role as a major player in addressing infectious diseases as a federal agency resulted from the passing of the National Quarantine Act of 1878 and "federal obligations for the regulation of interstate and international commerce."[38]

Pointing to "four elements of the neoliberal project: 'post truth,' disaster capitalism, individualism, and the dumbing down of society," Wesley C. Marshall declares "Donald Trump as man of his times, in many ways a singularly precise personification of today's

---

36. Aaron Baker, "Global Cinema and Contagion," *Film Quarterly* 66, no. 3 (Spring 2013): 12.

37. Shah, *Contagious Divides*, 121, 125, 145–46; Guenter B. Risse, *Plague, Fear, and Politics in San Francisco's Chinatown* (Baltimore, MD: Johns Hopkins University Press, 2012), 168–69, 171–73.

38. Risse, *Plague, Fear, and Politics*, 99–100.

neoliberal inspired zeitgeist."[39] Despite Trump's populist and protectionist rhetoric, there is, therefore, a consistent implementation of the neoliberal project in every sphere of life, as well as both within and beyond United States soil. As Maria Ryan points out, "Trump's most ostensibly radical commitment . . . to economic protectionism . . . was not a wholesale rejection of neoliberal trade in all circumstances."[40] As Trump's comments about taking or keeping the oil in Iraq and in Syria show, military might and money are for him interrelated if not exactly interchangeable. After all, the "freedom" that the United States is protecting and promoting always involves the freedom of capital to move around the globe and the freedom to consume mindlessly. The basic blueprint for the Trump regime—including neoliberal privatizations, corporatization, deregulation, subsidies of transnational businesses but withdrawal from the service sector by the state, suppression of labor unions, predation of public and common goods, emphasis on "individual responsibility," and elevation of the market as the ultimate standard for measuring and organizing societies—was already laid out by Friedrich Hayek and the Mont Pelerin Society in the 1940s, and actively implemented later by Margeret Thatcher and Ronald Reagan in the 1980s as well as through the so-called Washington Consensus of the mid-1990s.[41]

Risse insightfully points out that using the war metaphor against threatening diseases is understandable but problematic, since it is likely to "elicit aversive emotions that translate into demands for belligerent responses."[42] We have certainly seen the allusions to war with Trump, when he called himself a "wartime president" and the coronavirus "kung flu," as well as the results of his rhetoric.

---

39. Wesley C. Marshall, "The Trump Administration and the Neoliberal Project," *Theory in Action* 11, no. 3 (July 2018): 58.

40. Maria Ryan, "'Stability Not Chaos'? Donald Trump and the World—An Early Assessment," in *The Trump Presidency: From Campaign Trail to World Stage*, ed. Mara Oliva and Mark Shanahan (Cham: Palgrave Macmillan, 2019), 214.

41. Wendy Brown, *In the Ruins of Neoliberalism: The Rise of Antidemocratic Politics in the West* (New York: Columbia University Press, 2019), 17–18.

42. Risse, *Driven by Fear*, 11, 200.

Citing the 2006 amendment of the National Defense Authorization Act that gives authority to the United States president to deploy the National Guard for "natural disaster, epidemic or terrorist attack, or serious public health emergencies" and referencing the movie *Contagion*, Risse further suggests that utilizing the military against threatening diseases has become a "new normal."[43] Again, while the size and scale of military involvement may be different today, resorting to military forces was not exactly new. Writing about San Francisco's Chinatown during the bubonic plague of the 1900s, Risse himself states that measures to contain the public health threat "were achieved through the employment of police and military forces," and, describing the Marine Hospital Service as "a paramilitary organization," identifies public health as having an "early martial character."[44] National guards were called out to enforce the quarantine of Honolulu's Chinatown during the bubonic outbreak, and "men were taken as if prisoners of war by lines of military guards" whenever a site was condemned, with one person remembering on that fateful day when Chinatown was burned down that it was "just like a war zone."[45] In San Francisco, health department inspectors were not only accompanied by "club-wielding police escorts," but they also "broke down the doors with their axes and sledgehammers" if they were not granted admission by the Chinese residents there.[46] Even earlier, when syphilis was becoming a public health threat, there was a movement to follow France and administer a kind of "police medical regulation,"[47] or government-enforced inspection that would be compulsory for prostitutes. In San Francisco, where syphilis was immediately attributed to Chinese prostitutes, the editor of *California Medical Gazette* wrote in 1869 that San Francisco should "be the first city in our broad Union to adopt the French police system of examination

---

43. Risse, *Driven by Fear*, 198–201.
44. Risse, *Driven by Fear*, 2, 3, 99.
45. Mohr, *Plague and Fire*, 57, 95, 133.
46. Risse, *Plague, Fear, and Politics*, 127.
47. Cited in John C. Burnham, "Medical Inspection of Prostitutes in America in the Nineteenth Century: The St. Louis Experiment and Its Sequel," *Bulletin of the History of Medicine* 45, no. 3 (May-June 1971): 203.

of prostitutes."[48] A prominent New York physician, Dr. William Sanger, even suggested that the compulsory inspection of prostitutes for syphilis should be done by "a special medical department of the police."[49] Note that this movement eventually failed not because people were opposed to the use of police and force, but because of the "moral outrage" that such inspection would end up "legalizing and licensing" prostitution rather than working to eliminate it as an avoidable social evil.[50]

Trump's "wartime" presidency was not only directed against the coronavirus but also continued this long national tradition of global militarism—whether through military aid and training or direct military interference—under the pretext of promoting "development" and protecting "democratic freedom."[51] Besides authorizing bombings in Afghanistan, Iraq, Syria, Yemen (though often without releasing any airpower summaries), the Trump administration, following a long-established pattern, carried out military operations on United States soil. In ways similar to the militarization of the police in its (anti-Black and anti-brown) war against drugs, the Department of Homeland Security militarized its agents to fight—and terrorize—"enemies within"—undocumented migrants and terrorists (and often, undocumented migrants *as* terrorists). It is little wonder why Trump and his supporters have continued to condemn Colin Kaepernick's kneeling gesture as disrespect of both the national flag and the United States military.[52]

Conclusion

A national narrative of development and progress enables the powerful to emphasize closure and their ability to get over and move on from, perhaps even transcend, a less-than-desirable past. As

---

48. Burnham, "Medical Inspection," 205.
49. Burnham, "Medical Inspection," 205.
50. Burnham, "Medical Inspection," 211.
51. See Andrew J. Bacevich, *The New American Militarism: How Americans Are Seduced by War* (New York: Oxford University Press, 2013); Rosa Brooks, *How Everything Became War and the Military Became Everything: Tales from the Pentagon* (New York: Simon & Schuster, 2016).
52. Brown, *Ruins of Neoliberalism*, 14.

Joseph R. Winters writes, "The pervasive commitment to the idea of progress in American culture . . . mitigates experiences and memories of racial trauma and loss."[53] We see this, for example, in the white and dominant perspective that slavery is "over," that the internment of (Japanese American) citizens is "no more," that affirmative action is "obsolete," or that the Cold War has "ended." Referring to this cultural habit to "repress" and "forget troublesome details of the national memory," Ralph Ellison proposes that "more than any other people, Americans have been locked in a deadly struggle with time, with history."[54] By denials, disguises, or deflections, various wreckages and numerous wounds are written out of our country's narratives and collective memories, even or especially if those damages are fundamental and foundational to the building of our "forgetful nation" and its myths.[55] With what Diana Taylor calls "percepticide,"[56] we as part of the general population may willfully blind ourselves to disavow or (dis)miss not only sights and scenes of past and present injustice but also the continuations of past discriminatory tactics into the present.

With Trump's defeat in the November election and disgrace after his failed attempt to incite a coup in January, there will be those who want to celebrate and say that we can finally move on from a bad chapter of US history. However, not only does Trump's practice of making those of Chinese or Asian ancestry scapegoats for the coronavirus pandemic have a long history, but the ideologies associated with this practice are also in the DNA of this nation.

---

53. Joseph R. Winters, *Hope Draped in Black: Race, Melancholy, and the Agony of Progress* (Durham, NC: Duke University Press, 2106), 4. Commitment to this progress idea is, for example, consistently present in the rhetoric of President Obama, Trump's predecessor; see Winters, *Hope Draped in Black*, 187–207.

54. Ralph Ellison, *Shadow and Act* (New York: Random House, 1964), 250.

55. Ali Behdad, *A Forgetful Nation: On Immigration and Cultural Identity in the United States* (Durham, NC: Duke University Press, 2005).

56. Diana Taylor, *Disappearing Acts: Spectacles of Gender and Nationalism in Argentina's "Dirty War"* (Durham, NC: Duke University Press, 1997), 119–38.

The close connection among capitalism, militarism, and racism in the United States—a kind of "unholy trinity," if you will—have long been recognized by people of color, so Trump's regime in the United States is more a symptom or a mutated virus than a new virus. These ideological forces will not disappear even though they may function differently and more subtly with a different person in the White House.

Akin to the threat of terrorism's so-called invisible enemies and of the pandemic's unsuspected contagion, white supremacy, neoliberalism, and imperialism—by portraying Blacks as a menace, widening the wealth gap, and weakening national sovereignty with permeable borders—trigger a social sentiment of fear that also allows a more authoritarian culture of oppression, colonization, and exploitation to develop. As many media pundits have pointed out, Trump's election in 2016 had partly to do with his self-projection as a "strong man" who could alleviate people's anxieties about terrorism, offshoring job loss, queer sexuality, Roe v. Wade, and/or "illegal" immigration (though the media are themselves by no means innocent when it comes to the spread of fear with their many infotainments). Trump's rally cry—"you're not going to have a country anymore"—is, like the "emotionology" at work in scapegoating people of Asian ancestry for a host of contagious diseases such as the coronavirus, a symptom of a syndrome that Martha C. Nussbaum calls "the monarchy of fear."[57] What Trump did, from scapegoating of Chinese Americans to his manipulation of a general politics of fear and of division, was not new. Neither were his specific policies that promoted white supremacy, neoliberalism, and militarism. He was merely the *extreme* or the *most explicit expression* that proves the rule.

---

57. Martha C. Nussbaum, *The Monarchy of Fear: A Philosopher Looks at Our Political Crisis* (New York: Simon & Schuster, 2018).

CHAPTER 13

Black Lives Still *Matter*

Joshua S. Bartholomew

Introduction

Black Lives Matter (BLM) has achieved the greatest support for racial justice since the civil rights movement. The summer of 2020 produced the largest protest movement in American history. The tragic deaths of Breonna Taylor, Ahmaud Arbery, and George Floyd radicalized millions of people who were previously inclined to dismiss systemic and structural racism. BLM carried forward a long tradition of political action for Black freedom, continuing a movement for liberation that helps us reckon with the aftermath of Trump's administration. The surge in public support for BLM appears to be an expression of approval for the movement's most basic demand: that the police stop killing Black people. But how did we get here? Even before the Trump years, BLM had been showing up for racial justice and condemning white supremacy, but not nearly as many people took heed to its message and admitted that Black lives do indeed matter. So, what has changed? And where do we go from here? The answers have to do with the evolution of BLM, and a mass awakening to the truth that white supremacy has not ever served *the people*.

How Did We Get Here?

What is BLM? Founded in 2013 as a response to the acquittal of Trayvon Martin's murderer, BLM represents a global network with local chapters whose mission is to eradicate white supremacy and to intervene in state and other forms of violence against Black communities. By countering and fighting acts of violence, carving out space for Black thriving, and centering Black existence, BLM reflects a collective of inclusive activists who believe in a liberation movement that affirms the most marginalized within Black communities. It is an international movement with a local focus, with branches in towns and big cities targeting different areas, practices, and modes of societal transformation. BLM both organizes and mobilizes people. It has been the people's voice of social change and resistance, fighting to hold the US system of anti-Black racism accountable.

BLM first emerged to challenge colorblind racism among other sociopolitical tools used for the maintenance of today's racial order. During Barack Obama's presidency, there was a general consensus among many Americans that Obama's election meant that we lived in a postracial society. The activism of BLM, the Movement for Black Lives, and the constant testimonies of those lost to police violence articulated a clear counternarrative to the trend to believe that racism no longer existed. When Trump ran for office, he used the ambivalence of many Americans concerning the reality of anti-Black racism, stoking sentiments toward white voters that were antithetical to the goals and aims of BLM. His campaign promised to restore a fictional past in which white supremacy was unquestioned. Trump created and empowered a backlash of white supremacy in spite of cries for racial liberation and social justice.

Trump's election was a setback to some of the achievements and conversations BLM had begun to foster. It was a pivotal moment for activists to look inward and to reevaluate methods and objectives. In the moment, Trump's election proved that BLM did not have what it took to elect the type of courageous and visionary leader the times warranted. Trump forced BLM to confront opposing forces during an administration that was intolerant, and even dismissive, of BLM's advocacy and resistance to white supremacy. BLM had to revisit its political options and deal with the disillusionment of having to now face even more racist policies on policing, immigration, and access to jobs. BLM rightly turned to its communities for empowerment and stability with a focused look on the substantive actions that people in the highest political offices were making to represent the most marginalized. BLM built power on local levels, marking an important change in its course of political action that would prove to be a necessary foundation for its eventual resurgence.[1]

BLM's activism after Trump's election cautions us to be wise about what it means to engage people who have no stake in all of humanity, especially the humanity of Black people. Instead of negotiating with hate and injustice, BLM continued to contest anti-Black racism and empowered Black people and all people to remain committed to the struggle for liberation. During the Trump years, activists built protective measures for the most vulnerable members of our society, developing connections for youth empowerment, affordable housing, and access to employment. Large majorities of Americans supported reforms such as requiring the use of body cameras, banning choke holds, mandating a national police-misconduct database, and curtailing qualified immunity, but many people still viewed racism as largely a personal failing rather than a systemic force. Until something unprecedented happened.

Trump's assurance to usher in a return to the cultural conservatism of the 1950s became enveloped by overlapping national crises. The Covid-19 pandemic exposed Trump's inability to reach people beyond the limits of his overwhelmingly white and conservative base. And, as with other issues, including the coronavirus pandemic, the Trump administration's governing strategy did not reflect the country's broader interests and current political realities. Statistics emerged showing that Black and nonwhite people disproportionately filled the ranks of essential workers, the unemployed, and those most vulnerable to the virus. Numerous experts from different fields from politics to medicine derided Trump's downplaying of the virus and his urging of Americans to return to work no matter the cost. All the while, the state's apparent apathy to the rampant racist killings continued unceasingly. The coalition of people sympathetic to BLM's cause could now see much more eas-

---

1. An example of similar institutional transformation from another local movement is Kayla Reid's Action St. Louis; see https://actionstl.org.

ily and clearly the ways in which Trump was not a president for the people. The United States erupted last summer with a message that was loud and clear: Black lives *still* matter!

Where Do We Go from Here?

Throughout BLM's lifespan, there are lessons we can take away for how to sustain hope in the struggle for Black liberation and for how to build power in the politics of race. BLM has made people grapple with the fact that we are not actually in a postracial society. This shift in public opinion partly uncovers discontent with social and economic systems that have led to ongoing conditions of racial and political unrest. While retiring the name "Aunt Jemima," tearing down Confederate statues, and painting the street with BLM is necessary and opens up important conversations, Black people still need, and collectively want to live in, a system that holds police accountable and prevents state violence from ever happening again. Fostering a culture of liberation involves transforming deep-rooted structures of racism embedded within American society. Now more than ever is the time for a collective, community-centered, antiracist plan for interventions and policies that eliminate white supremacy as the social evil of our time.

For the first time in US history, there may be an antiracist majority in the racially and socioeconomically diverse coalition of voters radicalized by the blunt transition from the hope of the Obama era to the malice of the Trump years. BLM's preparation in meeting the moment creates an opportunity for activists to lead the first antiracist majority in the United States, and maybe even in the world. The work of generations of Black activists, thinkers, scholars, and organizers such as Angela Davis, Kimberlé Crenshaw, Michelle Alexander, and others has gotten us here. Society is in a place where expressions like *systemic racism* are readily accessible to people from varying demographics and occupations, and more and more people are becoming aware of the need for social change. We are at a turning point, with implications for economic justice and Black self-determination. But how far will the possibilities of the times extend, and how can BLM and Black activists effectively continue the abolitionist project of making people aware of the need to eradicate anti-Black racism and white supremacy once and for all?

We could consider two potential endings—one aimed at police and prisons, and a broader outcome, focused on the elimination of entrenched systems that suppress the agency and full equality of Black people. Some of BLM's more radical remedies, like defunding the police, have yet to be fully embraced. Although there is no universal, definite consensus on how to end America's tradition of racism, there is a general agreement that police are not the solution to problems like systemic poverty, mental-health challenges, and being displaced from a home, and that we should use public resources to meet the needs of communities. Many want to see the existing systems of policing and carceral punishment abolished and replaced with social mechanisms that actually rehabilitate and restore justice and keep people safe inside and outside of their homes. Believing in racial equality in the abstract and supporting policies and practices that would make it a reality are two different things.

What we have needed for some time is a coming together in Black communities of two forces of liberation that have had the same goal in mind but have not been working together throughout BLM's existence: BLM and Black churches. Once the fortress of abolitionist advocacy and one of the original sites of Black people's awakening to the evils of white supremacy, Black churches have been noticeably absent from the center and development of BLM. Historically, Black churches served as a bastion for spiritual and civil activism. However, as the civil rights generation aged, church became less relevant to a generation raised on technology and increased global connections. As the deaths of unarmed Black people continued, the millennial generation sparked BLM on social media, changing the landscape of how to generate awareness for racial justice. Consequently, BLM activists have found different ways to connect not just to the struggle for freedom but also to spirituality, sometimes cutting ties altogether with organized religion and Black churches. If collective progress is going to be made in the struggle for Black liberation, then BLM and Black churches will have to address their differences. A united front against racism is much better than a divided one.

Black congregations have been involved in the Underground Railroad, the abolitionist movement, and the civil rights movement. While that may be the view of Black history with which we are most familiar and told to emulate, Black churches should support BLM, given that the struggle now looks different and includes innovate tactics and calls for radical change. We should remember that many Black churches during Martin Luther King Jr.'s public ministry were against what he was doing and wanted him to serve communities differently. We owe much of where we are today because King chose to press onward. The goal here is not to bash Black churches or its impact on our communities but to highlight that churches are made up of imperfect human beings who sometimes need their perspectives to be challenged and fine-tuned for the greater benefit of and service to the people.

What is missing from an approach to collective liberation in Black churches is the ability to form *common connections* with movements like BLM. We can no longer assume that the tradition of hope within Black churches will be passed down through generations of churchgoing families. Increasing diversification of faith options makes it imperative that intentional effort be devoted to keeping the common connection between BLM and Black churches going. But even more crucial than the retention of ideals is the healing of the wounds of generations past. The coming together between Black millennials and Black churches in the Black freedom movement entails the need for Black churches to confront barriers within its institutions that present problems for BLM. BLM was created and has been sustained primarily by Black women and queer persons. Enduring conservative attitudes in Black church cultures can oftentimes clash with ideals of radical, inclusive hospitality that range from inappropriate to downright oppressive treatment and training regarding LGBTQ people. Black churches must be liberated from bad habits of patriarchy, internalized racism, misogyny, homophobia, transphobia, queerphobia, class fragmentation, and Christian triumphalism in order to be able to effectively work together with BLM.

Although justice seeking is intergenerational, BLM activists identify clear differences between their organizations and those of the civil rights generation that preceded them. In contrast to the patriarchal leadership model of King and the civil rights movement, BLM is a decentralized, leader-full network of local organizations. BLM replaces the charismatic male figure with many voices, especially those of Black women, inviting the gifts of the community and the emergence of unlikely local leaders. BLM's social media platform has become a way for its members to tell counternarratives. BLM actions disrupt everyday life, shutting things down and putting the bodies of its supporters at risk. BLM also works with allies, but from vanguard positionalities, engaging not in interracial but in cross-racial collaborations that focus on undoing the systematic denial of Black humanity by the schemes structured to support oppression.

Institutionalized religion is steeped in tradition, but Christian churches need to evolve. "Every change that has happened has come as a result of mass movements."[2] Therefore, Black churches should do everything possible to remain relevant within movements and strategies to uplift Black communities, even when it means they must be constructively critical of their own legacy. Black churches can articulate more concrete approaches to social justice by supporting BLM as a way to offer practical guidance for Black and marginalized communities. Black religious leadership can make an enormous contribution to these shifting times by contributing to antiracist culture and structural social change in American society. Black preachers and pastors are in charge of the most numerous and continuous gatherings of Black people, those who are the worst victims of America's racism and whose churches are financially, culturally, and politically independent of corporate influence. Whether organized religion plays an important role in one's life, the centrality of Black churches in Black communities and in the United States has been and continues to be monumental to the fight for freedom. But until Black churches and BLM can establish cohesion, it will not be easy to find a central locus of spiritual awakening and support for Black freedom.

---

2. Angela Y. Davis, *Freedom Is a Constant Struggle: Ferguson, Palestine, and the Foundations of a Movement*, ed. Frank Barat (Chicago: Haymarket Books, 2016), 36.

Conclusion

From its inception, BLM nurtured the power of Black communities in the face of social and political challenges. In spite of major setbacks and unforeseen circumstances, BLM developed community-oriented strategies of resistance that reenergized the spirit of US democracy when it was most needed. BLM's activism, determination, and commitments to racial justice raised the consciousness of millions of people during a time of contemporary racial division and unreliable political leadership. While BLM weathered the Trump years and increased the general public's awareness of racism, the fight for racial equality is far from over. The next phase of the struggle involves cultivating antiracist sentiments, institutions, systems, and practices to shape society and its appreciation that Black lives matter.

Black communities are not a monolithic people, but Black people are a collective. Black churches that have not been supportive of BLM should reevaluate their politics of Black liberation and examine how much power has been given to harmful aspects of their belief systems. Much like when Black churches did not join the Black Power movement, Black churches are again in danger of missing an opportunity to evolve and to support the most relevant voice of Black resistance to white supremacy. In order to confront realities of systemic racism and foster antiracist interventions, Black communities can contribute to BLM and continue to establish common connections that denounce oppressive tactics in the struggle for liberation. The point is for Black churches to provide better choices and to create a political culture that is more inclusive and democratically conscious. No other community can do so as effectively. To followers of Jesus the Christ, such praxis is a quintessential social Christian project.

As important members in the struggle for liberation, white people and non-Black people have much work to do. The work of antiracism is not solely a project for Black communities; in fact, non-Black, especially white communities, have just as much at stake in their humanity. Racism dehumanizes the oppressor just as much, if not more, than the oppressed. What we do not want is for the people's demand for social justice to give way to complacency or be eclipsed by another white, racist backlash. Given that the coming of more opportunities for racial awakening is uncertain, the time to act is now. Great strides toward self-determination and equality are possible for as long as they are rooted in the collective, anti-Black racist efforts of liberation for Black people, and for all people around the world, because Black lives *still* matter.

CHAPTER 14

"*I Can't Breathe*": *Neocolonial Geotrauma and Violence in the Age of Trump*

APRIL M. WOODSON

> Trauma reminds us that there is literally no place outside of research—and conversely, no research that is "beyond" the body. Such conclusions demand critical reworking of the academic voice and an openness to the vulnerability of living in times of "crisis ordinariness."
>
> —Lauren Berlant[1]

Senate Uncertainty Induces Historic Memory and Geotrauma

The years of the Trump presidency were traumatic for many Americans, especially African Americans. A narrative of white exceptionalism and neo-Nazi friendliness was the tone of the Trump administration. For some Americans, the Biden–Harris victory was a cause for celebration; however, many Americans knew that a Biden–Harris victory needed House and Senate majorities to help America move toward, instead of away from, its potential for great-

---

1. Lauren Berlant, *Cruel Optimism* (Durham, NC: Duke University Press, 2011), 4. See also Kate Coddington and Jacque Micieli-Voutsinas, "On Trauma, Geography, and Mobility: Towards Geographies of Trauma," *Emotion, Space and Society* 24 (August 2017): 52–56.

ness. Despite the Trump administration's mantra "Make America Great Again," it is debatable if and when America was "ever great." Thus, the evening of January 4, 2021, the night before the Georgia Senate runoff, was anxiety filled for many Americans, just like the eve of election night 2020.

As someone who lived in the Atlanta metro area for many of my adult years, I sat on the edge of my bed, vacillating between praying to God for a miracle and wondering if my old home state would deliver this country from another impending congressional nightmare. God, I trust; however, I also knew that the state of Georgia could fail to deliver a two-seat Senate victory, which is what was needed to restore the executive-congressional balance of power that could give America a fighting chance to get through the Covid-19 pandemic. Regardless of how the Senate runoff election turned out, I knew that I had to find peace on the other side of it. That night, I wondered how many other Christians were praying for the outcome that I was, or had white evangelical Trump supporters so usurped Christianity that many Christians were praying for 45's legacy to continue through a Republican Senate majority alongside a conservative Supreme Court constructed by both Trump's hand and the Republican majority Senate. I specifically pondered, "What were African American Christians in Georgia praying for the night of the Senate runoff?" Many may have been praying for the victory of Rev. Raphael Warnock, whose victory would make him the first African American senator from Georgia and "the one" who could carry the legacy of the social gospel from Ebenezer Baptist Church, where Rev. Martin Luther King Jr. was baptized, ordained, preached his first sermon at nineteen years old, and pastored with his father until 1968, all the way to the halls of Congress. More importantly, I knew that Atlanta Mayor Keisha Lance Bottoms and other Georgia public leaders were praying for peace on January 6, regardless of the runoff election results.

Blackness and Christianity are not mutually exclusive; yet they have felt conflicting and tumultuous (for me)[2] during the Trump

---

2. I want to make clear that I am not speaking for all Blacks, nor am I speaking for all Black Christians.

administration because Trump has utilized, promoted, and endorsed white nationalism as a method to court and keep his evangelical Christian base. Christian, American, Black, and female. All these adjectives define me—and *all* are nonnegotiable parts of my identity. But whose Christianity and whose idea of democracy would I be forced to live in after the 2020 election? The past four years have been the only time in my life when I have weighed the gravity between Matthew 5:44, which states, "Love your enemies and pray for them who persecute you," and Matthew 11:12, which states, "From the days of John the Baptist, the kingdom of God suffers violence and the violent take it by force." Would my Christian beliefs guide me to "turn the other cheek" or would my Black nationalist tendencies emerge from my racial fatigue and current and generational geotrauma. "Geotrauma describes multiscalar, intersecting and mutual relations between trauma and place."[3]

Well past midnight and pacing the floor, I realized that I was "there" again. I was back in an anxiety-filled state with a flurry of emotions of impending doom, and I began to struggle to breathe. I knew that this was not a self-induced panic attack or a mental fit of terror because I could feel the pull of ancestors on my spirit, and I began to sense generational trauma beginning to rise to my consciousness. Black scholars have theorized slavery in the United States as a psychic event, the memory of which is passed down through generations of African American communities and how the frequent reenactment of racist violence impacts collective and individual psychology.[4] During the Trump years, Americans have witnessed a series of reenactments of white nationalism with its roots in white colonizing Christianity heralded by our commander-in-chief.

While the mantra "I Can't Breathe" has become a rallying cry for the Black Lives Matter movement, it was first uttered eleven times by Eric Garner on July 17, 2014, in Staten Island, New York, when he was unlawfully put in a choke hold by Officer Daniel Pantaleo

---

3. Rachel Pain, "Geotrauma: Violence, Place and Repossession," *Progress in Human Geography* (August 2020): 3.

4. Pain, "Geotrauma," 5.

while two other NYPD officers tackled him to the ground for selling loose, untaxed cigarettes, or "loosies," cigarettes sold individually, as they are called in the "hood," where the cost of a pack of cigarettes is often inflated at local bodegas and corner stores in low socio-economic neighborhoods. The Eric Garner case was the first death of a Black man at the hands of the police where civilian video of the incident was introduced to the nation by news media outlets. Many Americans, myself included, were certain that justice—the firing and conviction of Officer Pantaleo—would be served because the disturbing videotape revealed the unauthorized and unlawful use of a choke hold, which is a police practice that was prohibited by the NYPD in 1993. According to the NYPD, this blatant use of excessive force was deemed "necessary" to subdue Mr. Garner, the 395-pound, obese, chronic asthmatic with an enlarged heart, husband and father of three children. "I can't breathe" were his dying words.

Now these words haunt me and many other African Americans into a trauma-induced state of anxiety, fear, depression, and racial fatigue that was re-ignited in the summer of 2020 when for nine minutes and twenty-nine seconds, with a knee pressed against his neck, "I can't breathe" became the dying words of yet another Black man. George Floyd, with the knee of Officer Derek Chauvin on his neck, died, as three additional Minneapolis police officers watched him beg for his life and call for his mother, and as civilians watched and videotaped the event.

The trauma of the 2014 Garner case lingers for many Americans, especially African Americans, who assumed that because this case had cell-phone video, unlike the deaths of many other Black people at the hands of law enforcement, there would be swift disciplinary action and a conviction of the officers involved. The video of this "gang" of Staten Island officers who gave the narrative that Mr. Garner was "resisting arrest" will never leave my psyche, particularly because New York is the state of my birth. Born in the Bronx and raised on Long Island, I still have flashbacks to my teenage years of the subway vigilante Bernard Goetz in 1984 and the 1989 Bensonhurst riots that occurred after the killing of sixteen-year-old Yusef Hawkins. State provisions and actions compound trauma in the normalization of violence such that the state is complicit with individual abusers (Pantaleo) in "institutional betrayal" (NYPD), in failing to ensure justice, and through the effects of austerity on the possibilities for healing and rebuilding.[5] Yet, places like Bensonhurst and Staten Island have never been considered as places in need of healing.

Frantz Fanon said, "We revolt simply because . . . we can no longer breathe."[6] My scholarship argues that the African American historical experience is a colonized experience in the United States through the interplay of the doctrine of Manifest Destiny that guided the political system, the social/domestic system of white-male patriarchy, and the institutionalized economic system of slavery—all of which were co-signed and endorsed by "the colonizers," white Christianity.[7] "Postcolonial trauma theory identifies the roots of many collective traumas to lie in the violence of colonialism, racism and capitalism."[8] Open, ongoing, and institutionalized contemporary racism against Black bodies is what I am calling neocolonialism. The social and political problem of trauma is the interplay of embodied experience with spatial context. This includes the ways that trauma may be reflected back, compounded and manipulated, or challenged and transformed by the environments that it inhabits.[9] Institutional racism in the criminal justice system has allowed and even condoned neocolonial violence against Black bodies. On this issue, the Trump administration remained silent.

There is an interwoven line between the events of January 6 at the Capitol by white insurrectionists and the colonial-to-contemporary tapestry of US colonial systems that function to keep knees on the necks of African Americans (and other marginalized people). The criminal justice system that took five years to fire Officer Pantaleo and justified the choke hold that fatally killed Eric Garner, the unlawful

---

5. Pain, "Geotrauma," 6.
6. Christina Sharpe, *In the Wake: On Blackness and Being* (Durham, NC: Duke University Press, 2016), 108.
7. April Woodson, "'Dialogical Offense': A Postcolonial Womanist Deconstruction of the Colonial Experience of African American Women through U.S. Institutional Apparatus Known as Criminal Justice Policy" (PhD diss., University of Denver and Iliff School of Theology, 2020).
8. Pain, "Geotrauma," 5.
9. Pain, "Geotrauma."

use of a no-knock warrant resulting in the death of Breonna Taylor in her bed in her own home, and the endorsement of neo-Nazis as "fine people" from the president are a few examples. The Capitol insurrectionists continue to use their god of whiteness to suppress the democratic values that need to emerge, must emerge, in order for America to become an America for all people.

Vacillating between Hope and Hopelessness

On January 3, I celebrated as Cori Bush was sworn into the US House of Representatives and embraced the hope that Congresswoman Bush, six years my junior, would be a symbol for many Christians and Black Missourians particularly. Why? Because as a pastor who has been an activist since the Ferguson riots, Rep. Bush is the first African American woman to serve in the US House of Representatives representing the state of Missouri. I recently became a Missourian and recognize the magnanimity of this accomplishment by a Black woman who was born and raised in the congressional district that represents Ferguson, Missouri, which became infamous for the 2014 fatal shooting of Michael Brown by the Ferguson police. I currently live approximately twelve miles from the site where the body of Michael Brown lay in the street for four hours. Missouri is now added to the list of my states of residency; all the places that I have lived are associated with high-profile police crimes against Black bodies and racial unrest. "*I Can't Breathe!*" I live in perpetual trauma by geography. A growing field of scholarship called geotrauma studies calls psychological trauma, rather than physical trauma, "the disease of our times."[10]

How can I and other African and Native Americans find peace in a land that cries out with the breath of our dead ancestors and the loss of breath by our contemporary brothers and sisters—especially in the wake of a national pandemic where Native, Black, and Hispanic lives have been disproportionately lost to this respiratory disease called Covid-19? Contrary to Trump supporters who believe that Covid-19 is a hoax, "the dead, take up space." Many

---

10. Pain, "Geotrauma," 1.

faith traditions and worldviews believe that "absent" from the earthly realm does not mean "absent." "Indigenous explanations of intergenerational trauma do not see relationships with ancestors as closed off after death, but intergenerational transmission as having spiritual dimensions."[11] Even America's civil religion recognizes this principle. Why else would this nation honor two dead presidents and celebrate both Memorial and Veterans Day with such great fanfare? What about the cries of my ancestors from the Middle Passage, slavery, reconstruction, segregation, and the Black Power and civil rights eras who lost their lives fighting "to breathe" but were lynched, gunned down, hosed, and even executed? Did their Black lives matter? Under the Trump oligarchy and its associated evangelical, cultic Pence Christianity, the breath of my people was silenced by the neofascist political rhetoric and unchecked neocolonial violence against Black bodies under the rhetoric of "we are the party of law and order."

What were Christians praying for on the eve of the Georgia Senate runoff? What were African Americans praying for? These two groups are not mutually exclusive; there is overlap. I know because I live, move, and have my being in this overlap. I breathe in this overlap. Am I being asked to choose between the cry of my racially fatigued embodied self and the wrath of the righteousness of my God? America was founded on Judeo-Christian principles, which say in Acts 17:28, "for in him, we live, and move and have our being," with the "him" being Jesus Christ, Savior, Lord, and Liberator. Many African Americans embrace Jesus as the liberator who came to set the captives free at the cost of his own blood and not a sanitized version of white liberalism that wants comfortable "liberation."

Trumpian Neocolonial Trauma Produces New "Voices" and New "Praxes"

Writing as a Christian ethicist gives this chapter academic location, but it does not necessarily reflect its context. In this chapter, I join

---

11. Pain, "Geotrauma," 7.

those scholars who investigate trauma as a chronic ongoing condition often situated in collective histories of violence. Historically, conceptualized as a wound or physical injury to the body, modern psychologists have since theorized trauma as emotional wounding or psychic forms of distress.[12] This is especially true for Black, postcolonial, and indigenous analyses. Feminist and queer scholarship also place oppressive social and political relations at the heart of trauma.[13] The Trump years have had distinct implications for the characteristics of my research and academic voice, and I think that they should for other academics as well. For example, Latinx Christian ethicist Miguel De La Torre states, "Nationalist Christianity not only manifests itself in our political structures (the current Trump administration); but also impacts how our academic disciplines construct knowledge."[14] De La Torre invites his reader to "embrace hopelessness" as a praxis.[15] He states that the hopelessness that he advocates is neither despairing nor disabling; rather, it is a methodology that propels the marginalized toward concrete actions.[16] De La Torre's hopelessness is one form of praxis that should be embraced. However, given recent geotrauma in the United States (not just for African Americans), "Is it possible to imagine hope as a '(geo)space' where hopelessness and a sense of God's sustaining presence somehow coexist?"[17] As a Christian, I say, perhaps; as an African American, I'm not so sure. Because of the geotrauma of violence during the Trump presidency our voices and praxes as scholars and activists *should* sound and look different.

The praxis that I advocate is one that I have named "dialogical offense," "dialogical" being the adjective describing the noun "offense." Athletes are expected to operate from a posture or posi-

---

12. Pain, "Geotrauma," 5.
13. Pain, "Geotrauma," 5.
14. Miguel A. De La Torre, "Embracing the Hopelessness of Those Seeking Pastoral Care," *Journal of Pastoral Theology* 30, no. 1 (2020): 4.
15. De La Torre, "Embracing the Hopelessness." Also see Miguel A. De La Torre, *Embracing Hopelessness* (Minneapolis: Fortress Press, 2017).
16. De La Torre, "Embracing the Hopelessness," 7.
17. Leanna K. Fuller, "A Pastoral Theological Response to Miguel De La Torre," *Journal of Pastoral Theology* 30, no. 1 (2020): 17.

tion of offense as necessary to their victory, but so should everyday Americans. I am advocating "embracing offense" as a conscious necessary praxis of living in an unstable America. "Dialogical offense" is the nomenclature that I have designated to collectively describe strategies of resistance by scholars on the margins (and our allies) who take the posture to destabilize the center, canon, or status quo. The Trump years have left marks of geotrauma on the African American psyche, particularly when President Trump said that the 2017 Charlottesville neo-Nazi demonstrators were "very fine people" yet failed to make any national statement about the countless incidents of violence against Black bodies at the hands of the police that occurred all over this nation during his presidency. More importantly, as a moral leader President Trump never addressed the idea that every human life is precious.[18]

The insurrection at our nation's Capitol and other horrific acts against our democracy of "We the people" should have heightened the awareness of all Americans that domestic terrorists are operating openly and under cover in our midst. So too should the praxis of Americans on the side of justice. What I am claiming as acts of dialogical offense have varied based on the historical era for Black Americans. For example, to cope with their geotrauma, a psychic posture of dialogical offense for Africans started when they hit the shores of America. Another historic praxis can be seen in Nat Turner's bloody slave rebellion, in 1831, which Turner saw as prophetic from "the colonizer's" religion that he learned to preach; yet this slave rebellion was viewed as a horrific insurrection in its time, when approximately fifty-one white people lost their lives. Turner's insurrection returns us to the writings of Fanon, who discussed the thoughts of the colonized during their insurrectional stage as "It's them or us."[19] Another example of what I am claiming as dialogical-offense praxis was when Sojourner Truth bared her breasts at the Women's Rights Convention in 1851 and said, "Ain't

---

18. Here I am utilizing Jeremiah 1:5(a) (NIV), "Before I formed you in the womb, I knew you," to make this claim.
19. Frantz Fanon, *The Wretched of the Earth* (New York: Grove Press, 1963), 43.

I a woman?" Both are examples of direct opposition or "positions of offense" to the lie of white male superiority, colonizing paternalism, and economic and physical exploitation. "Histories of violence can be put in a dialogical relationship with each other; psychic and political struggles must go hand in hand lest political action be haunted by an unprocessed past."[20] African Americans particularly must process the past of the Trump presidency. A praxis of dialogical offense does not have to include violence, but Fanon's words remind us that revolt may be necessary—to breathe. A posture of offense that demands dialogue between Americans caught between democratic ideals and demagogic leadership must find a way to mend itself—its systems and its soul. My hope is that the Biden–Harris team will operate like a John the Baptist preparing the way for an American future yet to be known, even a future that may incur more violence from both sides. As America seeks to move post-Trump, we must be prepared.

As I stated earlier, God I trust. I trust that, like the Bible story of the tumultuous transition from King Saul to King David's kingship,[21] God put President Joseph R. Biden, a devout Catholic, in the White House, "for such a time as this."[22] Learning from our contemporary events, Americans must incorporate into their American democratic understanding that "breath" is given by "the Divine" but it must also be given by our democracy. As a nation, if we have learned anything from Garner's and Floyd's last words and the Covid pandemic, it is that breath is precious. When all Americans, regardless of party affiliation, incorporate the right to breathe into our democratic nonnegotiables and begin to live from this idea as a praxis of dialogical offense, then America may be on its way to becoming great—maybe for the first time.

---

20. Pain, "Geotrauma," 8.
21. See 1 Samuel 18–24 and 2 Samuel 1–5.
22. See Esther 4:14.

CHAPTER 15

"Chickens Coming Home to Roost": American Muslims in the Aftermath

AMIR HUSSAIN

If you stick a knife in my back nine inches and pull it out six inches, there's no progress. If you pull it all the way out that's not progress. Progress is healing the wound that the blow made. And they haven't even begun to pull the knife out, much less try and heal the wound. They won't even admit the knife is there.

—Malcolm X[1]

On January 4, 2021, California Republican Congressman Devin Nunes was awarded our nation's highest civilian honor, the Presidential Medal of Freedom. The last words of the award citation stated that Nunes had "uncovered the greatest scandal in American history." I begin with this incident not simply because I live in California but because I believe it best captures the end of the past four years. An elected representative who spread disinformation that benefitted the president was awarded, I repeat, the highest honor

---

1. Malcolm X, interview ninety days after controversial statement about "chickens coming home to roost" (March 1964): https://www.youtube.com.

our nation can give to a civilian.² The treasonous storming of the Capitol that occurred two days later on January 6 was an effect of that disinformation campaign. So let us return to the beginning of those four years.

The weekend after the 2016 presidential election, American Muslim comedian Dave Chappelle hosted *Saturday Night Live*. During his monologue, four days after the election and three days after the concession by Hillary Clinton, Chappelle said, "You know, I didn't know that Donald Trump was going to win the election. I did suspect it. It seemed like Hillary was doing well in the polls and yet—I know the Whites. You guys aren't as full of surprises as you used to be." Chappelle continued, "But America's done it. We've actually elected an Internet troll as our president." He ended by describing an event he attended at the White House during the last few weeks of the Obama administration, with a largely African American crowd in attendance where he "saw how happy everybody was. These people who had been historically disenfranchised. It made me feel hopeful and it made me feel proud to be an American and it made me very happy about the prospects of our country. So, in that spirit, I'm wishing Donald Trump luck. And I'm going to give him a chance, and we, the historically disenfranchised, demand that he give us one too."³

I write this chapter as a Muslim scholar of Islam, who became an American citizen in 2013. The 2016 election was my first chance to vote in a presidential election. Like Chappelle, I also did not predict the winner of the election, but I suspected it would go to a Republican. America has a forced binary choice of parties, Democrat or Republican. This is not to discount independents or parties like the Green Party or the Libertarian Party, but they have no hope of winning a presidential election. In full disclosure, when I first registered to vote on that day in 2013 when I became a citizen, I

---

2. For a thorough investigation of the issues related to Nunes and his memo, see Russell Spivak and Benjamin Wittes, "About That Presidential Medal of Freedom: Revisiting the Nunes Memo," *Lawfare*, January 12, 2021.

3. Dave Chappelle, "SNL Monologue," *Saturday Night Live*, broadcast November 13, 2016.

declared no party preference. Therefore, I do not mean to disparage one party or elevate another.

I moved to the United States from Canada in the second term of the Clinton administration. Eight years of Clinton were followed by eight years of Bush, and then eight years of Obama. The pattern I had lived through, Democrat, Republican, Democrat, meant that a Republican would be the next president. Astute readers will note that I have not used the name of the forty-fifth president when I describe his administration. I come from a theological tradition that says that to speak the name of evil is to give it power. Moreover, I mean no hyperbole with the term "evil," I use it simply as a descriptor. As a theologian, I remind my students that the theological opposite of good is not bad, it is evil. The last four years have shown us much of the evil in our land.

Muslims, both within America and around the world, were the religious community that was most affected by the forty-fifth president. These difficulties, to be sure, were not new or unique to that administration. And like Dave Chappelle, I was willing to give the forty-fifth president the benefit of the doubt at the beginning of his term. But I was also mindful that no other presidential candidate had publicly declared his hostility to the second largest religious tradition in the world, saying very famously on *CNN* on March 9, 2016, "I think Islam hates us."[4] So I was not surprised by the effects of his administration on Muslims.

We saw the open intolerance to Islam in opposition to new mosques proposed throughout the country. We saw seven states (Alabama, Arizona, Kansas, Louisiana, North Carolina, South Dakota, and Tennessee) passing anti-sharia laws when not a single Muslim group in America had asked for the implementation of sharia laws. Oklahoma also voted for such a law, but it was struck down in 2012 and never implemented. We saw Lt. General Michael Flynn, who became President Trump's national security advisor, tweet that "fear of Muslims is RATIONAL" and heard him claim that Islam is a political ideology (and not a religion, and therefore

---

4. Theodore Schleifer, "Donald Trump: 'I Think Islam Hates Us,'" *CNN*, March 10, 2016.

not protected under the Constitution) which has become a "malignant cancer."[5] However, he resigned on February 13, 2017, not for his comments about Islam and Muslims, but for misleading Vice President Mike Pence about his telephone calls with the Russian ambassador. It is important to remember that on Election Day, Lt. General Flynn penned an op-ed in *The Hill* supporting Turkish President Erdoğan against one of his critics, American resident Fethullah Gülen. Flynn described Gülen as "a shady Islamic mullah," "a radical Islamist," and the head of "a dangerous sleeper terrorist network."[6] Only later was it revealed that Flynn had been paid over half a million dollars by the Turkish government and that he did not register as an agent working for a foreign government until March of 2017.[7] Think about that one for a second. The man chosen as the national security advisor was secretly working for the interests of a foreign government. Fortunately for Flynn, he was preemptively pardoned by the forty-fifth president on November 25, 2020, while in the middle of a criminal trial. On December 8, the judge dismissed that case because of the president's pardon.[8]

We saw Islam-haters such as Steve Bannon, Mike Pompeo, John Bolton, and Sebastian Gorka come and go in the administration, while Stephen Miller remained until the end. We saw the forty-fifth president retweet anti-Muslim videos from a right-wing fringe British group on November 29, 2017, to the dismay of British Prime Minister Theresa May. However, we also heard the president's press secretary, Sarah Huckabee Sanders, defend the president by saying that it didn't matter if the videos were real or not, as "the threat is real."

On Friday, January 27, 2017, a week after his inauguration, the

---

5. Matthew Rosenberg and Maggie Haberman, "Michael Flynn, Anti-Islamist Ex-General, Offered Security Post, Trump Aide Says," *New York Times*, November 17, 2016.

6. Lt. Gen Michael T. Flynn, "Our Ally Turkey Is in Crisis and Needs Our Support," *The Hill*, November 8, 2016.

7. Rebecca Kheel, "Turkey and Michael Flynn: Five Things to Know," *The Hill*, December 17, 2018.

8. Rohini Kurup, "Judge Dismisses Michael Flynn's Case after Trump's Pardon," *Lawfare*, December 8, 2020.

president ordered that the United States ban travelers and refugees from seven Muslim-majority countries (Iraq, Syria, Iran, Libya, Somalia, Sudan, and Yemen). He did this in the afternoon, after making comments that morning for International Holocaust Remembrance Day that made no mention either of the Jews or of anti-Semitism. Thousands of people protested the ban at airports across the country in the following days. I flew back to Los Angeles from Washington, DC, on January 29, and those protests were quite powerful to see, people standing up for us not just or only as refugees or immigrants, but as Muslims. That was extraordinary. What has also been amazing to see is the response from the American Jewish community. They have been at the forefront of the protests, both because they know that the commandment that is repeated more than any other commandment in the Torah is to not oppress the stranger, and because they know with the painful history of the Holocaust where the road of prejudice and intolerance ends. And with the rise of hate crimes against Muslims, it is important to remember that over half of the hate crimes committed against a religious group in America were against Jews.

That first travel ban was rejected by the United States Court of Appeals for the Ninth Circuit on February 9, 2017. The forty-fifth president introduced two subsequent versions of the ban, and it was the third version that was upheld by the Supreme Court. President Joe Biden, on his first day in office, issued Presidential Proclamation 10141 revoking the travel bans.

To discuss the problems caused by the forty-fifth president and his administration would require more space than this entire book. This chapter is not intended to catalogue all of the issues that affected American Muslims during the past four years. But one has to address the issues of racial injustice. George Floyd was murdered by police on May 25, 2020, in front of Cup Foods, a store owned by an Arab American Muslim, whose teenage employee—also a Muslim—had earlier reported to police that Mr. Floyd tried to use a counterfeit $20 bill to buy cigarettes. Muslim American businesses are common in lower-income areas, such as the part of Minneapolis where Mr. Floyd was killed. This puts stores in a precarious position—catering for the community while also duty-bound to report crime to the police, sometimes under the threat of being closed down if they do not comply. The circumstances of Mr. Floyd's death hint at the proximity and complex relationship that different sections of America's Muslim community have with law enforcement and with the Black Lives Matter movement.

Since Mr. Floyd's killing, Muslim Americans have mostly shown solidarity with the Black Lives Matter movement. Mahmoud Abumayyaleh, the owner of Cup Foods, has said that the store will no longer call the police on customers. Nationally, there have been numerous statements from groups such as the Muslim Public Affairs Council, the Council on American Islamic Relations, and the American Muslim Institution. A joint announcement by over thirty-five national Muslim civil rights and religious groups and more than sixty regional groups noted that Black people were "often marginalized" within the broader Muslim community. It continued: "And when they fall victim to police violence, non-Black Muslims are too often silent, which leads to complicity."[9]

There have been Muslims of African descent in America for almost five hundred years. Estevanico the Moor was brought as a slave to what is now Florida in 1528 and is memorialized on the Texas African American history monument at the state capitol in Austin as the first African to enter Texas. At least 10 percent of the slaves brought from West Africa were Muslim, and the National Museum of African American History and Culture tells some of their stories as part of its collection.[10]

In the last century, many African Americans came to Islam through the Nation of Islam, which wove a Black nationalist element into their religion. Black Muslims played a crucial role in the civil rights movement. Even today, quotes and images of civil rights activist Malcolm X, who converted to Sunni Islam in 1964 after leaving the Nation of Islam, remain potent in the current protests. I chose a phrase associated with Malcolm X as part of my title.

---

9. "Joint Statement against Anti-Black Police Violence," *Muslim Advocates*, https://muslimadvocates.org.

10. "Collection Story: African Muslims in Early America," *Smithsonian*, https://nmaahc.si.edu.

In describing the murder of President John F. Kennedy, Malcolm talked about the hate in America, and how this was an incidence of "chickens coming home to roost." There is violence in America, and we have for decades ignored the dangers of white supremacy. Nonwhite Americans were not surprised at the violence that took place on January 6, 2021, at the US Capitol. The chickens, once more, came home to roost.

Organized groups of dangerous white people are called militias, not gangs. We do not rewrite our laws for them, do not punish them the way we do with gangs, do not create specialized teams or units of law enforcement to deal with them. And there has been a danger from them for decades. Think back to the first attempt by a white Christian supremacist group (The Covenant, the Sword, and the Arm of the Lord) to attack the Alfred P. Murrah Federal Building in Oklahoma City, which took place in 1983. Then think of the attack that succeeded in 1995, where the attacker had with him a copy of *The Turner Diaries*, a Christian, white supremacist novel that talked about an attack on the US Capitol and a race war that led to the extermination of Jews, nonwhites, liberals, and politicians. We need to remember these things. They are not only part of our past but also part of our present reality. We ignore them at our peril. So it was heartening to see during the inauguration no reference to Muslim violence but an emphasis on domestic terrorism.

Muhammad Ali, who at one time was perhaps the most recognizable Muslim in the world, gained fame as much for his political stances as his boxing prowess. Ali led the way for other Muslim American athletes who have pushed for social change, including NBA great Kareem Abdul-Jabbar, who was involved in discussions with the Olympic Project for Human Rights for Black athletes to boycott the 1968 games. And twenty years before Colin Kaepernick, NBA player Mahmoud Abdul-Rauf refused to stand for the national anthem while playing for the Denver Nuggets because of his "Muslim conscience." Polling shows many of these protests were greeted with disdain by the majority of white Americans.[11]

---

11. Carrie Dann, "NBC/WSJ Poll: Majority Say Kneeling during Anthem 'Not Appropriate,'" *NBC News*, August 31, 2018.

Today, at least 20 percent of Muslims in the United States are African Americans. But starting from the 1965 Immigration and Nationality Act, there has been a growth in immigrant Muslims coming to America. While increasing overall numbers of Muslims in the United States, immigration has created a dividing line in the American Muslim community—between Muslims with an American heritage that stretched back generations and newer arrivals. Immigrant Muslims were often assumed by American Muslims to know more about Islam as they came from Muslim majority countries, and so they were given more authority in Muslim organizations and as Islamic leaders. They also built mosques that served their own ethnic communities, with immigrant Muslim communities often worshiping separately from African American Muslims. There is also a split in the economic status of American Muslims. According to the Pew Forum, 24 percent of American Muslims have an annual income above $100,000, while 40 percent have an income below $30,000.[12] Many of those who are wealthy—like billionaire Shahid Khan, an immigrant from Pakistan who now owns the NFL's Jacksonville Jaguars—are from immigrant Muslim communities.

The intersection of race, class, and national identity means that views vary on issues such as police, protests, and discrimination. A 2019 Pew survey found that 92 percent of African American Muslims believe there is a lot of discrimination against Black people, compared with 66 percent of non-African American Muslims.[13] Nonimmigrant Muslims are more likely to have lived out the history of the United States, including the horrific legacy of slavery. As Americans, they were also taught early on and often that the right to protest is protected under the Constitution. Immigrant Muslims may have a very different experience with protest if they come from a country where dissent can lead to imprisonment or death. They

---

12. "Demographic Portrait of Muslim Americans," *Pew Research Center*, July 26, 2017.

13. Besheer Mohamed and Jeff Diamant, "Black Muslims Account for a Fifth of All U.S. Muslims, and about Half Are Converts to Islam," *Pew Research Center*, January 17, 2019.

may also be more wary of being seen as "anti-American." Immigrant Muslims expressed more pride in being American than US-born African American Muslims, according to a 2017 Pew poll.[14] Both communities, however, share a complicated history with US law enforcement. For African Americans, police violence dates back to slavery. Since the terrorist attacks of September 11, 2001, police in cities like Los Angeles and New York have tried to infiltrate and surveil American Muslims.[15]

In vowing to stop calling the police on its customers, the Muslim-owned Cup Foods in Minneapolis is standing in solidarity with the largely Black community it serves. In a similar fashion, the soul searching that has followed Mr. Floyd's death provides an opportunity for Muslim Americans of all backgrounds to unite and side with the oppressed, many of whom share their religion. Under the Biden administration, we need to begin the healing. We need to know the wounds that many of us carry. To this end, we can continue to encourage more Muslims to enter the media in order to properly and honestly tell our stories. We also need to be more involved in the political process, not just to vote but to contact our elected officials about our concerns and where possible to run for office. We, too, as the blessed Langston Hughes reminded us, *are* America.

---

14. "Identity, Assimilation and Community," *Pew Research Center*, July 26, 2017.

15. "Factsheet: The NYPD Muslim Surveillance Program," *ACLU*, https://www.aclu.org.

CHAPTER 16

Rebuilding Jewish Orthodoxy after Trump through Interfaith Humanism

JOSHUA SHANES

Donald Trump entered American politics through the racist birtherism conspiracy and ruled through four years of unprecedented cruelty, hate-mongering, corruption, and incompetence. The damage of the Trump administration—from the degradation of our political discourse and norms to the lives lost through his response to the Covid-19 pandemic—as well as the relationship of Trump and his political cult to fascism will both be the subject of extensive research for many years to come. The latter is of particular interest to me as a scholar of twentieth-century Jewish history, nationalism, anti-Semitism, and the Holocaust, and in fact I have joined leading specialists in these fields publishing (hopefully nuanced) comparisons between our era and that one.[1] Neither topic, however, is the

---

1. See Joshua Shanes, "This Was the Week American Fascism Hit a Tipping point," *Slate*, August 28, 2020; Joshua Shanes, "Trump Republicans Love Candace Owens Because She Sells Their Brand of Fascism," *Haaretz*, April 14, 2019; Joshua Shanes, "Why We Must Keep Looking at Politics Through the Lens of the Holocaust," *Haaretz*, June 28, 2019. See also, among others, Robert Paxton, "I've Hesitated to Call Donald Trump a Fascist. Until Now," *Newsweek*, January 11, 2021; Christopher Browning, "The Suffocation of Democracy," *New York Review of Books*, October 25, 2018; Robert Steigmann-Gall, "One Expert Says Yes, Donald Trump Is a Fascist," *Tikkun*,

subject of this volume. Here we are concerned with the crisis that Trump and Trumpism engendered in religious communities split between their majority who swooned after Trump's cult and the minority left alienated from their religious homes. This was dramatically the case among Orthodox Jews and for the minority of Orthodox voices that opposed him.

A deep chasm of values, identity, and even a sense of reality has ripped across the Jewish world since the rise of Trump. While American Jews disproportionately opposed Trump—with nearly 90 percent of the non-Orthodox voting against him in 2020—Orthodox Jews like white evangelical Christians moved in the opposite direction. Voting records show bright red islands in Orthodox neighborhoods like Borough Park and New Square, which already voted heavily for Trump in 2016 and where support for Trump reached over 90 percent and even higher in 2020. Meanwhile, for the past four years, Orthodox rabbinical bodies and prominent rabbis made regular public pronouncements in support of the administration, swooning over Trump's gifts to the Israeli Right, while refusing to criticize his hate-mongering, praise and pardon of violent criminals, separation of families, evisceration of the environment and social welfare, and more.

In short, political tribalism trumped decency as Orthodox Jews—and their evangelical allies—turned out in droves for a man who ran on xenophobic hatred, gross misogyny, race baiting, calls for violence, ignorance and conspiracy paranoia, an alliance with neo-Nazis and white nationalists, and a narcissistic cult of personality unlike anything in American history. As a result, progressive Orthodox Jews and white evangelicals—isolated and even ostracized in their communities—face a crisis of religious identity, namely, the apparent inseparability of immoral political beliefs that comes with identifying with those communities. How might faith heal these divisions? Perhaps it cannot. Political divisions between those who advocate racist hate-mongering, misogyny, and cruelty

---

January 5, 2016; Eric Weitz, "Weimar Germany and Donald Trump," *The Tablet*, July 18, 2016, and countless publications by the historian Timothy Snyder.

and those who advocate for humanism and equality cannot be bridged. Only communities can be healed—and these groups no longer constitute a single faith community. For this division to heal, the core value system that currently dominates Orthodox Jews must be exposed as a perversion of God's truth, especially by open members of these communities who reject it.

Interfaith dialogue can, however, forge new ecumenical communities to defeat this heresy. The ecumenical fraternity of those camps worshiping the golden calf of Trump can be fought by a competing fraternity of Jews, Christians, and Muslims—as well as atheists and others—dedicated to the ethical humanism demanded by our shared prophets, even as we respect each other's ritual and theological differences. In other words, we have to reimagine religious community to form around shared theological commitment to humanism and human equality. By this definition, my tribe is formed by people committed to these values and not necessarily Jews—even Orthodox Jews—who share my strict observance of Jewish ritual.

One of the founders of modern Orthodoxy, Rabbi Samson Raphael Hirsch, once wrote that he would sooner be buried with Christians—traditionally something strictly prohibited—than in a cemetery controlled by Reform Jewish leaders.[2] I suspect he meant it hyperbolically, but when asked by a colleague if I agreed with his sentiment, my answer came so fast I surprised myself. I would sooner be buried next to a saint like Rev. William Barber—I should be so lucky—than in a field full of evil men only because they happen to be Sabbath-observant Jews. How do we build such a community? Perhaps scholarship can lead the way.

In 1967, Robert Bellah published his path-breaking essay on the "civil religion" of Americanism, to my knowledge the first scholar to apply Jean-Jacques Rousseau's category of civil religion to nationalism.[3] The argument was compelling. Traditional religion

---

2. Saemy Japhet, "The Secession from the Frankfurt Jewish Community under Samson Raphael Hirsch," *Historia Judaica* 10, no. 2 (October 1948): 99–122.

3. Robert Bellah, "Civil Religion in America," *Dædalus, Journal of the American Academy of Arts and Sciences* 96, no. 1 (Winter 1967): 1–21.

forged communities through defining its boundaries, sacred narratives of the past and destined future, holy dates, holy places, holy ideals, and rituals intended to realize those ideals. Nationalism—the ideology that nations exist and that one's own nation demands primary allegiance over all other identities—offers most of these sacred truths as well.

Bellah's student Robert Wuthnow developed this idea further, describing two competing civil religions in America, one conservative—grounded in a "myth of origin," "Judeo-Christian" values (which typically manifest as prosperity gospel, opposed to gay rights, a Christian public sphere, and Islamophobia), manifest destiny, xenophobia, and extreme chauvinism—and one liberal, grounded in secular humanitarianism and voices of the prophets seeking global peace and justice.[4] Both scholars were careful to distinguish between the official churches and this "well-institutionalized civil religion of America," but as Jose Santiago put it, "when the civil religion of nation and the civil religion of humanity stopped being [so] intimately united ... the idea of nationalism as the religion of modern times was born."[5]

Indeed, this has happened in the United States. A sizable camp of white evangelicalism, a religion[6] based on personal salvation through Christ and biblical obedience, has evolved into a political theology defending white, Christian America against its perceived enemies, internal and external.[7] We saw this most shockingly in the January 6 insurrection, but it has been developing for quite some time. Today, its battle against the competing civic nationalism of secularism and equality includes opposition to gay equality

---

4. Robert Wuthnow, *The Restructuring of American Religion* (Princeton, NJ: Princeton University Press, 1988).

5. Jose Santiago, "From 'Civil Religion' to Nationalism as the Religion of Modern Times: Rethinking a Complex Relationship," *Journal for the Scientific Study of Religion* 48, no. 2 (June 1, 2009): 397.

6. National Association of Evagelicals, "What Is an Evangelical?" https://www.nae.net.

7. Daniel Steinmetz-Jenkins, "The Nationalist Roots of White Evangelical Politics, *Dissent* 67, no. 2 (Spring 2020), https://www.dissentmagazine.org.

(under the guise of "religious freedom") and support for unfettered capitalism, gun rights, highly restricted immigration, the Israeli right, and strict opposition to abortion access.

Nearly all of the Orthodox camps—"modern," centrist, and Haredi (i.e., ultra-Orthodox)—increasingly see these political views as a central part of what defines Orthodox boundaries. This highlights how Orthodoxy is now constituting itself increasingly as a religio-political identity and affiliation. Public opposition to these political positions brings negative consequences; support reaps social rewards. Today, tragically to my mind, the wide spectrum of American Orthodoxy—from its most acculturated iterations to the ultra-Orthodox communities—is likewise being redefined, in part by its commitment to an ethno-nationalist theology, both as group boundary markers and markers of religious expression. Like evangelical Christians, Orthodox Judaism evolved from its theoretical focus on Divine service through study, prayer, and ritual observance into a denomination that increasingly places the values of the civic religion of ethno-nationalism at its center.

This political tribalism blends in new ways with the growth both in Israel and the United States of ethno-nationalist strands of Zionism, which is particularly pronounced among Orthodox Jews. The overwhelming anti-Zionist consensus of Orthodox Jews a century ago has almost totally evaporated in favor of a technical anti-Zionism among some ultra-Orthodox but a de facto "Israelism" among almost all of them; and therein lies the rub. The postwar division until recently had fallen largely between Haredi and centrist Orthodox Jews who accepted the reality of the secular Israeli state and worked with it, but insisted that it carried no theological significance, and modern religious Zionists who insisted that the state was the manifestation of messianic redemption, or at least a holy endeavor whose religious character must be ensured. The distinction between these groups increasingly grows dimmer, even if it formally remains, in part because both share similar political sympathies, even if only some incorporate innovative Zionist ritual and liturgy into their religious faith and practices such as reciting the prayer for the State of Israel in synagogue. Indeed, paradoxically, it is the more liberal Orthodox—who pursue progressive religious views on gender for example—who, because of their more pronounced Zionist vision, often express more radical and *illiberal* views about Israel, which has translated to similarly illiberal politics and alliances in America.[8]

And this is where it comes together. Ethno-nationalist prejudice against Palestinians brings together the progressive wing of Orthodoxy with centrist and ultra-Orthodox Jews absorbing Rush Limbaugh, Ben Shapiro, and Rabbi Avigdor Miller, a leading voice in the Orthodox world who for decades spewed racism, misogyny, homophobia, and hatred against liberals as a key tenet of Orthodox Judaism. "Progressive" Orthodox Jews unwilling to shed Jewish supremacism in Israel/Palestine (and all too often letting this "color" their attitudes about race here in America) make a Faustian bargain with evangelicals and other white nationalists (including open antisemites) while meeting Haredim who every day grow more Israelist, adding the Greater Israel project and anti-Palestinian animosity to their value system already sharply predisposed against the values of science, humanism, and reason. And all the while they are getting their news from talk radio and Jewish newspapers and WhatsApp groups reinforcing and accelerating these values. In short, Jewish supremacism—even when mitigated by voices on the fringe bemoaning widespread racism in the Orthodox world—makes Orthodoxy a natural bedfellow of a religio-political theology grounded in notions of American and Jewish exceptionalism, "Judeo-Christian" supremacy in America, and religious war, even when spouted by open Jew haters.[9]

The solution may be to build an ecumenical community grounded in a competing national religious narrative. I believe it has been a terrible mistake allowing the white nationalist Right to claim ownership of "national pride" and "religious values." America is a religious country. France's discriminatory secular national-

---

8. Joshua Shanes, "Book Review: Journey to Open Orthodoxy by Rabbi Avraham Weiss," *Tikkun*, July 31, 2019; Joshua Shanes, "In Pain . . . Calling Out Our Beloved Rabbi Avi Weiss," *Tikkun*, January 5, 2021.

9. Michael Schulson, "How an Orthodox Rabbi Became an Unlikely Ally of the Christian Right," *Religion and Politics*, February 14, 2017.

ist religion—which bans kippas and hijabs in public spaces—would not fly here, and nor would I want it to do so. People need transcendent community, to belong to something bigger than themselves, and in our age this is going to express itself (to my chagrin) as a national community. We need to nurture the liberal nationalist religion described by Wuthnow and reclaim the mantle of religious values based on its values.

I understand why many liberals—secular and religious—are so interested in separating church and state in matters of public education, control of our bodies, and more. But the liberal nationalist religion described by Wuthnow also wants to accomplish that goal. It can do so better by insisting, for example, that religious values mean providing health care for every American, without which many women (and men) do not have control over their bodies' health. Can you even imagine the civil rights movement without the call to faith? I believe the religious faith of men like President Biden, Senator Warnock, Rev. Barber, and Stephen Colbert is precisely the path forward to accomplish this goal. (I could add Mr. Rogers to that list.) It is a call to recognize the dignity of all women and men and to care for their needs. It is a faith built on the divinity within each human being, on the call to help them, on justice in every sense (economic, racial, social, environmental), and with no call to convert anyone to the religion or God that guides you to this light. For that reason, I celebrate their faith and their calling upon it at Biden's inauguration and into the future.

In response to the failure of Orthodox institutions such as the Orthodox Union, the Rabbinical College of America, Yeshiva University, and Agudath Israel—let alone Hasidic courts and heads of *haredi yeshivot*—to respond appropriately to the events of January 6, as well as the general rapture of Orthodox Jews behind Trump and Trumpism, a very small number of rabbis (mostly congregational) have stepped up to the plate. And yet almost none offered the simple message unequivocally condemning Orthodox Jewish support for Trump and calling for serious self-reflection to understand how we failed the most important moral challenge of our generation. While mostly well intentioned, the statements almost universally spoke about "both sides," some failing even to mention Trump, and almost none addressing the overwhelming support for Trump and Trumpism within the Orthodoxy communities these past years. The distinction between voting for Trump and supporting Trumpism in 2016 stretches credulousness in my mind, in light of Trump having been so open about his ideology and program. In 2020 that distinction is totally collapsed, particularly in light of the overwhelming enthusiasm behind him and his movement, even until this day.

I certainly understand that a rabbi wants to appeal to a wide audience and probably does not want to seem partisan. I do not envy their positions, and I applaud their courage in saying anything at all. However, if we want to uproot this scourge from our communities, we need to be honest about the extent of the phenomenon. We need to admit the extent of support without feeding narratives that undermine repentance from it. Yes, there are bad people and ideas on the "both sides"; and, yes, Trump is himself a terrible person who cheats on his wife and speaks crudely, but neither of those are especially relevant here. They are both excuses used to avoid grappling with the attraction of most of Orthodoxy to an American fascist movement that was not only grounded in racist hate-mongering ignorance, violence, and cruelty—and building up the neo-Nazi and other movements that support them—but also implemented policies toward that end. In other words, we have to grapple with the attraction of most of Orthodoxy to a white nationalist movement that included even antisemites. Moreover, in some ways this was the culmination of a decades-long process, not a sudden aberration. Indeed, European Orthodoxy in the nineteenth and twentieth centuries regularly allied itself with right-wing, even fascist elements in opposition to even moderate social democratic forces.[10] This too needs to be addressed. And yes, unfortunately, we are going to have to grapple with the relationship of that support to Orthodoxy's views on Israel, on Palestinian lives, and on the demand for Jewish supremacy in that land.

Moreover, faith leaders must be prepared to engage these topics from the pulpit with the full understanding that these are religious

---

10. Eliyahu Stern, "Anti-Semitism and Orthodoxy in the Age of Trump," *The Tablet*, March 12, 2019.

issues without fear of violating political "neutrality" or offending constituents. There is no neutrality in politics, any more than there is neutrality in Sabbath observance. The Sabbath comes, and one observes it or not in whatever way one chooses. "Political neutrality" is itself political. It is support for those in power, or for those destined to be victorious without the voice of the clergy. Too often faith leaders insist that they do not take stands on political issues but then happily support various causes that they understand to benefit their communities, such as rabbis advocating for a particular policy vis-à-vis Israel. This is a circular argument that labels such actions as "nonpolitical" because they seemed so self-evidently beneficial. Those were, in fact, political actions that reflected the Jewish values of the rabbis in question, and their refusal to advocate for other issues is equally a political act.

Faith leaders may not be versed enough in American law to speak to every political conflict or crisis. They can, however, speak to our faiths' basic values to vociferously oppose rhetoric or policies that they recognize violate God's will, and they can forge new communities across denominational and religious boundaries that share this worldview. The message must be clear. All blood is holy. All humans are holy. All life is holy. Only a religion or worldview that nurtures this sensitivity warrants God's name attached to it. Personally, I seek a Jewish community that is as committed to the prophets as it is to the minutiae of ritual law, and vice-versa. I need a community that is committed—as Jewish values—to condemning racism and hate-mongering, that is committed to legislation and social policy that protect the vulnerable and improve economic and environmental equality, but also supports Sabbath and kosher food observance, among other ritual pillars. It needs to recognize the evolution of Judaism but still find meaning in its various competing homiletic expressions, to remain committed to observance of ritual "between man and God," while taking texts and textual learning very seriously.

Most difficult of all, I need a community that does all of this without setting those values aside when it comes to Israel and without replacing any of those core pillars of Judaism—Torah study, ritual observance, and humanism—with the civic religion of nationalism, which so easily becomes a form of idol worship, elevating land and stones over people and God. It can recognize the importance of Israel and its legitimacy, but it must understand the Zionist project as a secular enterprise without exploiting Jewish symbols and eschatological language out of their original context for secular purposes. And while condemning arguments that privilege Palestinian sacred narratives over Jewish ones, it must also recognize the validity of Palestinian narratives, their right to equal treatment, and the immorality of their military occupation. In the meantime, those religious communities that fell into this racist cult need a process parallel to Germany's de-Nazification after 1945, in which each admits its past sins and works to purge those values from its midst. And this can only happen without pussyfooting around hard truths. May the seeds planted hesitantly by these few voices grow to a groundswell that truly transforms our communities into the holy bodies they claim to be.

CHAPTER 17

Much Ado about Nothing

TINK TINKER
(WAZHAZHE, OSAGE NATION)

No, the joe biden administration is not a shakespearean comedy.[1] For American Indian Peoples, however, it has to be considered a tragicomedy at best. I know that for many eurochristian[2] folk, the turnover in whitehouse occupancy is pure romance, proof of the superiority of the american system of governance—after four years of a horror show. The horror show saw eurochristian american men and women (White folk) in a bizarre dance with fascist autocracy, as rank and file eurochristians sought to preserve the only absolute advantage they have in reality over the persistent voices of American Indians and the rising tide of People of Color generally; that is, their property ownership in Whiteness, their perceived skin color.[3] And suddenly, american democracy is only good as long as the self-avowed White eurochristian wins. Anything else is open to recounts and rigorous challenges that seem to wax naturally into

---

1. This article preserves the author's personal conventions for capitalization, which carry significant authorial and political intentionality and are intended to cause rethinking of readers' categories of normativity.

2. See my recent essay, arguing for using eurochristian instead of "White." Namely, I argue that the color code needs to be recoded. Tink Tinker, "What Are We Going to Do with White People?" *The New Polis*, December 17, 2019.

3. Derrick Bell, "Property Rights in Whiteness: Their Legal Legacy, Their Economic Costs," *Villanova Law Review* 33 (1988); Cheryl I. Harris, "Whiteness as Property," *Harvard Law Review* 106, no. 8 (1993). Also see my article disavowing the color code: "What Are We Going to Do with White People?"

rampant White Supremacist violence and the threat of violence both in individual and mob manifestation. trump has, however, now been replaced with joe biden, to the relief of many. One late-night comedian quipped after the formal inauguration moment: "It feels good to only have to worry about a deadly pandemic all day." Many American Indian folk are not quite so star-dazed, even if our votes made a significant difference in key swing states. For us, the new normal is the old normal. "Envisioning praxis in a post-trump era" means going back to the ordinary struggle of just fighting ongoing colonialism every day. Across Turtle Island,[4] particularly in canada and the u.s., the movement is called Land Back!

So, we, the authors in this volume, have been instructed to assess the damage of the past four years to "our" democracy, to reflect on what this moment reveals about the state of christianity, and to explore the role that "faith" might play in reconciling a divided nation. As an American Indian, each of those poses particular and insurmountable obstacles to my own critical thinking processes. In order to fully buy into american democracy as our democracy, Indian folk must pretty much give up on any claim to Indian Land and abandon the Land Back Movement; we necessarily then subordinate any notion of Native sovereignty to the sovereignty of the conquering eurochristian state.[5] From the beginning of the conversion process to the present the eurochristian religion requires Indian folk to abandon the bulk of their Native worldview in favor of the up-down/hierarchical worldview of our colonizers. So, the language of Native folk has to be reshaped around the religious discourse of the colonizer.[6] And finally, to impose

---

4. Turtle Island is the general American Indian name for what eurochristian folk call the north american continent, from central america to the arctic.
5. I argued much of the case I am merely outlining here a decade ago in "American Indians, Conquest, the Christian Story, and Invasive Nation-building," in *Wading Through Many Voices: Toward a Theology of Public Conversation*, ed. Harold Recinos (Lanham, MD: Rowman & Littlefield, 2011), 255–77.

inker, "Why I Don't Believe in a Creator," in *Buffalo Shout, Conversations on Creation, Land Justice, and Life Together*, nrichs (Harrisonburg, VA: Herald Press, 2013), 167–79.

the eurochristian category of "faith" means that we must further abandon our Native languages in favor of some colonized version of those languages in which the missionaries have selected words in our language to signal their words, discourse, and worldview.[7] The questions themselves automatically presume the normativity of the eurochristian colonialist whole that is now trying to erase its own history of violence toward Native Peoples, its history of American Indian Genocide.

As an American Indian, then, I have little commitment to american (i.e., u.s.) style democracy, a procedural democracy at best. Nor do I have a commitment to eurochristianity or a concern for the state of christianity generally. I am a critical observer of both of these phenomena, so I do pay attention and have developed my own critique of both. And since the Osage language (i.e., wazhazhe) has no word for "faith," I will find it difficult to project what role faith might play in reconciling a divided nation. Indeed, as I clarified in an earlier essay, I find the whole notion of the u.s. as a "nation" to be entirely artificially constructed, a social imaginary based on a borrowed metaphor that in the final analysis erodes the source-domain meaning of the word nation—people born together.

Again, identifying as a non-christian I can indeed comment on the state of christianity in the u.s., but it might also be helpful for me as a Native scholar to comment on the state of American Indians following four years of trump and now looking to four years of biden. And, of course, we cannot look forward to biden without looking back at the obama–biden whitehouse and their track record before trump. While trump was quick and vicious in implementing elitist policies that returned new wealth to the already hyperwealthy, obama and his team were eventually just as oriented toward authorizing and implementing extraction policies. At the same time, it might be important here to state clearly that christianity, the eurochristian colonialist religion, has from the begin-

---

7. Tink Tinker, "jesus, the gospel, and Genocide," in *The Colonial Compromise: The Threat of the Gospel to the Indigenous Worldview*, ed. Miguel A. De La Torre (Minneapolis: Lexington Books/Fortress Academic, 2020).

ning been part of the problem in the Colonization and Genocide of American Indians. It has single-handedly ripped Indians out of their collateral-egalitarian worldview, attempting to replace Native community-ism and cosmic balance with the new normativity of a radical individualist and hierarchical goal of personal salvation.

Faith, in this context, seems to me to lead us astray, quite apart from the lack of the whole notion of any concept of faith in the traditional structures of Indian languages and cultures. Indeed, racism and White Supremacy are so deeply embedded in the american terrain that there does not seem to be any prospect that something called faith can bridge that divide—especially since both sides of the divide call on their religion and their bible for support. While White Supremacy is not at all new, the decidedly new twist introduced by the trump regime was the overt social licensing of all forms of eurochristian racism and xenophobia. White Supremacy suddenly became overtly mainstream (again) on Turtle Island almost overnight under trump and established a solid platform for White Supremacy in the twenty-first century. trump may be gone (for the moment), but trumpism is around now for the long haul. A whole cadre of eurochristian (White) folk are angry, and they are angry both at the rising tide of People of Color generally and those eurochristian folk whose sense of ethic and well-being bend them toward supporting that rising tide of People of Color. And these White supremacists are summoning "faith" as a source of support.

The theologian of hopelessness, the editor of this book, asks the authors here whether there are signs of hope in this shift away from donald trump, even as he acknowledges that we cannot move easily beyond trump-ism. But, of course, all sorts of people are clamoring to press me and every other Indian with any public profile to acknowledge that there is hope when, for instance, biden nominates a Pueblo Indian woman as secretary of the interior: Deb Haaland (Laguna Pueblo citizen). At least that much must be hopeful, they say.

At the time of writing this chapter, we do not know yet how tough Haaland's confirmation hearings will be in the u.s. senate or what her prospects are, but the truth is that we Native folk have very high expectations of Haaland, even as republicans are generating considerable opposition. It has been a long while since we have had a Native person climb that high in the u.s. government hierarchy, and this time we do want it to work in our favor—in ways that it certainly did not in the vice presidency of charles curtis (Kansa Nation). curtis served thirteen years in the u.s. house of representatives (beginning in 1893) and twenty years as a republican senator from kansas, including the last four and a half years as the senate majority leader; then he became herbert hoover's vice president for four years (1929–1933)—a very powerful politician indeed. It should be noted, however, that curtis's agenda for Indian people was pure assimilation to eurochristian culture! And curtis himself was the ideal model of that political platform that shaped more than half a century of liberal republican ideology with its severe colonialist ideas of Indian reform and social engineering. These liberal republicans, no less than their hyperright-wing counterparts today, always knew what was best for the poor Indians; yet, of course, Indians were never consulted unless they had already made the massive assimilative conversion engaged by people like charles curtis, especially when they were blessed with lighter skin color through miscegenation.

Haaland is certainly not curtis, but my fear is that expecting too much from Deb Haaland may be a recipe for disappointment. Haaland is a pure democratic politician, and a very effective one at that. That is both a plus and a minus from a Native perspective. She was elected to the u.s. house of representatives in 2018 and generated a genuine ripple of excitement across Indian Country. Yet it needs to be clarified that Haaland was elected in a district that consists of some three-quarters of the city of albuquerque. The district is more than 91 percent urban with a population of about 700,000. It is majority White (eurochristian), heavily hispanic, and only 3.5 percent Native. Unlike the rest of the state, the albuquerque district tended to be solid republican for half a century until the 2008 election. While the district does not include kirkland air force base, it virtually surrounds the military base, and it certainly does include a huge quotient of military and defense industry employees since kirkland is the home of the air force "nuclear weapons center." The weather is perfect for making bombs, evidently. What this means is that any candidate for public office in this district must walk a tight line paying some direct homage to the military industrial complex. Add to that the fact that a big chunk of new mexico's economy revolves around energy production and in no small measure around fossil fuel production. Even as a proponent of the new green deal, Haaland must pay political attention to these realities—both in new mexico and nationally in her presumed role with interior.

Haaland is a citizen of the Laguna Pueblo, a small reservation just to the west of albuquerque. Yet Haaland's strongest political identity has been shaped by the new mexico democratic party. She was the obama campaign coordinator in new mexico in 2008, then went on to become the chair of the state democratic party. When she won a seat in the house of representatives, the strength of her political base was in the city of albuquerque and not Indian people—who undoubtedly voted for her. All this is to say that Haaland understands american politics and is capable of playing in that field where one learns the art of inter-party compromise that becomes far more important to political survival than simply pressing Native issues. Indian folk are glad she will be at interior. At the same time, they know full well that her job there is to satisfy the political needs of the democratic party machinery first and foremost and to help ensure future electoral success for the party. In this regard, the post-trump democratic machinery needs to cover its bases with the military-industrial complex just as much as trump's republicans did before them. Remember that was the obama agenda and the agenda of biden's whole career as a politician.

How will Haaland or her boss joe biden react when they run headlong into conflicts of political and economic interest, desires, and presumed needs? In the final analysis will they pay attention to Native Peoples' needs and the force of Treaties signed with the u.s.? Or will they bend to the will of politically powerful forces whose wealth might dictate the next election cycle? In this scenario, I would think that Indian Peoples could expect to lose nine out ten contests—even with a Native placed in the secretary of interior position.

biden has stopped the keystone xl pipeline. He seems to be signaling the looming end of fossil fuel extraction. He issued a "temporary moratorium" on the pending oil and gas leases in the arctic national wildlife refuge, Land sacred to Native Peoples in alaska. And he seems to be signaling that he will reverse trump's executive order on the national monuments in Utah that are Lands so important to Native Peoples across Arizona and Utah: Bears Ears and Grand Staircase-Escalante both look like their original protected Land base will be restored, something Indian Nations in that region have been agitating for ever since the trump administration took action to severely reduce the size of these monument Lands that the Natives hold sacred. That is welcome news for Native folk.

Yet we need to remember that these stoppages and turnarounds only come after years of Indigenous protest across Turtle Island. We can celebrate with all the eurochristian liberals because our Indigenous voice has finally, for once, been heard. But will biden stop line-3 across Indian Land in minnesota or the dakota access pipeline that was and is protested against by Natives in north dakota as an immediate threat to their fresh water supply, or will he find these projects too important to the national interest?

Even more importantly, however, what will biden and his interior secretary do about mineral extraction? Will he continue the obama-bush-clinton-trump minerals endeavor? What will Haaland do about australia's mining conglomerate rio tinto zinc,[8] and its "resolution copper" mining project with its horrendous plan to destroy a whole mountain, sacred to the San Carlos Apache People, in order to retrieve a billion dollars' worth of copper? Or what will she do with the permit generated by trump in his last days to allow a canadian mining giant, "lithium americas," to destroy traditional Paiute Land in nevada with a huge open-pit mine? Yes, "rio tinto" is australian and not american, but the political promise is to make the u.s. copper independent for the foreseeable future. And while "lithium americas" is canadian, it will likewise help make the u.s. lithium independent. We need to understand here that both metals are key for the production of twenty-first-century high-tech goods,

---

8. This is the very same corporation that willfully destroyed an Aboriginal People's 46,000-year-old sacred site last year (Juukan Gorge Cave) in order to expand its iron extraction project.

both military goods and consumer. Indeed, biden campaigned back in october promising miners "that he planned to increase domestic lithium production to wean the country from foreign sources like china." It will be nearly impossible, even or especially, for a Native interior secretary to say no. As Lower Brule Lakota scholar Nick Estes cautions: "Resource colonialism is a bipartisan affair."[9]

Here is the late colonialist situation American Indians find themselves in today. To this day in 2021, it is impossible for any American Indian to get elected to a position of significant power in the u.s. body politic without making substantial compromises in terms of the American Indian worldview, culture, and value system—no matter what that person may protest to the contrary. Even if an Indian candidate attempts to distance herself from the american romance and claim allegiance to Indian values, we simply do not have the voting population to elect someone who maintains that rigorously. The reality is that the Indian candidate must navigate through a non-Native, largely eurochristian electorate in order to secure election to office. In other words, to play the political game effectively, we are thrust back into the assimilation game that was foisted on Indian people by the eurochristian missionaries and boarding schools a century and a half ago. We can play. The body politic desperately wants us to participate. But we can only play if we learn to play by the eurochristian rules of the game! Increasingly, moreover, only people with access to obscene amounts of cash have any hope for consistent electoral success, which means that the successful candidate in most cases will need to court deep-pocketed funding agents embedded in the military industrial complex and its close subsidiary the extractive industries complex (think here in terms of fossil fuels, oil and gas pipelines, etc., as well as mineral extractions).

We should not think that somehow president joe biden will completely turn his back on a forty-year career of supporting both the military industrial complex and extractive industries. He certainly voices a new concern for the climate crisis at hand and gives carbon

---

9. Nick Estes, "Biden Killed the Keystone Pipeline. Good, but He Doesn't Get a Climate Pass Just Yet," *The Guardian* 28 (January 2021).

neutrality a new prominence that is certainly welcome. Nevertheless, we need to be cautious in our expectations. Appointing Haaland secretary of interior is a great first step in many respects, but the appointment does not quite even begin to rectify 528 years of eurochristian colonialism and domination. Native Peoples and Native Lands continue to be under enormous colonizing pressure to cave into the desires of the eurochristian political-industrial machine. Yet, knowing full well the complex economic and political issues biden and Haaland face, we need to ask the question Nick Estes frames: "why biden and his supporters can imagine a carbon-free future but not the end of u.s. colonialism."

One Native facebook pundit posted a simple response to the current american political scene. This Indian simply opined: "I'm saving my 'happy tears' for when we get the Land back."

CHAPTER 18

Option for Life:
Remembering the Body of Christ,
Re-membering *Our Catholic Body*

MIGUEL H. DÍAZ

In their recent book titled *Taking America Back for God: Christian Nationalism in the United States*, Andrew L. Whitehead and Samuel L. Perry argue that "At least since the early 1800s Christian nationalism has provided the unifying myths, traditions, narratives, and value systems that have historically been deployed to preserve the interests of those who wish to halt or turn back changes occurring within American society."[1] Christian nationalism thrives within a context that promotes cultural wars and fosters the fear that "America" is losing its distinct identity as a Christian, white, and heteronormative society. As a tool to face this so-called crisis in national identity, Christian nationalists promote the meta-narrative that misinterprets America's exceptionalism in ways that single out our nation above all other nations. In this narrative, only a few among us can be considered true "Americans."

Trump's mantra to "Make America Great Again" perfectly aligned with this nationalistic and socio-political ideology. Tragically, as the recent failed insurrection at our Capitol on the feast

---

1. Andrew L. Whitehead and Samuel L. Perry, *Taking America Back for God: Christian Nationalism in the United States* (New York: Oxford University Press, 2020), 151.

of Epiphany revealed, such distorted notions of American patriotism, whether driven by religious or secular ideology, often propel individuals to resort to whatever means are necessary to justify their particular ends. The ideology to Make America Great basically amounted to a multipronged assault on racial-cultural diversity. Instead of exercising the creative power of human words in a way that would encourage fellow Christian citizens to become co-creators of communal relations in the image of the God (Gen 1:1–26), Trump and his allies repeatedly misused words to "other" our neighbors, near and far away.[2] In short, the age of Trump unleashed hostile words that carried religious overtones that deepened our existing polarization. Words were manipulated with the sole purpose of constructing and/or sustaining racist, sexist, heterosexist, and xenophobic ideologies.[3] These constructions undoubtedly used Scripture as a way to foster a nationalistic agenda, but as Whitehead and Perry rightly conclude, Christian nationalism is ultimately not so much about religion itself as it is about misusing religion to maintain social power and privilege at all costs.[4]

Roman Catholics, and in particular white conservative Catholics in this country, have been no less responsible for cultivating and reflecting social divisions. Indeed, conservative white Catholics have been called the "New Evangelicals."[5] This group of Catholics overwhelmingly supported Trump, though President Biden man-

---

2. See Miguel H. Díaz, "Who Is My Neighbor? Catholics and the Trump Administration," in *Faith and Resistance in the Age of Trump* (New York: Orbis Books, 2017), 91–98.

3. Culturally speaking, American nationalism "glorifies the patriarchal, heterosexual family as not only God's biblical standard, but the cornerstone of all thriving civilizations." See Whitehead and Perry, *Taking America Back for God*, 152.

4. Whitehead and Perry, *Taking America Back for God*, 153. See also Miguel H. Díaz, "I Was a Terrified Child Immigrant Who Became a Theologian and U.S. Ambassador. I Want U.S. Officials to Stop Misusing the Bible," *Reuters*, June 22, 2018.

5. Tom Gjelten, "For Trump, Conservative Catholics are the New Evangelicals," *National Public Radio*, October 26, 2020; and Miguel H. Díaz, "A Latino/a Take: Vatican's 'Ecumenism of Hate' Essay Is Onto Something," *Crux*, August 7, 2017.

aged to pull away some of their support in the 2020 presidential election. The Catholic vote for Trump in 2020 can be summarized as follows:

> This year, Catholic voters accounted for 22% of the electorate, and there was a sharp rift within their ranks by race and ethnicity. Among white Catholics, 57% backed Trump and 42% backed Biden, according to VoteCast. In 2016, Trump won 64% of white Catholics and Clinton won 31%, according to a Pew Research Center analysis of voters. Among Hispanic Catholics, VoteCast shows 67% backed Biden and 32% backed Trump.[6]

I agree when David Gibson argues that the election results "show that the Catholic Church is as divided as our nation," and yet disagree with the part of his conclusion that states "the real divide is race and ethnicity, not theology."[7] Religion is never an a-cultural phenomenon. Religion impacts race and ethnic perspectives and vice versa. This means that differences between the vote of white Catholics and that of Black and brown Catholic voters cannot be simply explained by focusing on racial and ethnic differences. We must also consider the ways these communities of color understand, value, and prioritize particular teachings of Christian faith. For instance, as Gustavo Gutiérrez reminds us, teachings like the preferential option for the racially and/or cultural marginalized are theo-centric options at the core of Christian teaching.[8] Beyond race and ethnicity, our communal divisions also manifest the failure of evangelization to make this point crystal clear for all Catholics.

Regardless of how we interpret the divisions that exist within the Catholic body, the fact is that these divisions continue to adversely affect the ability of Catholics to speak along a united front and confront the challenges that face our nation. As a way to prompt

---

6. Elana Schor and David Crary, "AP Vote Cast: Trump Wins White Evangelicals, Catholics Split," *Associated Press*, November 6, 2020.

7. Schor and Crary, "AP Vote Cast."

8. Gustavo Gutiérrez, *A Theology of Liberation* (Maryknoll, NY: Orbis Books, 1988), xxvii.

some Christian theological reflection on the polarized Catholic body of believers, this chapter briefly explores Paul's First Letter to the Corinthians, highlighting his practical teaching on the body of Christ. Paul's teaching will provide a springboard to challenge Catholics in the United States to remember Christ's broken body and *re-member* their existing fractured human limbs by embracing an integral and inclusive approach to life.

Remembering the Body of Christ for the Sake of Christian Unity

Efforts to ensure the survival of America's "Christian" identity, for which conservative Catholic voices have played no small part in promoting,[9] have valorized conquest over compromise, idealized and enforced strict boundaries and borders, and justified erecting physical and relational walls to protect America from sociocultural contamination and demise.[10] Sadly, such efforts have led to displacing civility with intolerance. The ancient dictum "divide and conquer" (*divide et impera*), cited by Alexander Hamilton in Federalist Paper No. 7, as a warning against enemies foreign and domestic that would seek to profit from division, is today something that Catholics should heed.[11]

---

9. While I find problematic the failure to question the particular version of "natural law" arguments that have shaped conservative Catholics, politics, and the law in the United States, the following piece manages to highlight the tremendous influence Catholic conservative philosophers are having on the nation. The authors argue that "Traditionalists within the Church and the Republican Party have locked the nation into a legal framework that has solidified the assumptions of Thomist natural law." Peter Hammond Schwartz, "Originalism Is Dead. Long Live Catholic Natural Law," *The New Republic*, February 3, 2021. I would argue that what these thinkers have done is to attempt to lock us into *a* particular version of "natural" and of "law." See Miguel H. Díaz, "An Unfinished Project: John Courtney Murray, Religious Freedom, and Unresolved Tensions in Contemporary American Society," *Loyola University Chicago Law Journal* 50, no. 1 (2018): 2n3, 6–8.

10. Whitehead and Perry, *Taking America Back for God*, 152.

11. Alexander Hamilton, aka Publius, "The Federalist Papers, No. 7: Concerning Dangers from Dissensions Between the States," *The Independent Journal*, November 15, 1787.

Paul was no stranger to communal tensions arising from diverse Christian perspectives, factions, and divisions. He wrote his First Letter to the Corinthians sometime in the early 50s CE to a community that was struggling to address internal divisions (1 Cor 10:1–31). He tells us at the beginning of the letter that he has heard of divisions in Corinth from members of Chloe's household. This news presumably came to him from "her slaves or freedmen traveling on business (1 Cor 1:11)."[12] Paul goes on to describe the polarization that has taken place among the different members that comprise the community. Some he says claim to belong to Paul, others to Apollos, others to Cephas, others to Christ (1 Cor 1:12). Paul admonishes the community with the following words: "Has Christ been divided? Was Paul crucified for you? Or were you baptized in the name of Paul?" (1 Cor 1:13). The context and content of the letter suggest that these divisions among the Corinthians have arisen "from a false sense of status among individuals or groups" that selfishly put some individual interests over others.[13]

Paul also describes various unethical behaviors (1 Cor 5:1–6:20) and religious practices that he considers detrimental to the community (1 Cor 7:1–11). He laments over the fact that communal disagreements are not resolved internally and instead taken to the courts to be resolved (1 Cor 6:1–11). Examining the particular ethical behaviors and religious practices that Paul sees as the cause for communal divisions are not the main concern of my chapter. Though, clearly, doing so would shed some light on existing divisions among diverse Catholic communities related to religious practices and ethical behaviors. Rather, it is Paul's overall theological approach to Christian unity, which he roots in the Eucharistic ritual of remembering the Lord's Supper and its relationship to "*re-membering*" a divided community that I want to highlight for consideration. Simply put: Paul makes the question of Christian unity

---

12. Pheme Perkins, *Reading the New Testament* (New York: Paulist Press, 1988), 178.

13. Holly E. Hearon, "1 and 2 Corinthians," in *The Queer Bible Commentary*, ed. Deryn Guest, Robert E. Goss, Mona West, and Thomas Bohache (London: SMC Press, 1988), 609.

inseparable from the memorial that recalls Christ's body and as a result of this remembering, challenges the community to make real their comm-union, that is, their common unity.

Those among us who have experienced marginalization and exclusion in the church at the hands of sustained and systemically perpetuated oppressive social constructs have reason to question calls for communal unity, especially when such exhortations come dressed up in the name of Christ. Appeals such as Paul's in 1 Corinthians 10 "to be in agreement," to have "no divisions," and "to be united in the same mind and purpose" can land on deaf ears when dominant voices deploy God-talk as a way to maintain the status quo and keep those who have been marginalized in their "rightful" and "naturally" constructed place in society. For instance, as Hearon argues, many within the LGBTQ+ communities "will recognize this rhetorical strategy as a ploy to silence opposition by the suppression of differences for the sake of unity: for the good of the country, the church, the family or community."[14] That said, as she goes on to point out, "Paul's emphasis on interdependence, that is, a unity which is dependent upon a self-conscious recognition of and celebration of diversity, continues to challenge all communities of faith to examine the ways in which they have constructed hierarchies that threaten the life of the body rather than contribute to its health and function."[15]

This focus on the challenge to effect the real presence of Christ in community is what the late Pauline scholar Jerome Murphy-O'Connor underscores in his piece titled "Eucharist and Community in First Corinthians."[16] Murphy-O'Connor argues that "we tend to give Paul's concept of the Church as the body of Christ the status of a metaphor or image."[17] He pushes back on this metaphorical understanding and on embracing a monolithic approach

---

14. Hearon, "1 and 2 Corinthians," 607.
15. Hearon, "1 and 2 Corinthians," 611.
16. Jerome Murphy-O'Connor, "Eucharist and Community in First Corinthians," in *Living Bread, Saving Cup*, ed. R. Kevin Seasoltz (Collegeville, MN: Liturgical Press, 1987), 1–30.
17. Murphy-O'Connor, "Eucharist and Community," 3.

to Christian unity that fails to account for a true diverse community.[18] In other words, unity is not sameness.[19] Thus, for Murphy-O'Connor, Paul's letter proposes, above all, a practical approach to communal living. Paul invites his readers to think of ecclesial life as *coexistence*. Paul's communal vision favors sharing over possession and cooperation over autonomy. Murphy-O'Connor summarizes Paul's teaching on the communal existence of Christian life, that is, on the notion of the church as the body of Christ. Murphy-O'Connor underscores the distinction between coordination / cooperation on the one hand and coexistence on the other:

> When we reflect on the Church as the body of Christ we do so in the light of the parallel provided by the human body, as Paul himself did (12:12). But where we are tempted to see the point of the parallel in terms of coordination and cooperation, for Paul it was a question of coexistence in the strict sense of that much abused term. The limbs of the human body all share a common existence, since they are infused by the same life. Their very reality as limbs is conditioned by their being part of the body.[20]

Paul takes so seriously the theological nature of communal coexistence that he not only challenges the divisions of the Corinthian community but also charges the community of being guilty of participating in the ongoing "crucifixion" of Christ. According to Paul, the Eucharist, which remembers the words and actions of the Lord's Supper, invites us to become aware "not merely of his historical existence, but of the meaning of his life and in particular his death" for those who commemorate this event.[21] Or to put it another way,

---

18. Murphy-O'Connor, "Eucharist and Community," 4.
19. Elsewhere I have explored the trinitarian underpinnings of community, oneness, and diversity. See Miguel H. Díaz, "A Trinitarian Approach to the Community-Building Process of Tradition: Oneness as Diversity in Christian Traditioning," in *Futuring Our Past: Explorations in the Theology of Tradition*, ed. Orlando O. Espín and Gary Macy (Maryknoll, NY: Orbis Books, 2006), 157–79.
20. Murphy-O'Connor, "Eucharist and Community," 4.
21. Murphy-O'Connor, "Eucharist and Community," 20.

"Christian remembrance is concerned with the past only insofar as it is constitutive of the present and a summons to the future."[22] Within this Pauline theological realism, it is not hard to see why Paul rails against the Corinthian's community, which he feels has failed to "discern the body" (διακρίνων τὸ σῶμα, 1 Cor 11:29). In no uncertain terms, he lets the community know that when it comes together "it is *not really to eat the Lord's Supper*" but to participate in the Lord's crucifixion (1 Cor 11:20, 11:27, 11:33).

Paul's main point to the members of the Corinthian community is that their ordinary and daily relationships and actions fail to realize what their words signify. This community has failed to practically heed the words and actions of Christ, Christ's life given up *for* and *from the many,* especially those who have been marginalized and oppressed. It is clear that, for Paul, such remembering is not simply an act that engages the mind but is something that demands communal transformation. Commenting on 1 Corinthians 11:27 ("Whoever, therefore, eats the bread or drinks the cup of the Lord in an unworthy manner will be guilty of profaning the body and blood of the Lord"), Murphy-O'Connor points out the consequence of celebrating the Eucharist under these polarizing conditions. He argues that the failure of its members to reject their self-centered existence makes them guilty of continuing to perpetuate divisions and places them "among those responsible for his (Christ's) death."[23]

Re-membering Our Catholic Body

If Paul were writing a letter today to the Catholic community in the United States, I suspect that he would reprimand them for ways Catholics have been bought into the cultural wars and contributed to polarization within the United States.[24] As was the case in Corinth, various Catholic communities in our land are highly

---

22. Murphy-O'Connor, "Eucharist and Community," 21.
23. Murphy-O'Connor, "Eucharist and Community," 27.
24. María Teresa Dávila, "A 'Preferential Option': A Challenge to Faith in a Culture of Privilege," in *The Word Became Culture*, ed. Miguel H. Díaz (Maryknoll, NY: Orbis Books, 2021), 49–69.

polarized along religio-political lines. Like he did in his letter to the Corinthians, Paul would undoubtedly challenge Catholics in the United States to remember the mystery they celebrate at the altar and to live that mystery by *re-membering* their polarized Catholic body in accordance with this mystery.

In his recent encyclical *Fratelli Tutti*, Pope Francis has written eloquently on the need to overcome divisions within the human family and on the socio-political preconditions needed for persons to coexist justly and peacefully with one another.[25] There is no doubt that we are far from achieving in our Catholic communities the kind of social friendship that the pope envisions. That said, as Carmen Nanko-Fernández argues, "The social friendship of which Pope Francis writes in *Fratelli Tutti* begins not with the reconciliation of enemies but with the *re-membering* of those excluded, those whose dignity was demeaned, those whose blood cries from the ground."[26] To do this we Catholics must not only remember the broken body of Christ, but we must *re-member,* to borrow from Pauls' image, those broken limbs among us. In other words, as Catholics *we must make an integral option for life.* We must take into consideration not only the individual, but also socio-political aspects of this option. And at this time in history, we must take into account the ecological crisis that affects us all, following what Pope Francis calls an integral ecology of life.[27]

Sadly, a significant percentage of Catholic voters have become single-voter issues. Some make abortion the sole reason for their

---

25. Pope Francis, *Fratelli Tutti* (*On Fraternity and Social Friendship*), encyclical, October 3, 2020.

26. Carmen Nanko-Fernández, "The Dead and the Living Deserve Better than Rushed Reconciliation," *National Catholic Reporter*, November 18, 2020.

27. In using the phrase an *integral option for life*, I rely on the following central argument that pervades Pope Francis's writings: "Since everything is closely interrelated, and today's problems call for a vision capable of taking into account every aspect of the global crisis, I suggest that we now consider some elements of an *integral ecology*, one which clearly respects its human and social dimensions." Pope Francis, *Laudato Si* (*On Care for Our Common Home*), encyclical, May 24, 2015, IV:137.

political choices. These Catholics point to the number of abortions since Roe v. Wade to justify their complete opposition to pro-choice candidates, even when those candidates are practicing Catholics, as was the case with Joe Biden, who has now become the second Roman Catholic to be elected president of the United States. Others express concern over the defense of religious freedom, especially as it relates to sexual ethics and perceived threats to the "traditional" family. Lastly, some Catholics are divided on issues related to the proper role of government policies on behalf of the disenfranchised, such as the Affordable Care Act and justice for undocumented immigrants.[28]

An *integral option for life* requires Catholics to "discern" our Catholic body in an *evangelical* way that recognizes the real presence of Christ not only with respect to one issue but also with respect to a wide range of life issues that impact the least of our siblings (Matt 25:31–46). This *option for life* is both pro-life and pro-choice in the sense that it calls Catholics to discern life issues and make prudential choices with respect to the interdependence of all life.[29] It also calls Catholics to respect the freedom of conscience and religious belief, especially of those with whom we disagree. The ecclesial vision of John Courtney Murray, S.J., the Catholic champion of religious freedom who inspired *Dignitatis Humanae*, Vatican II's teaching on religious freedom, invites us to move from the position that "error has no rights to only people—not ideas—have rights."[30]

A faith-filled solidarity with those who suffer lies at the root of this integral approach to life. I'm thinking in particular of the lives of Black bodies threatened as a result of institutionalized racism; of brown bodies threatened as a result of preexistent social viruses

---

28. All of these views are expressed by Catholics in Don Clemmer, "Catholic Trump Supporters See Moment of Division," *National Catholic Reporter*, December 18, 2020.

29. See the article by the former president of Ireland, Mary McAleese, exploring the need for the church to recognize theologically the destiny of the unborn: "Flawed Defenders of the Unborn," *The Tablet*, February 11, 2021.

30. Díaz, "An Unfinished Project," 1.

that make them more prone to contracting the biological virus of Covid-19; of women's bodies threatened as a result of human trafficking; of LGBTQ+ bodies threatened from familial and institutionalized heterosexism; of Muslim and Jewish bodies threatened as a result of religious bigotry; of undocumented children's bodies and immigrant families threatened at our southern border; of disabled bodies lacking adequate protection; and of various species currently under the threat of extinction as a result of the environmental crisis. Catholics must "discern," as Paul asked the Corinthians to do, these threats to communal coexistence and *re-member* this broken social, ecclesial, and ecological body in the image of Christ.

To summarize, to act as a member of Christ's body necessarily means to reject the false concept of patriotism flown under the banner of Christian nationalism, embracing instead a "catholic" view, that is, more inclusive and just ways of being and acting in the world that contribute to the ongoing perfection of our union. This "catholic" *convivencia*, this personal accompaniment, will enable us to recognize and begin to heal the broken limbs within our social and ecclesial bodies. Finally, to embrace this integral option for the life of all human persons, especially those who have been marginalized and oppressed among us, will bring music to God's ears, for as St. Irenaeus proclaims: "The glory of God is the human being fully alive."

CHAPTER 19

Reinstating Catholic Faith in the Public Square after Trump

Simone Campbell

For the last sixteen years, I have worked in the midst of national policies and politics. As the leader of NETWORK, Lobby for Catholic Social Justice, we have promoted policies that prioritize marginalized people and communities. Our leadership helped to secure health care for over twenty million people in the United States through the Affordable Care Act, increased food security for people experiencing hunger, and funded critical programs in low-income communities. However, over the four years of the Trump administration, we witnessed an erosion of all of the communal commitments we hold dear.

Another factor that needs to be named, which I had not realized until after the inauguration of President Joe Biden and Vice President Kamala Harris, is that these last four years have taken an intense emotional toll. I have the feeling I have been holding my breath while strategizing how to counter the horrors of the Trump administration. In 2017, I held onto a small hope Mr. Trump could "grow into the office." This turned out to be a naïve Pollyanna view. Rather he consistently and deliberately eroded both the structures of government and our society. The emotional toll on our nation is just beginning to be recognized. I am surprised personally at the toll that it took on me. It is in this context of personal assessment I share the following reflections on our Catholic faith in the public square.

Factors in the Trump Administration

White supremacy, racism, and Christian nationalism have been at the heart of much of the Trump administration's policies. Everything from the initial "Muslim ban" prohibiting travel to the United States from Muslim-majority countries to the violent and cruel "zero-tolerance" policy to separating children from their parents at the southern border of the United States were, at their core, driven by racism and fear of the other. The lack of outrage from the White House in the response to the murders of George Floyd, Breonna Taylor, and so many others underscored the Trump administration's flagrant preference for white people. This was crystal clear when Trump directed the forced removal of peaceful protesters outside of St. John's Episcopal Church in Lafayette Park during the Black Lives Matter protests. The term of the forty-fifth president ended with President Trump's incitement of rioters to storm the Capitol building in an attempt to overturn the 2020 election. These violent rioters received a very different treatment from the police than did the peaceful protesters of the Black Lives Matter movement. This historical sin of white supremacy was alive and well in the Trump administration's policies.

The second sin that has been a hallmark of the Trump administration is hyperindividualism. I remember vividly in 2016 meeting an avid Trump supporter in his fifties. He was so angry that he had "worked hard and played by the rules" but he had not gotten ahead as his parents had promised. He was doubly angry because his adult children were having an even harder time than he was. They had moved home after finishing college because they could not find good-paying jobs. The whole family was trying to help them pay off their student loans. It came to me to say that it seemed like he was ashamed he had not measured up to his parents' expectations. Tears sprang to his eyes. We were both surprised at his reaction. We quickly ended the conversation because of our mutual embarrassment. In hindsight, I have many follow-up questions I wish I had asked. However, I am left to my own interpretation. I have come to see that this man had accepted the narrative of individualism that he was solely responsible for caring for his family. He did not see himself as part of a bigger social dynamic that had caused his wages to remain flat while the wealth of those at the top continued to grow by leaps and bounds. He did not see that our nation's economic policy was making this happen, and he was not personally to blame.

This sin of hyperindividualism masquerades as a "rugged independence." However, middle America, blinded by the rhetoric of individualism, has failed to see the reality lurking behind the rhetoric. The truth is that this dangerous rhetoric has masked the reality of policies in our nation that resulted in massive giveaways to those at the top of the economic ladder. This was exacerbated by the Trump administration's 2017 tax cut, which gave away huge amounts of needed federal revenue to wealthy corporations and individuals. It gave corporations an even bigger tax break than they were lobbying for. They were seeking a 28 percent corporate tax rate, but they received 23 percent as their base rate. The goal of this tax cut was allegedly to stimulate an economy that was already working at high capacity. This was simply an excuse to shift even more money to the wealthy. It has taken the pandemic to illustrate just how devastating this giveaway was. It undermined the capacity of the federal government to pay for what our nation needs for the common good. So many of our people are suffering because of reduced household income, lost employment, and social hardship. Some of the Trumpian legislators even have the nerve to say that our nation cannot afford to take care of our suffering people because of rising debt—which they caused by voting to pass the tax law!

This twenty-first-century sin of hyperindividualism is also seen in the basic response to Covid-19. The Centers for Disease Control has made it clear that wearing a mask and social distancing is the way to control the virus. However, the Trump administration failed to promote such simple behaviors. The virus, a communal experience, was addressed on an individualistic level. Many Trump followers will not wear a mask because of their "rights." This ultimate individualism denies the reality of the virus. The virus is no respecter of rights. It attacks anyone in its way. This is tragically played out in the accounts of some ICU nurses who say that even as some are dying of Covid-19 they do not believe that the virus is real. We as a nation are not able to prevent the spread of the virus because of this individualistic narrative that we do not share responsibility for protecting one another.

President Trump demonstrated this dangerous rejection of caring for the common good on January 6, 2021, when his lies about a "stolen" election came to a head. The mostly white men who rioted and attempted to overthrow the Congress and the election results had believed the "big lie." I think that they identified with the president because of their own anger seeking an outlet. Even though they were lied to by the president, they reacted without seeing any evidence of actual fraud. Their rage exploded into a violent attack on Congress.

Politically we came to the inauguration of the forty-sixth president with many in the Republican Party believing the president's lie that the election was stolen from him. At the base of this lie is racism and white supremacy, which says white people are entitled to privilege and they are denied that privilege by any commitment to the common good. This sense of entitlement is in a symbiotic relationship with the hyperindividualism of the Republican rhetoric that everyone is on their own.

Catholicism in Trumpian Times

The year before Donald Trump was elected, in September 2015, Pope Francis addressed a joint session of the United States Congress. At that time the Speaker of the House (John Boehner) and the vice president of the United States (Joe Biden) were both Catholics, as was the Minority Leader of the House (Nancy Pelosi). In his address Pope Francis stated: "It is my duty to build bridges and to help all men and women in any way possible, to do the same. . . . A good political leader always opts to initiate processes rather than possessing spaces." There was no political bridge building in the four years of the Trump administration. Rather, Senate Majority Leader Mitch McConnell refused to engage with the Democrats in the second half of the Trump term. His only interest was forcing through judicial nominations, even those candidates the American Bar Association had determined not to be qualified.

Such intransigence was not confined to just elected politicians. Unfortunately, many Catholic bishops had a similar approach to the administration. The one notable exception is the Justice for Immigrants (JFI) campaign of the United States Conference of Catholic Bishops (USCCB). The JFI staff did speak out against the Trump administration for their cruel immigration policies. Some Catholic bishops spoke against the administration's policy when Bill Barr, the US attorney general and a Catholic, started executing people on death row after a seventeen-year hiatus. Other than these exceptions, the USCCB was remarkably silent in the face of so many violations of Catholic Social Teaching. In fact, in the document "Faithful Citizenship," issued every four years in advance of the presidential election, a majority of the bishops of the United States voted to omit Pope Francis's teaching on the priorities that are "equally sacred" to the defense of the unborn. Such disregard for the pope's teaching combined with their embrace of President Trump's failure to care for the common good is an indictment on the leadership in the US Catholic Church.

This failure of church leadership was intensified when Archbishop Gomez issued a letter from the USCCB attacking President Biden and his administration shortly after the inauguration. It was shocking that after the corruption and cruelty of the Trump years, Archbishop Gomez attacked President Biden for his faith, without ever having a conversation with him. This is a prime example of how church leadership has fallen in with the Republican Party under the guise of being "pro-life."

Catholics as Multi-Issue Voters

The American Catholic Church is hindered by this inability to agree on the appropriate response to our faith mandates to both care for the unborn and for all of creation. In the spring of 2020, after prayer and discernment my organization discerned that we needed to oppose President Trump's reelection because of his violation of so many critical aspects of Catholic Social Teaching. This led us to use Pope Francis's "equally sacred" statement in the "Exhortation on Holiness" (paragraphs 101 and 102) as our guiding principle.

Pope Francis wrote:

> Our defense of the innocent unborn, for example, needs to be clear, firm and passionate.... Equally sacred, however, are the lives of the poor, those already born, the destitute, the abandoned and the underprivileged, the vulnerable infirm and the elderly exposed to covert euthanasia, the victims of human trafficking, new forms of slavery, and every form of rejection.

We had never spoken publicly about abortion as an organization, but this time we realized we could not be silent. For almost fifty years there has been the fight between "pro-life" and "pro-choice." It is a rigid binary as a result of the United States Supreme Court's ruling in Roe v. Wade. For too long, it's been impossible to find a shared way forward because these rigid positions are the organizing principle for numerous organizations and even engaging in the debate is seen as conceding. In the midst of this intransigent fifty-year fight, few people actually look at Catholic teaching for guidance on how to "care for the unborn."

Ironically, those who are most adamant in wanting to criminalize abortion are the same people who want to hurt the unborn by taking health care away from women and their children by repealing the Affordable Care Act. They also seek to undercut nutrition assistance for pregnant women and young children. It is those who are most in favor of abortion being a choice for a woman instead who champion many economic and health policies and programs that make abortion less likely.

At NETWORK, we came to talk about the need to care for the unborn and those who are already born, all the people whom Pope Francis named and more. We said that Catholics were not "single issue voters," as some of our leadership (and the media) would have us believe. We are instead "multi-issue voters." We trained hundreds of people in key states and regions to speak of being multi-issue voters. I realized that we had been silent too long and had ceded our moral voice in the debate. Our "Equally Sacred Scorecard" reported the positions of the presidential candidates on the issues Pope Francis named as "equally sacred." In this comparison,

President Trump got one point for his support of overturning Roe v. Wade and President Biden got seven points for supporting all of the other concerns Pope Francis said were "equally sacred." This commonsense approach to both our church's teaching and politics caught on with our members and many people "in the pews." We published it on our website in English and Spanish. A Vietnamese advocacy group reached out for permission to translate and use the scorecard in Vietnamese. We rejoiced in this request and immediately agreed. When they had finished the translation, we shared that on our website also.

The scorecard was downloaded thousands of times. It was wonderful to have people unconnected with NETWORK ask if I knew about it. A few of my Jewish friends said that they too had a "single issue problem" and were wondering about how they might have such a scorecard to break open the binary analysis! Much to our joy, this work to make the Catholic narrative broader—and more accurate—about being multi-issue voters is credited with helping shift the Catholic vote generally and more particularly in the critical states of Wisconsin, Michigan, Pennsylvania, and Arizona.

Potential Role of Faith

For now, we have survived the chaos of the Trump presidency. Our democracy almost crumbled in the attempted insurrection of January 6, 2021. Together, we witnessed a mob storm the Capitol in support of President Trump's big lie that the election had been stolen from him. While our democracy survived, we still have thousands of people in our nation who believe that the election was fraudulent, and even more who acknowledge the election was fair, but wish it had a different outcome. If ever there was a time for faith leaders to speak out and lead our people, it is now.

In the encyclical *Fratelli Tutti* Pope Francis sets out the mandate of political leadership in these challenging times. He calls for a "politics of encounter" as the way forward. He notes that gratitude, solidarity, and reciprocity mark such politics. If our faith leaders engaged in such encounter, then our church leadership might be more inclined to tell the stories of our people and invested in lifting up the ways we are connected. The bishops and the USCCB should look to the gospel for both the style and action of leadership. Jesus did not issue judgments and laws; rather he called on all to love and engage with those who are different from ourselves.

At NETWORK, we have done a variety of programs to meet "our people." In the fall of 2020, we did a "virtual" Nuns on the Bus tour. During that tour, we were able to record visits with people providing needed services and working for justice around the country. These virtual events allowed our members to share in this encounter. Two visits that stood out for me were our time with New Labor in New Jersey and the Angry Tias and Abuelas of the Rio Grande Valley. They are what the church can be.

New Labor is a large group of immigrant workers who have come together to ensure that their employers do not succeed in stealing workers' wages and, more recently, to help their members during the pandemic. They reported to me, and NETWORK members watching the event, that some employers had it written into their business plan not to pay workers their full salaries so that they could have a higher profit. Such disregard for the workers was shocking to me but was commonplace in New Jersey and New York restaurants and construction companies. By working together, these immigrant workers helped one another get the salaries due to them. They would go together to confront the employer. This solidarity was very successful in shaming an employer into doing the right thing. This model of solidarity and providing actual care for the needs of the community is a great role for the twenty-first-century church to play. However, it requires the leadership (including the bishops) to be interested and concerned in the actual needs of their people.

The Angry Tias and Abuelas of the Rio Grande Valley are a group of people who were outraged at the treatment of immigrants seeking to enter our country. When the Trump administration started separating children from their parents, they jumped into the chaos by just trying to help by responding to their very physical needs. The young people would be released from detention without shoelaces or belts. The "angry tias and abuelas" just started getting necessities for them. They started calling their friends to come help. They responded to people in need. This is the result of encounter and need. One of the women we spoke with told us she had never been involved in politics or policy. However, after seeing the needs of the children, she knew that policy mattered. She could not go back to ignoring politics because of the suffering that she had seen. This is the role for the church in the twenty-first century. Our church leaders need to have their hearts broken open by the needs of their people. Once they have allowed themselves to be touched by the need, then we cannot be idle or sanctimonious in the face of suffering.

Who Are "Our People"?

A few years ago I was giving an evening talk at Emory University. Before the talk, I had dinner with board members of the sponsoring center. In the course of the conversation, I talked about "my people" and told stories about the people I had met. One man was very upset that I spoke about "my people." He was a large donor to the university and was used to being included. He felt that my language was divisive. It took me a few follow-up questions to realize what he meant. Finally, it dawned on me that what he was upset about was that he thought he was not included in "my people." He wanted to belong. That insight has led me to a politics of inclusion. Everyone belongs if we are moved with compassion for the other. Pope Francis highlights this in his encyclical *Fratelli Tutti*. In his recounting the story of the Good Samaritan, Pope Francis points out that the Samaritan was the stranger who saw need and responded. The Samaritan identified with the victim and moved to action. He did not do the work alone. Rather, as Pope Francis notes, the Samaritan took the man to an inn—the service provided in that day for the care of travelers. The Samaritan used the social system to help heal the person attacked on the road.

For me, in the post-Trump era, I believe that our Catholic Church could be a leader if we return to the gospel and identify with the people. Our hope is in being open to hear the stories of our neighbors and responding with our care. To do this, I believe, we need a vibrant spiritual renewal that leads to action. Spiritually, we need to know that we are one body and cannot leave anyone out of our care. This means that progressives need to have an active care for those who disagree with them, and conservatives need to care for progressives as well as those who are marginalized in our nation. Love is the spiritual mandate of the gospel, and it is about time we started acting like it. Only a profound spiritual renewal will bring us to that Pentecost insight.

Once we know that we are one body, then we cannot leave anyone out of our care. The structural racism that gives me white privilege and oppresses people of color must be dismantled. The economic inequality increased by our legislation must be reversed. If our church follows this path, the silence of so many of our church leaders will end as the gospel mandate is absorbed into their lives. If we as a church come to "hunger and thirst for justice" then we will find our way forward out of the hyperindividualism and lies of the Trump administration. We will come to know that we are one people, and no one can be left out of our care. So let the measure of the leadership of our bishops be how they embody the politics of encounter. And let the measure of our fidelity to the gospel be how much we lift up the stories of our people so that hearts are broken open and healing can begin.

CHAPTER 20

Seeking Healing in an Age of Partisan Division: Reckoning with Theological Education and Resounding the Evangel for the 2020s

AIZAIAH G. YONG AND AMOS YONG

Four years ago (late fall of 2016), one of us (dad) was reeling from the American presidential election and contending with how to resist from his Asian American, pentecostal-evangelical location,[1] and the other (son) was just finishing his first semester of PhD coursework and on the front end of a sojourn that opened up to excavation of his mixed-race (Chinese-Mexican) ancestry.[2] Today, at the end of almost an entire year of pandemic quarantine that

---

1. For the results of that grappling, see Amos Yong, "American Political Theology in a Post-al Age: A Perpetual Foreigner and Pentecostal Stance," *Faith and Resistance in the Age of Trump*, ed. Miguel A. De La Torre (Maryknoll: Orbis Books, 2017), 107–14.

2. See "Multi/racial Experiences and Embracing the Many Tongues Within," *Made for Pax StoryArc*, issue 2, "Cultural Identity"; https://www.madeforpax.org/cultural-identity/motion, where Aizaiah describes his own journey of embracing his multiracial identity as a pentecostal Christian and the importance of considering our social location when it comes to theology and spiritual formation.

has not only further exposed the unjust racialization of late modern life but also been marked by the cataclysmic events of January 6, 2021, that rocked the foundations of the United States body politic, we are even more deeply troubled. The three parts of this essay (1) explicate that we are shaken to our core precisely because we are theological educators, (2) suggest postures for theological repentance, and (3) recommend a practical spirituality of redemptive healing for this next segment of our theological, political, and educational journey.

Theological Education in 2020: A Reckoning

The images of what happened in the Capitol building on Wednesday, January 6, will reverberate in our collective memory. We have heard the news reports, the commentary, the analysis, all *ad nauseum*, since that will neither change the facts of what happened nor return the lives lost that day. While not minimizing 45's role in what occurred, we recognize this administration has been as much a symptom of our imploding culture wars than a lone instigator. So, what we experienced was a judgment on our body politic. The rioting was a culmination of our collective incapacity to listen to one another, understand across differences, confess our errors, and work toward collective well-being.

The white evangelical church's backing of Donald Trump has been well documented. Critics would say this was a Faustian bargain, even as it is also surely difficult for nonevangelicals (and many evangelicals of color) to understand the reasons motivating this transaction: religious freedom protections, conservative judiciary appointments, opposition to abortion and LGBTQ+ inclusion, and support of the nation of Israel.[3] Of course, evangelicals and other Christians differ among themselves on these issues, and the events of the last four years have heightened these fragmentations. Whether part of the crowd or intended as evangelistic tools, evangelical slogans and symbols were found on Capitol Hill on January

---

3. E.g., Ralph Reed, *For God and Country: The Christian Case for Trump* (Washington, DC: Regnery, 2020).

6. The fact remains that there has been both public backing and support through silence from white evangelical churches when it comes to claims of the election being stolen, which has served to galvanize extremists, not to mention Christian white nationalists. Hence, if January 6 was a judgment on the nation, then the Scripture that insists judgment "begin[s] with the household of God" (1 Pet 4:17a)[4] would indict the evangelical community for its complicity in these developments.

As second and third generation pentecostal preachers, we have also been disheartened (to put it mildly) that so many pentecostal churches and leading personalities have participated in, if not also contributed to, our partisan divisiveness. In addition to the politicization of these communities and congregations, the pandemic has also brought forward the anti–medical-establishment strain of the classical pentecostal movement that has been among those at the vanguard insisting on gathering in person without adequate protective protocols. Here we find the combination of those believing in the protective power of divine favor and blessing wedded to the argument for free association and religious liberty perceived as under assault by "radical liberal" culture. But the more worrying part of what has been happening includes the thousands of "prophecies" that have been given over the last decade or more, leading up to and intensifying from 2016 to 2020, including putative divine assurances that Trump would serve two consecutive terms in office.[5] Yet even after certification of the electoral college and the inauguration of the new president, very few of these have been led to repent, recant, and admit they were wrong. Literally hundreds of thousands of faithful churchgoers have been reinforced in their convictions by these alleged "prophetic utterances," and if the US public had previously been skeptical about contemporary prophecy (and their prophets) for the many reasons we are familiar with,

---

4. Unless otherwise noted, all scriptural quotations are from the New Revised Standard Version of the Bible.

5. For fairly exhaustive documentation, see James A. Beverley, with Larry N. Willard, *God's Man in the White House: Donald Trump in Modern Christian Prophecy* (Pickering, ON: Castle Quay Books, 2020).

what has happened in this arena now is incontrovertible evidence that there is a reckoning due in the pentecostal-charismatic community about what it means to hear from and speak on behalf of God.

People of faith, especially those who claim the lordship of Jesus Christ, should be brought to their knees in the present moment, regardless of party affiliation. Aren't all of us siblings in Christ? If so, then, "If one member suffers, all suffer together with it" (1 Cor 12:26a). When families have been devastated, they instinctively seek to encourage one another. How might such mutual edification be possible without first being able to name these deep fissures, incapacities, and impotencies at the very core of who and what we are? It is too easy for "us" to say that it is "them" who are the problem, yet all of us claim the same savior and believe, at least in theory, that we share an invitation to the Lord's table.

If we were to be honest with ourselves about all of these matters, then, there is an even deeper level of interrelatedness in the present quagmire: that pertaining to the work of our theological institutions. We as theological educators ought to have an even profounder set of anxieties and concerns. In particular, for the elder among us (Amos), who has worked for over two decades in theological education largely within evangelical communities and now may be handing some of that work off to the younger (Aizaiah) and next generation, January 6 demands a further reckoning: recognition that the nation with the highest number of theological institutions and with the most material resources for the formational task has been producing church leaders and pastors of congregations that either have explicitly supported (or been in denial of their connection to) the events of January 6. If judgment begins in the house of the Lord, then to what degree did the riot on Capitol Hill also pronounce judgment on the theological institutions that have served these ecclesial communities?

Yet what does it mean to say that theological schools and seminaries might be under judgment? We would ask: What do the actions of churches and their members in the last few years up to these recent events tell us about our formational efforts, first in our hallowed schools and then through our graduates in our churches and communities? What does January 6 and the events leading up to it reveal about the values, priorities, and message of our curricula that have been internalized by our students and graduates, and through these, given to the churches, their members, attendees, and participants? What does it say that all of our expertise channeling two thousand years of biblical knowledge and theological wisdom and tradition has produced such a divided church willing to demonize fellow siblings to the point of violence? How is it that the most vibrant—if growing numbers rather than demographic decline is indeed a sign of vibrancy as sociologists might suggest—churches in North America, not to mention around the world, are of the evangelical, pentecostal, and charismatic type that have not only been enthusiastic in trading for some political gains (their agendas) at the expense of other political issues (e.g., immigration, poverty, racial and gender justice, environmental care, that have an equally substantive biblical basis) but also among the most susceptible to and persistent perpetuators of the fabrications that the election was rigged and that our democratic institutions are no longer trustworthy?

Theological Repentance as a Prelude to Redemption

As Asian American and mixed-race theological educators embedded within evangelical and pentecostal-charismatic movements,[6] then, our hearts are broken for our nation, for our churches, and for our theological institutions. In the following, we invite you to name the ways in which we have been complicit in the partisanship of our churches and the unraveling of our body politic. We present three sets of confessions to name our sins in order that divine redemption might be received on the other side.

First, our Asian American and mixed-race perspectives must name the white supremacy and normativity that we have been

---

6. The elder has carried ministerial credentials with classical pentecostal churches all of his adult life while the younger is, in the course of writing, in the process of transitioning his from a classical pentecostal to a mainline Protestant denomination.

racialized into, including through our theological formation, within our churches and our theological education.[7] This racialization has allowed us to give lip service to the many tongues of Pentecost, heralding the multicultural, multilingual, and multiethnic character of the body of Christ, while yet succumbing into the realities, at least in North America, of a "color-blind" society where the racial hierarchy remains uncontested. Colorblindness has been theologically justified from apostolic texts about there being neither Greek nor Jew but these have provided excuses for alignment with the dominant (white) culture—including ecclesial cultures—and alleviated responsibility for dealing with the historic injustices of Native American genocide and the scourge of African slavery in American history. If we are to fully embrace the promise of the New Heaven and New Earth, that it will be adorned with the gifts of those from many tribes, peoples, kings, and nations, then we have to go beyond simply enjoying the food, music, and worship of peoples of color and repent from our unquestioning embrace of a Euro-American colonial culture that has benefited and continues to profit politically, economically, and socially at the highest detriment of those un- or less-assimilated. Whereas many Asian Americans may be deferential to majority (white) culture as part of their survival and desire for upward socioeconomic movement, coalitions need to be forged first with those on the margins, surely beginning with indigenous and Black American communities but also with migrant sojourners, whether from south of the border or elsewhere around the world. Repentance here—we invite others beyond the Asian American and mixed-raced communities to consider—involves new solidarities: less cozying up with those in power and more communion with our siblings who have been on the underside of history, the poor toward whom the divine spirit has directed the proclamation of the evangel (see Luke 4:18).

Second, our lifelong inhabitation within pentecostal-charis-

---

7. Amos's own very gradual coming to grips with this reality is documented in various of his essays, some of them gathered in Amos Yong, *The Future of Evangelical Theology: Soundings from the Asian American Diaspora* (Downers Grove, IL: IVP Academic, 2014).

matic communities must name the Achilles' heel, so to speak, that represents the shadow side of the movement's strengths: its spiritual vitality has emboldened a triumphalism that denigrates those perceived as outsiders.[8] On the one hand, pentecostal-charismatic spirituality is presumptive about its full-gospel character (Jesus as savior, sanctifier, healer, Spirit-baptizer, and soon-coming king), spawning both (at best) an elitism that is less appreciative of other expressions of Jesus discipleship and (at worst) a rigid exclusivism that otherizes those not deemed born-again with the relevant markers. On the other hand, a spirituality that prioritizes the *charismata* to the neglect of the fruit of the Holy Spirit always risks a disembodied expression (which is a key way in which the oppression of bodies is then "conveniently" overlooked and then perpetuated), and this sensibility undermines any capacity for intersectional assessment, much less acknowledgment, of how our collective and personal identities are gendered, racialized, and historically-socially constructed. Those in the pentecostal-charismatic movement must repent from not persisting on the fine line between prophetic boldness on the one side and servant-like humility on the other. Our prophets must be cautious of the hazards of their vocation: as the Scriptures are clear that not all who call themselves prophets are true (e.g., 1 John 4:1–3). Our churches should continually test the prophets and ask if their words produce the fruit of the spirit or serve to perpetuate Christian political power, privilege, and domination. Repentance, for all Jesus followers who believe in and are open to spirit-inspired speech, must turn from the self-

---

8. David J. Courey, *What Has Wittenberg to Do with Azusa? Luther's Theology of the Cross and Pentecostal Triumphalism* (New York: T & T Clark, 2015), illuminates the triumphalism that infects pentecostal-charismatic spirituality. Put another way: pentecostal-charismatic supernaturalism understandably and even rightly emerged in reaction to the limitations of the immanentistic naturalism of the modern world, but precisely because subject neither to human manipulability nor rational comprehension, more often promises more than what is delivered, which in the end results in undermining rather than nurturing faith; see Amos Yong, *The Spirit Poured Out on All Flesh: Pentecostalism and the Possibility of Global Theology* (Grand Rapids, MI: Baker Academic, 2005), chap. 7, for more on this theme.

aggrandizement of the few to the recognition that the one body has many members, each with the spirit's gifts enabling edification of others (1 Cor 12).

Last but not least, while neither of us has made much of our having been situated, by and large, within the contemporary evangelical movement, we are surely children thereof, and we lament that this North American movement has embraced a partisan nationalism (pledging allegiance to modern-day Caesar) that has undercut its capacity to bear witness to the coming divine reign (under the rule of Christ) for the sake of the entire world. The problem here is not the *evangel* that is the good news of Jesus Christ who sets the captives free, but the *-icalism* that thinks we are building an earthly kingdom of comfort wherein we decide who is included and who is not.[9] United States citizenship (which includes an assumption of US history as neutral at best and thus denies the oppressive realities foundational to the expansion of power therein) has trumped (pun intended) commitments to the coming kin-dom (Heb 11:13–16, 12:18–28); modernist individualism has not only elevated and focused on individual rights while marginalizing and even ignoring altogether social justice; and neoliberal capitalism has sucked us all into the never-ending quest for economic growth that overlooks our interdependence with the environment, driven our accumulation of property instead of apostolic giving (Acts 2:42–47), and prioritized an ethic of productivity that ignores the call to sabbath and the need for personal and planetary rest and renewal.[10] In all of this, our evangelical (and pentecostal-charismatic) piety has overemphasized an individualized outworking of God's redemptive work, which lacks the interpersonal, ecclesial, and communal character of the divine intention for life's flourishing. Repentance will require

---

9. See Mark Labberton, ed., *Still Evangelical? Insiders Reconsider Political, Social, and Theological Meaning* (Downers Grove, IL: IVP Academic, 2018).

10. One set of constructive responses by evangelical-friendly voices can be found in Jonathan P. Walton, Suzie Laboud, and Sy Hoekstra, eds., *Keeping the Faith: Reflections on Politics and Christianity in the Era of Trump and Beyond* (Middletown, DE: KTF Press, 2020).

acknowledgment of how our theological education has not inoculated us from all these seductions, resulting in our cultural captivity instead of a church of Jesus Christ capable of speaking truth to power and co-creating a world of mutuality where all thrive.

Spiritual Formation for the 2020s: A Call to a Spirituality of Redemptive Healing

What shall we do with broken heartedness and the brokenness of our churches, institutions, and even body politic? For both of us as pentecostal theological educators and ministers, our intention is to seek redemptive healing, and to work in this direction requires that we focus on the core, spiritual dimension of the issues. In pentecostal-charismatic traditions, healing is one of the primary manifestations of the *evangel,* and if there was ever a time for US pentecostal-charismatic and evangelical churches to heal and do so by renewing our spiritual identities, it is now amidst such widespread division and confusion. In this concluding section, we are inviting a return to the *evangel* by offering a practical-mystical spirituality of redemptive healing that includes but goes beyond the individual level and extends to the entire world.[11] Our starting place is the admission we are a people in need of redemptive healing and that this healing is not a quick-fix solution but rather a lifelong pursuit that deepens within us (and flows beyond us) as we open our lives to receive it at personal, collective, and cosmic dimensions. Redemptive healing happens by way of faith wherein we prepare ourselves with trust and openness to embrace the divine spirit's work in us in ways that necessarily disrupt our assumptions and bid us to lay down our "dreaded and cherished illusions."[12]

---

11. We combine here the spiritual and the mystical that is deeply embedded within the pentecostal-charismatic imaginary: e.g., Mark J. Cartledge, *Encountering the Spirit: The Charismatic Tradition* (New York: Orbis Books, 2007); Daniel Castelo, *Pentecostalism as a Mystical Christian Tradition* (Grand Rapids, MI: William B. Eerdmans, 2017).

12. Christian mystic and spiritual teacher James Finley, *The Contemplative Heart* (Notre Dame, IN: Sorin Books, 2000), 208–9, describes spiritual healing as discovering our true identity and "learning from God how to let

This spirituality of redemptive healing we present does not just correlate with pentecostal spiritual and mystical sensibilities but, particularly given the need to attend to our institutions, churches, and also the extant body politic, extends to seekers from other traditions as well. On the one hand, we must embrace our own historicity along with our unique and many embodiments (at the various dimensions of our relationships), and yet, on the other hand, we are also invited to respond to the intercultural challenges of our contemporary globalized era.[13] The latter could involve synthesizing wisdom from across cultural and spiritual traditions in order that we might experience the collective renewal so needed in our time.[14] We imagine this spirituality offers us profound transformation at the personal and collective levels to empower us to meet our precarious moment. Its four steps proceed from four foundational questions that are key to the spiritual life and can be practiced individually or in a small group or as a larger institution such as a congregation or theological school. The first movement is one of *setting intention*; the second movement is *creating space*; the

---

go of and die to your dreaded and cherished illusions that anything less than infinite union with the infinite love of God has the authority to name who you are." This reality is of utmost importance if we are to heal the ways our hearts are easily given to despair amidst the contemporary crises.

13. The following builds particularly on the younger's multiracial experience that has generated and benefited from a spirituality of synthesis designed to heal from (and resist) racial oppression as well as nurture the religiosity needed for the twenty-first century; see Aizaiah's doctoral thesis, "Living in the Compassionate Presence of Life: Spirituality and Care for Multi/racial Experience(s)" (PhD diss., Claremont School of Theology, 2020), esp. chap. 1, "Catching Our Breath from Racial Oppression," which draws from a range of sources, most importantly Christian mystic and spiritual teacher Raimon Panikkar. For the elder's treatment of Panikkar, see Amos Yong, *Hospitality and the Other: Pentecost, Christian Practices, and the Neighbor* (New York: Orbis Books, 2007), 94–98.

14. Some of the theoretical foundations for interreligious spirituality have been laid in the elder's work on Buddhist-Christian comparative theology—e.g., *Pneumatology and the Christian-Buddhist Dialogue: Does the Spirit Blow through the Middle Way?* (Studies in Systematic Theology 11; Leiden and Boston: Brill, 2012)—and this portion of our essay moves us in the praxis dimension.

third movement is *waiting for insight*; and the fourth movement is *integrating life anew*.

The first movement, *setting intention,* originates in the spiritual question "What is desired?" The truth is that the core of our spiritual formation is inexplicably bound to what we desire. If we as pentecostal ministers and theological educators desire and wish to lead others to heal by the *evangel,* setting our intention begins with the kind of repentance from all the things we have desired other (and more) than the *evangel*. We hope to have begun modeling this movement in this essay. Setting intention also allows us to gauge how open we are to take the risk of spiritual (trans)formation because it requires us to be radically honest with ourselves to confess where we are truly at. What is the truth we carry deep in our bodies? What is the truth that must be named in our collective memory that resides below the surface? What is the truth carried in the land? Our intention must be informed by noticing our resistance to these questions, admitting where sadness and rage lie, and professing what we desire instead. Even if we do not know what we want or need, this movement invites us to admit our own confusion and set an intention to find clarity about ways to live that promote flourishing instead of perpetuating the untruths that lead inevitably to suffering. Setting an intention can also involve symbolic acts we take that help us to remember our desire for wholeness, such as lighting a candle and or reciting a phrase of Scripture that will reground us in this awareness.

The second movement, *creating space,* stems from the foundational spiritual question "Where is our devotion?"[15] So much of our suffering is not due to a lack of time but rather misplaced priority. In the US evangelical church particularly, we have named how devotion has been placed in endeavors that perpetuate collective suffering rather than alleviate it. This movement invites for our devotion to be reconsidered and instead placed in activities that cultivate

---

15. James K. A. Smith describes the centrality of longing and desire when it comes to transformative theological education and personal spiritual formation and devotion in *You Are What You Love: The Spiritual Power of Habit* (Grand Rapids, MI: Brazos, 2016).

connection with oneself, with other beings (human and more than human), the larger institutions we inhabit, and the entire cosmos. This movement helps us to establish daily or weekly rhythms that renew us and awaken us to a deeper sense that we are interwoven with all of Life, no exceptions. This movement contrasts the commercialized and individualized "self-care" culture centered on toxic consumeristic habits of binge watching, information greed, and entertainment. Instead, creating space calls us to respond to the following question: What are the foundational activities that we are devoted to engaging in that provide nourishment and restoration for all our relationships: personal, interpersonal, communal, social, and cosmic? A good way to gauge if this movement is effective is to ask: How does the way in which we are creating space enable us to stay present to and feel the suffering in the world, including the suffering of those in churches on the other end of the spectrum from where we are theologically, or of those in the other political party? If this practice does not equip and empower us to compassionately respond to suffering, then it is actually part of the problem causing us to use spirituality to bypass issues rather than face them in love.[16]

The third movement is *waiting for insight*. The movement is fed by the spiritual question "What is the divine inspiration for today?" If we admit our need and open ourselves up to activities that reconnect us to the Whole, then what ensues next is divine revelation about how we are being called to live differently amidst our particularity and in our collective space and time. This movement helps us to transcend our limitations by embracing them. This movement also demands us to reallocate our resources in more expansive ways than we had previously done, institutionally, ecclesially, and communally. This new insight will often contrast with our convention-

---

16. The spirituality we have created is also inspired by our understanding that spirituality is personal but only as powerful as it cultivates compassion for all who are experiencing suffering and oppression; see also Aizaiah G. Yong, "Critical Race Theory Meets Internal Family Systems: Toward a Compassion Spirituality for a Multireligious and Multiracial World," *Buddhist-Christian Studies* 40, no. 1 (2020): 439–47.

ally programmed responses, and stretch us, requiring immense courage because they surpass any ability we have to achieve them through willpower, the rationalistic mind, or effort alone. This movement does not ask us to do everything that is required to heal our churches, our national life, or the cosmic Whole, but asks us to contribute to healing in practical and actionable ways that promote Life's flourishing at every level. Often the insights we receive do not show us every future step but the next faithful step.[17]

The fourth movement is *integrating life anew*. This movement brings the *spirituality of healing* into a full circle and is built off the question "Who is my neighbor?" Extending from the insights from the third movement, this step is one of dialogue and mutuality, where the previously received revelations are tested in the face of loving relationships with the world. How does that which we have received in our particularities serve or call forth a greater compassion for self, others, our communities, our churches, and for *all* the world's inhabitants? Are we co-laboring as theological educators and pentecostal ministers endeavoring to "disciple" people in our image with our language and our ethnic/racial cultural bias? Or are we leading with a servant's heart that approaches the world—including others so very different from us—with a cautious conviction, one endowed with humility, curiosity, reciprocity, and vulnerability? This last movement confirms that the ultimate sign of the spirit is love, a love that seeks to be in communion with all of Life, starting with those who are most vulnerable due to injustice and oppressively marginalized from white majority cultural centers.[18]

---

17. See Dori Grinenko Baker, Matthew Wesley Williams, and Stephen Lewis, eds., *Another Way: Living and Leading Change on Purpose* (St Louis: Chalice Press, 2020).

18. For more on how spirituality can be used to foster solidarity with diverse others experiencing racial and other oppression, see Aizaiah G. Yong, "All Mixed Up: Multi/racial Liberation and Compassion Based Activism," *Religions* 11, no. 8 (2020), https://www.mdpi.com; see also Amos Yong, *Spirit of Love: A Trinitarian Theology of Grace* (Waco, TX: Baylor University Press, 2012).

This *spirituality of redemptive healing* we have presented embraces our human contingency as well as finds hope and confidence in the Spirit that cannot be contained or tamed by any one individual, family, cultural group, institution, or spiritual tradition. Thus, although our hearts are broken, as theological educators, pentecostal ministers, and fellow human beings, we invite you to join us in these movements of formation and abide steadfast in the promise of the Psalmist: "The Lord is near to the brokenhearted, and saves the crushed in spirit" (Ps 34:18).

CHAPTER 21

Unite and Conquer: Cutting Taxes, Religion, and Relationships of Race and Class

Joerg Rieger

Resenting taxes and questioning government both have long traditions in the United States, going back before the Revolutionary War. In recent history, however, these topics have been appropriated by conservatives in order to push particular political agendas. The tax cuts of the Trump administration, the so-called Tax Cuts and Jobs Act of 2017, are just the most recent example of this, and they need to be seen within this context in order to understand the full range of implications. In this chapter, we will take a look at the logic that guides recent efforts to cut taxes, beginning with economic and political motivations, and drawing out parallels to developments in religion as well as possible alternatives.

Economic-Religious Logics

The economic logic behind cutting taxes is fairly simple and has consistently been embraced by Republican administrations since Ronald Reagan's tenure as president in the 1980s: tax cuts are supposed to benefit the economy by providing economic stimulus. While there is considerable disagreement among economists, those who favor tax cuts argue that lowering taxes for corporations and businesses invariably leads to economic growth. These economists believe, against evidence provided by many studies,[1] that lowering taxes guarantees economic progress, manifest eventually in the creation of new jobs and rising salaries. One little-known feature of the Trump tax cuts of 2017 confirms the preferential treatment of corporations: while income tax cuts and other tax cut provisions were set to expire in 2025, corporate tax cuts were permanent.

While the idea of paying lower taxes appeals to a broad base of voters, what is commonly overlooked is that the direct financial impact of tax cuts is most pronounced at the top, because this is where the largest sums of money flow, while the lowest incomes tend to see no gains or experience losses.[2] In addition, tax cuts that reduce progressive tax rates, according to which higher incomes are taxed at higher rates, work to favor higher incomes as well. Progressive taxes have been lowered to such an extent that the marginal tax rates for the highest incomes are at 37 percent after the 2017 tax cuts, down from around 90 percent between 1944 and 1963.[3] The common argument that a rising tide will lifts all boats—that as the rich get richer everyone benefits—remains unproven, as I have argued in detail elsewhere.[4] Numbers published in October of 2020 state that US billionaires gained almost $1 trillion during the Covid-19 pandemic,[5] a time when many others suffered economically and many lost their jobs. There is a rising tide, but it lifts fewer and fewer boats, and tax cuts that disproportionally benefit the top further contribute to growing inequality rather than mitigate it.

At first sight, it may seem as if the economic logic at work here is unrelated to any religious logic. But there are some interesting

---

1. Center for Budget and Policy Priorities, "Tax Cuts for the Rich Aren't an Economic Panacea—and Could Hurt Growth," https://www.cbpp.org.
2. Erik Sherman, "CBO: The Senate Tax Bill Is Even Worse for Low-Income People Than Thought," *Forbes*, November 27, 2017.
3. Tax Policy Center, "Historical Highest Marginal Income Tax Rates," February 4, 1010, https://www.taxpolicycenter.org.
4. See Joerg Rieger, *No Rising Tide: Theology, Economics, and the Future* (Minneapolis: Fortress Press, 2009).
5. Aimee Picchi, "U.S. Billionaires Gained Almost $1 Trillion in Wealth During the Pandemic," *CBS News*, October 20, 2020.

parallels. At the most basic level, tax cuts that are most beneficial for corporations and higher-income groups are linked to common assumptions that power and agency are most consequential when located at the top. This matches widespread images of God as operating from the top down, linked with implicit or explicit assumptions that those at the top of society are closer to God. Such assumptions might shed light on why there is still so much faith in economic top-down schemes and why many Americans are more likely to question government support for the needy than massive government support for wealthy corporations. Even self-declared "fiscal conservatives" are more likely to question the government spending money on welfare programs rather than government spending that supports corporations. That considerably more money is spent at the top than at the bottom, and that this goes often unchallenged, points toward a deeper religious logic, according to which actions at the top trump actions at the bottom. If this assessment is correct, we can also identify a place where religion and theology can make a difference: rethinking images of God from the bottom up, as various liberation theologies have done in consultation with social movements, may present promising alternatives.[6]

Political-Religious Logics

At first sight, the political logic behind tax cuts appears to be simple. Self-interest, it is commonly assumed, is what motivates people to resent paying taxes. Who would want to give up some of their hard-earned income to the government? Nevertheless, it might also be argued that self-interest could justify paying more taxes. The majority of people would likely benefit from raising taxes to some degree, as they would benefit directly if tax monies were spent on better infrastructure like roads, sewers, and cleaner air, and they would benefit indirectly if tax monies were spent on better education of their children, improved care for their aging parents, the flourishing of their neighborhoods, support for their beloved communities, and so on. The American revolutionaries of the eighteenth century

---

6. For a sampling, see *Introducing Liberative Theologies*, ed. Miguel De La Torre (Maryknoll, NY: Orbis Books, 2015).

understood this logic when they coined the well-known motto "No taxation without representation." Strangely, in the current American situation where conservatives like Trump and the Tea Party have consistently pushed back against taxes, the motto seems to have been reduced to the first part: "No taxation—period." Political representation for the interests of the majority of taxpayers is not at the center of the conversation anymore.

Many who support the politics of lower taxes typically fail to understand that tax reductions tend to benefit disproportionally higher income levels, and particularly corporations, in a way similar to the economic logic of tax cuts. As a result, the habitual assumption that lower taxes are in the interest of all taxpayers is wrongheaded. The self-interest of taxpayers who are part of the working majority might be served better if taxes were raised and taxation became more progressive again. This is even more true if the matter of democratic political representation of all taxpayers (the second half of the American revolutionary motto "no taxation without representation") is taken into account.

The dominant political logic of tax reductions as a matter of self-interest is connected to certain religious logics as well. Even though an overemphasis on self-interest has traditionally been called into question in religious discourse, in conservative religious circles the focus on so-called family values, assumed to be religious values, provides a justification for selfishness. Religious support for the modern nuclear family and its self-interest, taking for granted that families are supposed to look out for themselves, has played a significant role in upholding the dominant status quo. As British socialist feminists observed in response to the politics of British Prime Minister Margaret Thatcher in the 1980s, which closely resembled the politics of presidents Ronald Reagan and later Trump in the United States, society is divided into families in competition with each other and exploiting each other, rather than made up of families supporting each other, as conservatives would have it.[7] The result of a certain religious emphasis on the family,

---

7. See Michele Barrett and Mary MacIntosh, *The Anti-Social Family* (London: NLB, 1982).

very similar to religious emphases on the nation, is increased selfishness; yet this selfishness does not benefit everyone equally, as it favors the elites rather than the majority. Once again, religion and theology can make a difference here when efforts are made to rethink dominant religious discourses from alternative points of view. Queer theologies, for instance, not only reexamine the nature of conservative family values but can also provide compelling alternatives for rethinking other relationships, including political and economic ones.[8]

Unite and Conquer: Race and Class

While the strategy of divide and conquer is well known, there is also a less-reflected-upon but common strategy that I have come to call "unite and conquer." In the United States, this strategy can perhaps best be observed in the legacies of white supremacy and racism, but it also applies to conservative tax policy as manifested in the Trump tax cuts. Here, elite leaders employ the tools of racist populism in order to coax the white population into believing that it has more in common with them than with others. In the United States, this time-honored tool has been brought to bear even before the founding of the country, when white landowners successfully employed racism to suggest to white sharecroppers that they had more in common with their white masters than with their fellow Black sharecroppers.[9] Who is conquered here, of course, may come as a surprise: white supremacist unite-and-conquer methods not only conquer racial minorities but white racial majorities as well. This becomes clearer when it is understood that the interests of the white majority, who all have to work for a living, differ substantially from the interests of the elites, represented by a white male billionaire president such as Donald Trump. Things become even clearer when it is seen that the interests of white working people—

---

8. See, for instance, Marcella Althaus Reid, *From Feminist Theology to Indecent Theology: Readings on Poverty, Sexual Identity, and God* (London: SCM Press, 2004).

9. See Lerone Bennett, *Before the Mayflower: A History of Black America* (New York: Penguin Books, 1984).

like some modicum of respect, power at work, adequate salaries and benefits—are closer to the interests of Black working persons than to the interests of white elites.

A similar strategy of unite and conquer is at work in conservative tax policies, including the 2017 tax cuts of the Trump administration. It is no accident that Trump successfully employed both white supremacist and conservative tax policy in order to further his political agenda. Cutting taxes appealed to large parts of the population and unified them behind a president and his politics that would ultimately benefit the few rather than the many. Uniting the masses behind tax cuts covers up who really benefits and who does not, as explained above. As a result, working people who do not understand what is going on are united with corporations whose mandate is to serve stockholders rather than working people, and are thereby conquered. In other words, members of the working majority who embrace the economic or political logic of conservative tax cuts are working against their own interests without being aware of it. This goes a long way toward understanding why so many people seemingly vote against their own interests.

Both forms of unite and conquer depend primarily on the invisibility of class differentials. More specifically, both kinds of unite and conquer thrive by actively covering up the realities of class exploitation, according to which the few profit from the labor of the many,[10] thereby misleading those who stand to benefit less from either white supremacy or the cutting of taxes. For those who are being misled in these ways, life and death are often at stake. As research has shown, some white people would rather die from lack of medical care than support access to medical care for all if it were to benefit Black people.[11] The current status quo can only be upheld if those who benefit less by unite-and-conquer schemes are mis-

---

10. This dynamic has become more pronounced since the 1970s, when productivity began to continue to rise but wages stagnated. See Economic Policy Institute, "The Productivity-Pay Gap," Economic Policy Institute, https://www.epi.org.

11. See Jonathan Metzl, *Dying of Whiteness: How the Politics of Racial Resentment Is Killing America's Heartland* (New York: Basic Books, 2019).

led: how else would a self-centered white billionaire president like Donald Trump have been able to hold on to power and even been able to incite a mob to storm the Capitol building toward the end of his tenure,[12] and how else could the ongoing dominance of large corporations over the economy and the global political atmosphere be maintained?

Religion has played its own role in this logic, as it often employs unite-and-conquer methods as well. The function of Christian notions of God in the United States is a case in point. When US politicians refer to God, they can expect the majority of Christians to assume that they are talking about the same God, thereby uniting Christians against people who do not believe in God. In reality, of course, there is a substantial and often irreconcilable difference between images of an imperial God and the God of Jesus Christ who resists empire. Not only does religion function in producing a misleading unity that, once again, favors those in power; it also divides those who may have more in common than they realize. Progressive Christians, for instance, may have more in common with progressive Buddhists who are not interested in God questions, or with progressive agnostics or even atheists who also reject images of an imperial and tyrannical God. Religious and theological discourses can contribute to rethinking God images, relationships, and the question of self-interest in inspiring ways.[13]

Religious Logics and Antidotes

These reflections afford a closer look at popular and widespread religious logics tied up with economic and political logics. After what has been said so far, it should not be hard to see how the Religious Right as well as the gospel of prosperity have their own unite-

---

12. For a statement addressing this final major act of Trump's presidency, see the Vanderbilt Wendland-Cook Program in Religion and Justice's Statement in Response to the Events of January 6, 2021, https://www.religionandjustice.org.

13. For the difference of the imperial God and the God of Jesus Christ as well as constructive alternatives, see Joerg Rieger, *Jesus vs. Caesar: For People Tired of Serving the Wrong God* (Nashville, TN: Abingdon, 2018).

and-conquer schemes going. To start with the latter, proclaiming that the wealth of the wealthy is within the reach of all who follow certain religious rules and demands is not only misleading but leads people to identify with the wealthy rather than with the rest of humanity; this is also the result of believing in the American dream. This move unites people who otherwise may have very little in common, and it conquers both outsiders and insiders: those who adhere to the gospel of prosperity, often at great sacrifice to themselves and their communities, but who do not strike it rich only have themselves to blame. To be sure, this pertains to the majority of the faithful, and so the emphasis of unite and conquer is on conquer, as unity in this case is ultimately an illusion in service of controlling the masses.

The Religious Right's unite-and-conquer schemes would merit being studied in greater detail, beginning with the fact that the driving forces behind it are linked with big money and well-documented ongoing corporate efforts to move Christianity to the right, dating back to the first half of the twentieth century.[14] The faith that is proclaimed by the Religious Right, including its moral commitments, tends to feed into unite-and-conquer schemes. The way in which images of Jesus are bent into their opposite may serve as an example. Turning Jesus into a supporter of conservative family values and into the champion of the wealthy and powerful serves to unite the faithful with the dominant status quo and covers up who Jesus really was. Recall that the Jesus of the New Testament Gospels not only refused to shore up conservative family values but challenged them at almost every turn (see Mark 3:31–35, Matt 10:34–39, and others). Moreover, the Jesus of the New Testament was not only closer to the poor, minorities, and women, but challenged the privileged, preaching woe to those who are rich and full (Luke 6:24–25) while challenging those who identify with the schemes of dominant power (Mark 10:35–45).

These considerations point to religion as a possible antidote to unite and conquer. Both ancient and sacred traditions as well as

---

14. Kevin Kruse, *One Nation under God: How Corporate America Invented Christian America* (New York: Basic Books, 2015).

current religious practices and lived religion provide alternatives. The famous passages in Acts 2:43–47 and 4:32–37 are often referenced as promoting alternative ways of life where communities share their wealth rather than compete against each other. This throws another light on tax policies that might be tailored to serve the common good rather than the privileged few, exemplified to some degree in the United States starting with the New Deal in 1933 until well into the 1970s. Of course, these ways of life have never been without tensions and problems (Acts 5:1–11), but religion continues to inform alternative ways of life, challenging and reshaping dominant ones. In particular, these considerations require another look at places where fundamental relationships are shaped, including places of work, where most people spend the bulk of their waking hours. Since work is arguably the place most marked by the absence of democracy, any efforts to reclaim more democratic relationships in this context carry significant weight. Emerging conversations between religion and labor movements as well as religion and cooperative efforts among workers can help reclaim not only religion but also politics and economics.[15]

Conclusions

The surprising insight of this chapter is not that Trump's 2017 tax cuts were troubled, and in many ways misleading, but that most of those who supported them and continue to support similar policies never really benefited from them and are unlikely to benefit in the future. Similarly, the kinds of conservative Christianity that resonate with these political and economic moves are not beneficial for the many who continue to embrace them but only to the few who, in Trump's case or in the case of major corporations, are probably not even that interested in these (or any other) forms of religion.

---

15. See, for instance, the work of the Wendland-Cook Program at Vanderbilt University Divinity School (www.religionandjustice.org) and the Southeast Center for Cooperative Development (www.co-opsnow.org). See also Joerg Rieger and Rosemarie Henkel-Rieger, *Unified We Are a Force: How Faith and Labor Can Overcome America's Inequalities* (St. Louis: Chalice Press, 2016).

Nevertheless, this chapter confirms that there are real alternatives and that religion, including progressive forms of Christianity, can provide some inspiration. At the most basic level, there is a sense that democratic governments cannot function without a democratic tax system that ties together taxation and representation. Moreover, democratic governments and tax systems can also benefit from, and feed into, democratic religious and interreligious relationships. This is a matter worth exploring and deepening in the era that is beginning after Trump, and much remains to be done.

CHAPTER 22

Enough of Us Came Together to Carry All of Us Forward

John Fife

Beginning to contemplate the task of writing on immigration and border security for *Faith and Reckoning after Trump*, I found a few lines from President Biden's inaugural address inspiring:

> Our history has been a constant struggle between the American ideal that we are all created equal and the harsh, ugly reality that racism, nativism, fear, and demonization have long torn us apart. The battle is perennial. Victory is never assured. Through the Civil War, the Great Depression, World War, 9/11; through struggle, sacrifice, and setbacks, our "better angels" have always prevailed. In each of these moments, enough of us came together to carry all of us forward. And we can do so now.

"Enough of us" is an apt description of the 2020 election, which was won by seven million votes nationally, but in which a grand total of fewer than a hundred thousand votes in total in just five battleground states could have elected Trump in the Electoral College. Just enough of us in five key states! It surely seemed over the four years of the Trump administration that all of those who organized to resist the avalanche of anti-immigrant policies and executive orders were never going to be enough. Upon reflection now, and only because of the extraordinary commitment and sacrificial resources provided—it may be enough to end what Biden called our "uncivil war" against immigrant families and workers.

The early sign of hope for what was to come occurred shortly after the inauguration on January 25, 2017. Trump issued an executive order that became known as the "Muslim Ban." Far beyond "enough of us," airports became jammed spontaneously with lawyers, paralegals, civil liberty organizations staff, and resisters to the Muslim Ban. That resistance evolved quickly into a restraining order in federal court, upheld in the court of appeals, upheld twice by the Supreme Court—until it was approved on the third rewrite. At the same considerable time, on the local level throughout the nation, Muslim, Jewish, Christian, and other faith congregations came together in renewed grassroots relationship to lead local communities in common defense of the First Amendment and religious freedom.

Each time during the Trump administration that a new anti-immigrant strategy was unveiled by Stephen Miller and Trump, the same broadening coalition of law firms, civil liberties attorneys, faith leaders and congregations, grassroots immigrant organizations, human rights organizations, Latinx allies—all responded with organized resistance. Remember the response to early ICE raids on workers at meat-packing plants? Local congregations protected immigrant families in church buildings while lawyers mounted a legal defense for workers and business lobbyists worked to end any more raids. Remember churches, synagogues, and mosques declaring sanctuary for immigrant families in record numbers while over 542 cities, counties, and states declared themselves sanctuary governments, issuing new law enforcement policies to provide public safety for immigrant families? Remember the public-resistance rallies, their size and diversity, when the attorney general Jeff Sessions issued a zero-tolerance policy at the border and began separating infants and children from their parents? Remember the response of faith leaders, congregations, grassroots immigrant organizations, civil liberties organizations, lawyers, and medical teams on both sides of the border when ICE and US Border Patrol agents (under court order) began to dump asylum-seeking families on the streets of border cities? City leaders, churches and synagogues, volunteer doctors and nurses, and faith-based organizations took responsibility when ICE claimed they were overwhelmed. Remember when asylum seekers were turned away at the border and ordered to "Remain in Mexico" on the streets of border cities? Remember the aid and protection that flowed across the border from international aid organizations, medical teams, and legal defense teams? This list could easily become book length, and I trust that soon these stories of active nonviolent resistance will be told.

A closer look at just one of these examples, sanctuary, may be illustrative of the greater phenomenon. Sanctuary in sacred sites is an ancient tradition common to the writings and practice of all major faiths—Judaism, Christianity, Islam, Buddhism, Hinduism, and indigenous spiritual practice globally. Recently, in the United States, in the 1980s, the sanctuary movement revived that ancient tradition to protect refugees fleeing for their lives from death squads, torture, massacres of hundreds of villagers, and civil wars in Central America. The movement was based in faith communities and connected by a New Underground Railroad. It was supported by secular cities, universities, the state of New Mexico, and faith-based organizations in Mexico and Canada. Eventually, it succeeded after eight years in forcing the US government to end all deportations to El Salvador and Guatemala, and to grant Temporary Protected Status to over half-a-million refugees.

The new sanctuary movement was revived in 2007 to protect migrant families threatened with deportation of a parent by ICE agents under the newly formed Department of Homeland Security. Faith communities formed coalitions with immigrant-led organizations and legal defense teams in each impacted community. When the Obama–Biden administration took office in 2009, they increased the ICE enforcement and deportation capacity to a record three million deportations during their two terms. The campaigns of coalitions of immigrant-led organizations, Latinx organizations, human rights and civil liberties organizations, faith leaders and the new sanctuary movement in congregations forced the Obama administration to issue two memoranda in 2011. One established a policy of "prosecutorial discretion," which gave ICE officials the discretion to defer deportations on an individual case and established priorities for deportation. The second established "sensitive locations" that should not be targets or sites of enforcement action.

One of those "sensitive locations" was places of worship. The new-sanctuary-movement congregations became organizing hubs vital to protect migrant families, while attorneys and community leaders negotiated with ICE and DHS to stay deportations. As in the sanctuary movement of the 1980s, the voices and stories of the immigrant families from the safety of sanctuary became central to public education and support.

Under the Trump administration, all of the priorities for deportation were ended and prosecutorial discretion abolished. The sanctuary movement based in congregations evolved again under these circumstances. The number of faith communities declaring public sanctuary increased to record numbers. Today, over 1,400 congregations are public sanctuaries, and an unknown number have protected immigrants and refugees from deportation. They have become an organizing hub for thousands of other congregations to join the broader movement for the legal defense of immigrant families, advocacy and resistance, and solidarity campaigns with immigrant communities. The first line of defense for immigrants has become the dramatic increase in sanctuary cities, counties, and states in the past four years. In the 1980s, faith-based congregations were the base of the movement, and seventeen sanctuary cities supported the movement by instructing public employees not to cooperate with federal immigration agents. In 2017, the number of cities, counties, and states soared to 564. Thus, secular governments have become the first line of defense for immigrant families and congregations of faith the strategy of last resort.

During the Biden–Harris campaign for the presidency in 2020, the campaign published their immigration policies. The first section on immigration was titled "Undoing the Harms of the Trump Administration and Righting the Wrongs." On his first day in office, President Biden signed a series of executive orders and administrative memos. The nonpartisan American and Immigration Council has provided the following summary:

- scaling back Trump's unchecked immigration enforcement
- one hundred day moratorium on most deportations
- the end of the Muslim and African travel bans

- protecting people with DACA
- expedited access to green cards for Liberians
- pausing construction on the border wall
- ending Trump's unconstitutional census order
- suspending new enrollments in the "Remain in Mexico" program for asylum seekers.[1]

Then, on the same day, Biden introduced to Congress and the American people, a sweeping immigration bill that will be transformational for an estimated eleven million undocumented immigrants. According to America's Voice, the bill would provide:

- a pathway to citizenship for DACA recipients, farm workers, and Temporary Protected Status holders
- a plan for undocumented immigrants to be able to apply for green cards
- assistance for reducing the visa backlogs created by the Trump administration
- funding for border technology
- improvements to the immigration courts across the country
- funding to help Central American countries to assist migrants seeking protection.[2]

There will of course, be a series of executive orders, administrative memos, and rule changes issued over the next four years. The Biden campaign initiative titled, "Building a 21st Century Immigration System," will be the heavy lift. There has been no immigration reform legislation that has passed Congress since 1986.

The George W. Bush and the Obama administrations both failed in their committed attempts at immigration reform. It is clearly one of the most contentious and divisive political issues in both parties,

---

1. Katy Murdza, "Biden Took Eight Administrative Actions on Immigration," *Immigration Impact*, January 22, 2021, https://immigrationimpact.com.

2. Frank Sharry, "Biden–Harris Roadmap on Immigration Reflects How the Tectonic Plates Have Shifted," *America's Voice*, January, 21, 2021, https://americasvoice.org.

marking decades of failure. It will take a rare bipartisan effort involving compromise and negotiation. For the purposes of this chapter, it is clear that righting the wrongs of the Trump administration and building a just immigration system for the twenty-first century will require enough of us joining together in the broad coalitions that joined to resist the wrongs of the past: immigrant-based organizations, human rights and civil rights institutions, Latinx, Asian, and Black Lives Matter movements, bipartisan political leadership, Chamber of Commerce and business leaders, educators, faith leaders and faith-based institutions.

What have we learned from the past four years about the role and unique contribution of faith-based organizations, leaders, and congregations in that broad coalition that formed the resistance, and must now become "enough of us to carry us all forward to immigration reform"?[3] I was a graduate student during the civil rights movement of the 1960s. What I saw, participated in, and learned then is as valid and valuable as today's struggle for immigration reform and justice. Every evening, after the marches, sit-ins, and rallies for civil rights, folks would gather at a church, sing the freedom songs, hear the old stories of God's liberation, and revive the spiritual strength to face whatever trials the next day might bring. Those same old freedom songs and sacred stories of liberation are being sung again today when faith leaders and congregations are part of the broad coalition for immigration justice. Cesar Chavez and Dolores Huerta were leaders who understood the centrality of the Mass to sustain the farm workers movement. The contribution of faith communities to nonviolence in the movement is, in my judgment, essential to the inevitable discussion of tactics and strategy in every broad and diverse coalition.

When I was growing up in the mountains and hill country of Appalachia, we heard a lot of preachin' about the Day of Reckoning. It usually referred to the time of accounting and judgment at death. But reckoning was also invoked for younger folks when we committed a sin within the family or community. That need for a reckoning is essential for the Christian family and community in

---

3. President Biden's Inaugural Address, January 20, 2021.

2021 in my judgment. The hard truth of the past election is that 81 percent of white, evangelical Christians voted for Trump and were essential to his party's base. This is not just a current problem for the predominantly white, evangelical church. It has its origins in finding theological and biblical support for slavery, then Jim Crow and segregation, and now white Christian nationalism. We must not forget that the KKK had two agendas. One was segregation; the other was anti-immigration. As a part of the family of Christianity, I believe it is the time of reckoning within the family. The only possible place for the family to gather is around the Bible, in serious and prayerful dialogue with one another. There is now a serious debate among evangelicals since the violent mob that stormed the Capitol on January 6, 2021, did so with many carrying crosses, flying flags with "Jesus Saves," singing Christian hymns, and praying alongside white supremacists, fascist symbols and banners, and even Camp Auschwitz hoodies. That debate is whether the evangelical branch of the faith should name white Christian nationalism for what it is—a heresy.

There is also a reckoning that must be done with all those in the Trump administration who ordered and carried out the zero-tolerance policy of the Justice Department and the Department of Homeland Security. A recent report of the inspector general of the Justice Department points the way to investigate what is a long and unresolved crime against humanity by the government. That seems to me to be the defining line between the "wrongs" of the Trump administration and the public reckoning and trial for those who ordered the separation of children from their parents as a deterrent to asylum seekers. On this moral criterion all faith traditions can find common cause. We know some, but not all, of the facts. At least 2,300 children, maybe thousands more, were forcibly taken from their parents' arms. The parents were deported as a deterrent to immigrants on the border. At least 611 of those infants and children have not been reunited with their parents after being ordered by the federal courts to do so. All faith communities must unite with the broadest possible coalition, led by the American Academy of Pediatrics, who termed the separation of children "torture." Enough of us must demand a public reckoning, evidence, and trial or we can never claim again to be a democracy that believes in "certain inalienable rights."

Among all of the recommendations of the Biden immigration Unity Task Force's detailed report (ten-pages, single spaced), there was one glaring omission. No mention was made about the worst violations of human rights and international law on the southwest border. That is the border enforcement strategy named "Prevention Through Deterrence" by the Border Patrol in 1994. It has remained the border enforcement strategy of the US government through all the administrations of Clinton, Bush, Obama, and Trump. The strategy is easily understood. Since the border was established in 1853, immigrants have crossed the line to work through the five urban areas between California and South Texas because they were the easiest and safest places to cross. The Prevention Through Deterrence strategy began by sealing off those urban areas with barrier walls, militarized Border Patrol presence, and technology. Then the same strategy was used and extended out from the cities until Border Patrol budgets and staff quadrupled and then quadrupled again. The purpose was to force migration into the most isolated and deadliest regions of the border lands—and then to use the thousands of deaths that would occur in desert wilderness as a deterrent to others seeking to cross. Thereby, the plan decreed, we will control the border. Over eight thousand human remains have been documented as the strategy has unfolded. Experts who have studied the evidence believe the death toll to be five times the number of remains found. The desert ecology is designed to clear any remains quickly, and the wilderness is vast.

As early as 2003, a six-judge panel of the Inter-American Court of the Organization of American States found unanimously that "Prevention Through Deterrence" was a violation of human rights and international law. The UN High Commission on Refugees and the UN Commission on Human Rights have concurred. This intentional strategy to use the death and suffering of tens of thousands of the poorest of the poor as border enforcement is not just a crime against humanity. It is a sin that requires a public reckoning by the community of faith. Faith-based organizations across the southwest border have responded for twenty years by taking humanitarian aid (water, food, and emergency medical care) into the desert to save lives and to document the violations of human rights by the Border Patrol. Faith leaders and institutions must demand that "Prevention Through Deterrence" be ended by our government or face our own reckoning some day for our crimes against humanity and sin of complicity.

Finally, communities along the southwest border, Native American tribal and spiritual leaders, and environmental organizations are demanding a reckoning by the Biden administration for the devastation unleashed on the southwest deserts and people by the construction of the border wall. Over the past four years, 455 miles of thirty-foot-high steel wall have been constructed at a cost of $15 billion of sequestered US taxpayer funds. Eighty-four federal laws that mandate protections for the fragile ecology, wildlife and endangered species, water resources, antiquities, burial grounds, ceremonial and sacred sites, public lands, and national parks have all been waived for the construction. Words like devastation cannot begin to describe the scope of this tragedy. While President Biden halted all the current contracts to build the walls, reckoning and recovery efforts are essential. Christian faith leaders and institutions have a particular responsibility to join the Native American spiritual and tribal leaders to reckon with and restore the devastation. Ceremonial sites and ancient burial grounds, sacred sites for Native peoples, must be recognized and preserved. Christian leaders must reckon with our own history of complicity with government policies to "Christianize and civilize" indigenous people and join with indigenous spiritual leaders to preserve sacred and cultural sites. Religious leaders of all faiths must join with environmentalists and border communities to reckon with the immeasurable damage to God's creation, which is sacred to all.

Faith and reckoning will require years, even generations to account for and repair the devastation to people and land, by not just the Trump years but by immigration policy and border enforcement for generations. Dr. King rightly reminded us, "The arc of history is long indeed, but it always bends towards justice." That is true "if enough of us come together to carry us all forward."

CHAPTER 23

Which God You Talkin'bout? Pastoring in a Divided Family, Church, Nation; Taking a Stand

JACQUI LEWIS

If we are going to pastor to this deeply divided nation, we're going to have to ask ourselves a really important question: Which God do we serve? Or better, *What God you talkin'bout?* Knowing something about the God we follow is a job for faith leaders. But also there is work for all of us who live in this nation as well. As people of moral courage, we must step fully into our leadership role, and join together in prophetic grief and sacred, righteous outrage to critique our white supremacist culture that masquerades as Christianity. We need to put down the puny, stingy gods to whom we have allegiance, gods who demand little of us, gods with whom we conspire to do little and to maintain the status quo and get comfortable with a God called Love.

What Children Learn

Martin's family could have taught him to hate white people, but they didn't. Their God wasn't having that. I wonder: Who taught that little girl, Lisa, who called me a nigger when I was five, to be racist, and who taught the one who taught her? While I was watching my Mom, learning what was good, right, and just; while I was observing the way Dad spoke truth to power, demanding reparations for us from Lisa and her father, what did Lisa observe as she watched her family? What did she hear? Were the lessons in her household stories of darkies who were inferior to white people; did she see evidence that they loathed our Black bodies, and take that feeling in as her own? Had her life in Mississippi as a child been shaped both by southern manners and the philosophies of white citizen councils or the KKK? When I was learning that Jesus loved all the little children, did a nice "Christian" pastor in the Mississippi church where Lisa grew up preach to her family that whites were predestined to be better than Blacks? Was it more subtle than that; did Lisa watch television, and, seeing no Black people to speak of, find us invisible? Or had she already seen, at the tender age of five, one of those postcards, where nice, white, church-going people stood alongside a tree, from which a Black body hung like "strange fruit," and smiled for the camera?

And every little girl and boy of European descent, nursed by a Black mammy; every child who came to understand that although that wet nurse was fit to feed them, she wasn't fit to live in a warm place or eat well or be in charge of her own destiny—each of them was being baptized into racial hierarchy. Each one of those children has ingested racial prejudice deep into their psyche, let it become code for their lives or let them reject the very premise of white superiority and do something about it. The answer to disrupting and dismantling racism is an every-person, every-day choice. And in this moment, my question is: Who will we choose to teach our children to be? What will we teach them about what is loving, just, and fair? What are they learning in our religious communities?

In the Name of Religion

As a clergy, I am ashamed that over time Christian theologians argued that the enslavement of human beings was justifiable from a biblical point of view. For much of Christian history, many saw no conflict between keeping the faith and keeping or trading enslaved human beings. Indeed, there was once such a thing as a *Slave Bible*, a version of the King James that contained only "select parts" of the Scripture. Its publishers deliberately removed portions of the text, such as the exodus story, that could inspire hope for liberation, and instead emphasized texts that justified the system of slavery, which was so vital to the British Empire. One theologian, Harvard-educated James Henley Thornwell, regularly defended slavery and promoted white supremacy from his pulpit in Columbia, SC. In a famous sermon, delivered in 1861, Thornwell preached, "As long as that [African] race, in its comparative degradation, coexists side by side with the white, bondage is its normal condition."[1] As Rev. Dr. Martin Luther King Jr. would note almost a century later in a handwritten letter from the Birmingham jail, the church has often been a defender of the status quo. King wrote, "The power structure of the average community is consoled by the church's silent—and often even vocal—sanction of things as they are."[2]

Before the fire that destroyed it in 2020, portraits of all the senior ministers who'd served in the history of the Collegiate Church of New York have hung on the walls at Middle Collegiate around our art deco social gathering space. Among them was a portrait of a minister who owned Africans, and one of me, with my dreadlocks shining and with my signature red lips. I am the first African American, the first person of color, and the first woman hired as a senior minister in charge of our church, which formed in 1628. I began my tenure at the Collegiate Church in 2004. It took a long time for this particular stained-glass ceiling to be cracked! I'm proud to be in this role, in a job I love, but I'm not proud of some parts of our history.

The Dutch colony of New Amsterdam (modern-day New York) legalized slavery in 1626. In that same year, the Dutch West India Company imported enslaved Africans to help build the infrastructure of the colony; those are the folks who began to worship together in 1628. Taking the company's lead, Dutch-speaking colonists purchased enslaved Africans from Dutch slave traders who landed in

---

1. R. L. Stanton, "The Ecclesiastical Disruption of 1861," in *The Presbyterian Quarterly and Princeton Review, Vol. V*, ed. Lyman H. Atwater and Henry B. Smith (New York: J. M. Sherwood, 1976), 344.

2. Martin Luther King Jr., "April 16, 1963 Letter from Birmingham Jail," in *Why We Can't Wait* (New York: Signet Classic, 2000), 80.

New Amsterdam. In time, the Dutch Reformed Church insisted that slaveholders seek the salvation of the people they counted as property and have them join the Dutch Reformed congregation. The Africans could marry under the sanction of the church and have their children baptized. Church membership conferred a special status, but there is no evidence that this led to freedom.

I'm embarrassed and ashamed to confess that my ecclesiastical ancestors not only engaged in the slave trade but are also the ones who bought *Manahatta*—the hilly land—from the Lenape people who lived and flourished on it. I find myself wondering about what lessons there are to learn today about calling, about vocation, about deciding before which god one should bow down.

Mark's Messiah

The Gospels all point to the ministry of Jesus of Nazareth; they each have their own point of view like news channels. In short, there's nothing about the baby here or in John. It's the oldest gospel, with a sense of urgency. Mark's Gospel is written to help citizens of the empire learn the hard truth about their world and themselves. Mark does not pretend to represent the word of God dispassionately or impartially, as if the word were innocuously universal in its appeal to rich and poor alike. His story is about and for those committed to God's work of justice, compassion, and liberation in the world; it's to those willing to raise the wrath of empire Mark offers a way of discipleship. Mark offers a way of being tutored, a way of living in the world with love of self, neighbor, and God. A way of living an ethic of love, period. Jesus brings the kin-dom of God, the reign of God nearby; those committed to God's work in the world, those who are willing to risk the wrath of the empire—they are enlisted to drop what they are doing and immediately follow.

Mark's Gospel is not the good news of private salvation; in fact, none of the Gospels are. But Mark almost dares you to read this good news as though the end game of faith is to get your personal relationship with Jesus Christ on. He dares you make your faith function as a way to avoid hell and damnation; to think that when the world comes to an end, when violence, oppression, and fear finally have the last day in this kingdom of the world, you can cash in your get-out-free card and be parachuted to heaven. No, Mark's Gospel is a call against empire. It is a call against oppression, a call against greed, a call against malice, a call against racial hierarchy and caste. It is a call to create the kingdom of God on earth. It is a call to all of us who would risk the wrath of neighbors and rulers to join Jesus as he makes the kingdom of this world become the KINdom God. Mark's Gospel is a manifesto, a call to radical discipleship rooted in love.

Not everyone reads it that way. In 1979, the Catholic bishops of Latin America gathered for a meeting in Puebla, Mexico. In his opening address to the gathering, Pope John Paul II said, "We find re-readings of the Gospel that purport to depict Jesus as a political activist, as a fighter against Roman domination and the authorities, and even as someone involved in the class struggle. This conception of Christ as a political figure, a revolutionary, as the subversive from Nazareth, does not fall within the Church's catechesis."[3] Yet I would submit that any depiction of Jesus that does not pit him against empire, against injustice; any depiction of a blonde, blue-eyed promoter of empire is blasphemy.

Speaking of being pitted against empire, travel with me back to first-century Palestine. Let go of the fact there are no demons. Jesus starts his ministry being tested by the devil, by Satan, by the adversary. He begins in spiritual warfare, Holy Spirit versus Evil Spirits. There are lots of places around the globe today in which the spirit world is viewed to be actively engaged with earthly beings and circumstances. Cuba, indigenous and aboriginal communities, African communities. I'd say one could make an argument for a connection between the battles on our national political stage and spiritual forces. So, let go of wondering if there was a devil or unclean or evil spirits. Also let's let go of whether or not this man had epilepsy. Mark is telling a story in which Jesus, the Son of God,

---

3. Ched Myers, *Binding the Strong Man: A Political Reading of Mark's Story of Jesus* (Maryknoll, NY: Orbis Books, 1988), 10.

brings the gospel of God into a space and time at odds with that gospel. Rome is at odds with God's agenda, at odds with God's son, and at odds with the promise of the reign of God on earth.

To be sure there were other gospels. The gospel of propaganda for the Roman Empire. The gospel of a king rising up, being installed as leader, as god. The propaganda of the *Pax Romana*. The gospel of Rome would have been a political document, declaring intention, declaring world view. And here Mark posits Jesus as the antithesis. His Gospel is for the poor, for the marginalized. This document—Mark's Gospel—is a gospel about God's economy, God's worldview. What is coming near can be seen and experienced in the person of Jesus. And the powers and principalities are set up and against what God is trying to do. The contest seen in the wilderness, the contest in this synagogue with the unclean spirits—this sets up the contest we will see on Palm Sunday. It's a contest that ends in death, or at least it seems to.

Jesus Messiah, the anointed one, is not the emperor. He is the bearer of God's vision for a healed and whole world. He brings news—good news—of liberation and freedom. He inaugurates a new world view. Mark's messiah brings glad tidings, yes, of a battle won, but not an earthly battle, a spiritual battle. It is a new beginning; this language takes us back to Genesis, and we sense that God is re-creating with peace—*shalom*—in mind. This good news is not eulogizing a Caesar; it is giving thanks in advance for God's salvation, for the ways God will make all things new in Jesus. That battle is on; lies versus truth; oppression versus liberation. Jesus takes his good news—God's good news—right into the center of religious life.

I think Ched Myers offers a convincing exegesis of one of Mark's basic themes, that from the start of his ministry Jesus demonstrated the coming of God's kingdom as the defeat and displacement of the power of Satan over the world. Jesus's first miracle is the expulsion of unclean spirits from a possessed man in the synagogue in Capernaum. Teaching a new teaching, not like the scribes, but as one with authority. Jesus is not blessing the status quo, but rather painting a picture of a preferred reality for God's people. He preaches in such a way that it challenges the people, basically panics the people.

And in his teaching, Jesus obviously has power over all evil spirits because he has defeated the Source of evil. Here is the man, filled with malevolent, unclean spirits. Hanging out in the synagogue. Recognizing Jesus, knowing where he comes from. Maybe playing the dozens a little bit with Jesus, a little verbal skirmish. Calls Jesus by name, trying to have a little power over him. Jesus demands he come out. This is a cosmic duel. Unclean Spirits versus Spirit of God. Reign of Rome versus Reign of God.

My question is, what kind of leaders were these with whom the unclean spirit felt comfortable kicking it? What kind of tepid, weak preaching was it that had the unclean spirit chilling and feeling just fine where he was. Some exegetes say the unclean spirit was speaking on behalf of the scribes when they said, "What have you to do with us?" Don't mess with us. Don't push buttons. Don't call foul. Don't hold us to the truth we say we believe. It's too much work to get well, make it whole, build a just community. Leave us alone!

Sometimes religious leaders don't like confrontation. That's foul, not OK, that's evil. We don't want to be judgmental. We want to build bridges. If we see something and say something, we'll make enemies. Our membership might drop. Our offering might go down. They won't like us, and we want to be liked. Plus there *are* good people on every side, right? Even in the face of crippling poverty, and violent xenophobia; even when they watch Confederate and Nazi flags waving during an insurrection; even when they see a man crushed to death by a police officer casually kneeling on his neck; even when children are snatched from their parents' arms and forced to live in sites of terror because they are trying to cross the border into safety—leaders are too timid, too often, to say, this is wrong. They proclaim a namby-pamby gospel. They say the word *love* and they mean something like weak tea. In the name of Jesus, in the name of God and God's Christ.

They hide behind their personal relationship with Jesus and don't believe it has any demand on their lives beyond personal piety. They hide in rituals and in prayer. They worship and fast in ways that bore God, displease God, because they do not liberate God's people. This is not new. These weak-tea-party people of faith are the kind who created the Klan, the kind who put their children on their shoulders while they watched lynchings for entertainment. No they're not, you say. You say those people were racists. I say every place on the spectrum in which lynching is on one end and silence is on the other—this is a place where God's gospel is not preached, not lived. Any space in which the poor are treated like they deserve their poverty, or in which climate science is denied, or in which anti-Black racism is fostered. Any place in which money is worshiped like a God—this is a space in which unclean spirits are comfortable. In the name of God.

On Insurrections and Revolutions

It probably sounds a little crazy to say that we are in a spiritual battle; it's perhaps not polite or politic to call out in the public square that we are in an ideological battle for the soul of America and for our souls. What we do instead is say we all worship the same God, which is to say we are not making any particular claims on God. On who God is, on what God wants, on what God requires from God's people. This abstract God is a screen on which we can make our projections, a concept that can be manipulated, created in our own image. This abstract God is not created out of nefarious intentions. This God comes to be in a society committed to tolerance and civility, on the one hand, coupled with universalist instincts born of an overwhelming awareness of the size and complexity and diversity of our world.

But the God to whom this text bears witness is jealous for us, claims us, wants to be known by us. Have you not known, have you not seen, have you not heard? The God who created you, who created the stars, who knows each star by name and can tell which one has burned out. The God who claims you, hears your cries, recognizes your voice, opens seas to free you, who liberates you. This God is speaking a word to you, a word that is old, a word that is new, a word that is timeless, that requires you to listen afresh, to open your ears and your heart to hear. This word is to be studied by you, reiterated by you, articulated by you, stewarded by you. It is precious, it is your privilege to have this word. It is given to you to make you holy because God is holy, to make you whole because

God desires your wholeness, to draw you to each other because God is the God of all the people and wants all of you redeemed, whole, living in peace.

This God wants to be in relationship with us, a personal relationship that has public implications. A personal relationship that leads to public acts of justice and peace. This has been God's desire, in the times of this old prophecy and in this new day, and in all the days in between. God claims us, claims all of us, not just the ones who claim God, and wants to be in relationship with us. Say there was a Christian pastor, maybe in the Dutch Reformed Church, maybe here in Manhattan. That pastor purchases people, makes property, chattel out of human beings who happen to be from Africa. That pastor is benevolent, almost kind to the people he owns. He doesn't brutalize them, he doesn't beat them, he allows them to join the church—encourages them to join the church—allows them to marry, to have children that they keep in the family, allows the children to be baptized. But the parents and the children remain the property of the Christian pastor. He has a personal relationship with God, he encourages the enslaved to have a personal relationship with God, to be comforted by that relationship, to be pious in that relationship, to stay in bondage, comforted by that relationship. The pastor, that master is having a relationship with some god, but not the God of liberation. That enslaved African has been evangelized into a relationship with some god, but not the God revealed in this text, not the God of this prophecy, not the God whom Jesus called Abba, Papa, Daddy.

To paraphrase Isaiah: Have you not known, have you not heard, have you not seen? The God of liberation, of justice, of mercy, of equity; the God of love, of fierce love, has given us a word to disrupt the false theologies, to defeat the demonic word of the god of greed, prejudice, and violence. This is the God *I'm* talkin'bout. A grown-up God demanding love. A demanding God requiring us to make some decisions, to declare ourselves, to denounce the weak gods and to tell them to get out! So we can get busy healing the world.

CONCLUSION

Is America Possible?

Miguel A. De La Torre

My former colleague Vincent Harding, scholar-activist and speechwriter for Martin Luther King Jr., would occasionally ask: "Is America possible?" In spite of the horrors he and his wife, Rachel Elizabeth, witnessed during their involvement in civil rights activism, he continued to believe and hope in the possibility of America, a nation where the aspiration of racial and economic justice could be achieved. Harding's question about the possibility of America continues to be relevant, especially today as the nation seems to be unraveling at the seams. At the start of 2021, after a presidentially inspired insurrection that led to a second impeachment, we continue to ask: Is America possible? As one side is fueled by verifiable facts and the other by alternative facts, Is America possible? Within a society that once argued over policy issues like tax cuts or immigration, now arguing over what is reality, Is America possible? How can America be possible when QAnon conspiracy theories thrive? Can two parallel universes occupy the same space? After a contentious seventy-eight-day transition period, how can one reconcile with an opposition that refuses to accept one's right to exist? Really. Honestly. Is America possible?

The nation may and probably will survive this moment in time. But is the hopeful dream that Harding believed in possible? True, there has always been division in modern American politics. But 2020 seemed and felt different. Before, in what now appears a simpler time, there were segments of the population who argued George W. Bush was not *their* president because of the Florida vote count in 2000, or that Barack Obama was not *their* president because he was Black. Even after revelations of foreign interference in 2016, most who saw the election as a travesty where the candidate who lost the popular vote nevertheless took the oath of office, still restricted themselves to simply declaring Trump as not being *their* president. But only the fringe elements of society would argue that 43, 44, or 45 was not *the* president. Yet with Biden, we saw this new phenomenon of repudiating the democratic process, egged-on not just by the fringe far right but also by the president whom he beat. Democracy is at risk when enough people are convinced that elections are fraudulent. Seventy-seven percent of those who voted for Trump, and 10 percent of those who didn't, marched to the constant drum beat of right-wing media outlets insisting the election was rigged, a claim made with no evidence whatsoever. Such delusions take a devastating toll. Lies have consequences, as witnessed by the storming of the Capitol on January 6. What can we expect when a sizable portion of the electorate rejects the democratic process, coupled with white militia (terrorist) groups calling for civil war and a president who instructs these hate groups (specifically the Proud Boys) during a national presidential debate to "stand back and stand by"? For the president of the United States to place hate groups on the ready is treacherous when we consider that, according to the FBI, hate crimes rose in 2020 to their highest level in more than a decade. The Southern Poverty Law Center tracked a 55 percent increase in the number of white nationalist groups between 2017 and 2019.[1] Have we entered a new way of being in which democracy is rejected, unless one wins?

Should anyone truly be surprised that Trump's legal offensive to overturn the electoral will of the people increasingly focused on disenfranchising the votes in the predominately Black cities? After all, one of the founding fathers of the modern conservative movement, the architect of the Heritage Foundation and the Moral Majority—Paul Weyrich—made it perfectly clear how the Religious Right can obtain and maintain political power. In a refresh-

---

1. Tim Arango, "Hate Crimes at Highest Since 2008, FBI Reports," *New York Times*, November 16, 2020.

ing moment of unadulterated honest candor during his address to the seminal Religious Right gathering in Dallas during the fall of 1980, he voiced his opposition to the democratic principle of one person, one vote. "I don't want everybody to vote," he told the audience; "As a matter of fact, our leverage in elections quite candidly goes up as the voting populace goes down."[2] The institutionalized voter suppression—voter purges, felony disenfranchisement, gerrymandering, and voter ID requirements—did not appear *ex nihilo*; it was and continues to be a strategy by which white supremacy is maintained. The only way white supremacy can remain in power is by short-circuiting democracy with apartheid legislation.

We really should not be surprised that the America in which we currently live had a president who clearly lost an election, stated the process was rigged, and sought to make his legal case by arguing that voter fraud was rampant among communities of color, specifically among African Americans. We win, according to the GOP playbook, as long as Black voters are not counted!

So, I must again repeat Dr. Harding's question: "Is America possible?"

In the end Trump lost, Biden was inaugurated, and so we may, with a sigh of relief, imagine that democracy was upheld, and all is well with the world. Or is it? Within two weeks of Biden's inauguration, Republicans in twenty-eight states proposed 106 bills to further suppress votes, specifically the votes of communities of color.[3]

Trump may indeed be gone, but like-minded political actors remain in all levels of society and government. The failure of America to repudiate the blatant racism of the Trump administration means Trumpism has laid the groundwork for a potential future in which a more sophisticated manifestation of white Christian nationalism will arise, better masking its xenophobia and its aversion for democratic principles. The Trump presidency's enduring legacy for the twenty-first century remains the normalization of an undemocratic morality rooted in racism.

---

2. Paul Weyrich, address at the Religious Right gathering, Dallas, Fall 1980: https://www.youtube.com/watch?v=8GBAsFwPglw.

3. "Republicans Want More Voter Suppression," *Washington Post*, February 3, 2021.

Trump's chaotic efforts to delegitimize the 2020 election in the eyes of his base seeded mistrust concerning the tradition of open and free elections. The spectacle played out between Election Day and the inauguration has created a metanarrative that will haunt future elections. Regardless of which party wins in future elections, neither side will fully trust the outcome. The destabilization of the fundamental means by which we carry out our democracy, coupled with a hyperpartisanship in which the opposing party is seen as the incarnation of evil, cannot end well if left to continuously fester. Can't we all just get along? My former colleague Vincent Harding would argue that even now, America is indeed possible. I, on the other hand, am not as hopeful.

We remain divided. Both sides of the political spectrum are furious. One side honestly believes the election was stolen, and in a way, it was. Racist voter suppression has legitimized and normalized electoral outcomes. The Voting Rights Act may have passed Congress over half a century ago, but the suppression of votes nullifying its intent went from overt means (asking prospective voters how many jelly beans are in a jar) to covert (demanding voter ID while closing facilities in communities of color at which to obtain the ID). The anger fueling the 2020 division went beyond which of the two old white men would get elected. The anger is that the racist voter suppression safeguards failed to work as they were supposed to—hence by definition the election was "stolen" from whites because democracy worked. And now, to the horror of many Trumpites, a Black woman is only a heartbeat away from the Oval Office.

So yes, an overwhelming voter turnout in communities of color in Detroit, Philadelphia, Green Bay, and Atlanta *stole* the election from those complicit with white supremacy because people voted. In white supremacists' minds, the only way to heal this division, to maintain the white America they envision, is to dismiss the votes of people of color, just as they did back when America was great! There can be unity for them when only legal votes—here legal is code word for white—are counted. So as votes from communities of color were being tallied in Philadelphia, and pointing toward a Democratic win, whites gathered at Philadelphia's convention center shouting "stop the count." Meanwhile, in Las Vegas, where it looked like the state might end up going for Trump (it didn't), a crowd of whites was shouting "count every vote."

Our disunity is not due to differences in political policies. The issues are no longer abortion, the Second Amendment, or trickle-down economics. Rather, only one issue exists: Fidelity to Trump and his unsubstantiated claim of a rigged election. Our division is fundamentally rooted in the white supremacist desire to erase, cancel, and dispossess marginalized groups. How can "united" states be possible when one side has no desire to unite with those whom they perceive at best as enemies, at worst, as satanic pedophiles?

The answer to "Is America possible?" cannot rest with those who have for centuries been repressed by white supremacy, but with those who have thus far politically benefited from the apartheid-based democracy. It is the abusers, the oppressors, the committed racists, the white supremacists who must first repent and then commit themselves through praxis to right the wrong in which they either participated or were simply complicit. America can never be possible when oppressors cloak themselves in victimhood, insisting on healing divisions as long as they can continue to benefit from the privileges associated with whiteness.

For America to be possible, the Republican Party must exorcise Trumpism. While many might prematurely cheer the demise of the Republican Party, I do not. Democracy works best when there exist several opposing political parties. I am no fan of one-party rule, not even if it's my party that is ruling. But an alienated nation cannot bind the tears that divide it as long as one party continues to weaponize racism to garner votes. When neo-Nazis and white supremacists become allies to one's political goals, maybe it's time to reconsider one's political positions. White nationalist Christianity's and the Republican Party's insistence on being the party for white supremacists (since Nixon's southern strategy) is not only suicidal for them, but for the nation.

As this manuscript goes to the publisher, we may ask whether we are now witnessing the last gasp of white supremacy or the resurgence of a new Jim and Jane Crow. Was the storming of the Capitol the last straw or the renaissance of an undemocratic movement in which the eventual white minority maintains political power? Trump is no longer needed. He was a useful tool to galvanize a white insurgence fighting against the emerging new America Harding believed was possible.

So—Is America possible? The flip side of this question is: What is the alternative? I choose to believe (belief is always a decision not something that can be proven) that America is possible in spite of white terrorism and centuries of oppression. But just because I am committed to reconciliation does not mean I am hopeful it will occur. Just because I believe America is possible does not mean I believe America will ever be able to live up to its rhetoric. The call for reconciliation, the praxis of applying balm to the wounds of division is not some religious attempt at being "holier than thou." Whether we are successful is not the question. In the final analysis, America may or may not be possible. But even if it is not possible, I will continue to struggle and strive for its possibility. What is important is that I live my life and act as if it is. The call to reconcile, to heal, to love is made because it is what shapes our very humanity and defines the faith we profess. Maybe the question is not if America is possible, but if *I believe* that America is possible. Hoping against all hope, regardless of whether or not it becomes a reality, I will choose to believe in the unbelievable.

Vincent Harding would often ask another question during times of seemingly irreconcilable divisions, such as during faculty meetings (where the battles are so fierce, because—as the saying goes—the stakes are so low). During difficult faculty meetings, when professors were figuratively at one another's throats, Harding would chime in, asking, "Colleagues, how can we turn this poison into medicine?" On Inauguration Day, Biden took the oath of office in a militarized zone. On the western front of the Capitol where he swore to "protect and defend the Constitution," a violent riot had occurred only two weeks earlier. Between the two events, Trump was impeached for a second time for his role in the January 6 riots. The damage caused over the four years of Trump contributed to a noxious environment. How then, choosing to believe in the different future Biden articulated in his inaugural address, do we turn this poison into medicine?

Contributors

Joshua S. Bartholomew is Assistant Professor of Ethics, Church, and Society at Saint Paul School of Theology. A former Postdoctoral Fellow at the Harvard T. H. Chan School of Public Health and Research Project Coordinator for the Institute for the Study of the Black Christian Experience, Bartholomew is the author of *Black Theology and the Black Panthers*. He is an Antiracism: Diversity, Equity, and Inclusion Interventionist, serves on the Applied Religious Studies committee at the American Academy of Religion, and is an Emerging Scholar in the Society of Christian Ethics. He was also a founding member of the Society of Race, Ethnicity, and Religion.

Simone Campbell, SSS, a member of the Sisters of Social Service, is a lawyer, lobbyist, and former executive director of NETWORK. She has led seven "Nuns on the Bus" tours to highlight social issues and the power of voting. Her most recent book is *Hunger for Hope: Contemplation, Community, and the Common Good*.

Aaron D. Conley teaches philosophy and religion at Regis University and is Adjunct Professor at Iliff School of Theology in the field of environmental ethics. His book, *We Are Who We Think We Were*, published in 2013 by Fortress Press, unpacks the symbiotic relationship between the fields of ethics and history by calling upon themes of liberation, womanism, and postmodern methods of deconstructing structural power dynamics.

Miguel A. De La Torre, an internationally recognized scholar, is Professor of Social Ethics and Latinx Studies at the Iliff School of

Theology in Denver. The American Academy of Religion bestowed on him the 2020 Excellence in Teaching Award and the 2021 Martin E. Marty Award for the Public Understanding of Religion. He has published forty-one books (six of which won national awards). A Fulbright scholar, he served as the 2012 President of the Society of Christian Ethics and was the co-founder/first executive director of the Society of Race, Ethnicity, and Religion. He also wrote the screenplay for the documentary *Trails of Hope and Terror* (https://www.trailsof hopeandterrorthemovie.com).

Miguel H. Díaz is the John Courtney Murray University Chair in Public Service at Loyola University Chicago. Dr. Díaz served as the ninth US Ambassador to the Holy See. He is co-editor of the new Orbis series Disruptive Cartographers. The series opened in 2021 with his volume titled *The Word Became Culture*. Díaz was recently awarded a grant by the Louisville Institute to work on a collaborative project that rethinks theology and pastoral practice from Queer and Catholic Voices of Color. He also contributes to writing a column for the *National Catholic Reporter* titled "Theology en la Plaza." As part of his ongoing commitment to advance human rights globally, he participates in a number of diplomatic initiatives in Washington, DC, including as a member of the Atlantic Council and the Ambassadors Circle at the National Democratic Institute (NDI).

Marvin M. Ellison, an ordained Presbyterian minister, is the Willard S. Bass Professor Emeritus of Christian Ethics at Bangor Theological Seminary. Founder of Maine's Religious Coalition Against Discrimination, he serves on the board of the Maine Coalition to End Domestic Violence and the Maine Action Fund for Planned Parenthood of Northern New England, where he has organized a volunteer chaplaincy service. Along with Tamara Torres McGovern, he co-hosts a community radio series called "Queer Spirit," ongoing conversations with LBGTQ leaders about the power of the sacred. He is the author of *Making Love Just* and co-editor with Kelly Brown Douglas of *Sexuality and the Sacred*.

John Fife co-founded in the 1980s the sanctuary movement to protect Central American refugees. He served as pastor of Southside

Presbyterian Church in Tucson for thirty-five years and as moderator of the Presbyterian Church (U.S.A.). In retirement, he is a founding volunteer with No More Deaths and Samaritans in the Sonoran Desert borderlands.

Juan M. Floyd-Thomas is Associate Professor of African American Religious History at Vanderbilt University Divinity School and the Graduate Department of Religion. He is author of *The Origins of Black Humanism* and *Liberating Black Church History* and co-author of *The Altars Where We Worship,* along with numerous other publications. Moreover, he is both a co-founder and an executive board member of the Black Religious Scholars Group (BRSG) and currently serves as the executive director of the Society of Race, Ethnicity, and Religion (SRER).

Stacey Floyd-Thomas is currently the E. Rhodes and Leona B. Carpenter Chair and Associate Professor of Ethics and Society at Vanderbilt University. She is a nationally recognized scholar and leading voice in Christian social ethics and womanist thought who provides leadership to several national and international organizations including Black Religious Scholars Group (BRSG), Society for the Study of Race, Ethnicity and Religion (SRER), and the American Academy of Religion (AAR). She has published eight books and numerous articles that focus on womanism, liberation theology and ethics, critical race theory, critical pedagogy, and postcolonial studies, including *Religion, Race and COVID-19: Confronting White Supremacy in the Pandemic.*

Elaine Nogueira-Godsey is Assistant Professor of Theology, Ecology and Race at the Methodist Theological School in Ohio. Her research focuses on the relationship between ecology, gender, race and religion, and in advancing decolonial methods of teaching. Her most recently published works are "Towards a Decological Praxis" and "Tangible Actions Toward Solidarity: An Ecofeminist Analysis of Women's Participation in Food Justice." Currently, she is working on a book entitled *The Ecofeminism of Ivone Gebara.* Dr. Nogueira-Godsey is co-chair of the AAR/SBL Women's

Caucus, treasurer of the International Society for the Study of Religion, Nature and Culture (ISSRNC), and an assistant editor for the *Journal for the Study of Religion, Nature and Culture* (JSRNC).

Trad Nogueira-Godsey is the Writing Instructor and member of the Adjunct Faculty at Methodist Theological School in Ohio. He holds a PhD in Religious Studies from the University of Cape Town and a Master of Theological Studies from Harvard Divinity School. His areas of focus are the sociology of religion, global Pentecostalism, and African Christianities.

David P. Gushee is Distinguished University Professor of Christian Ethics and Director of the Center for Theology and Public Life at Mercer University. He is the past president of both the American Academy of Religion and Society of Christian Ethics, signaling his role as one of the world's leading Christian scholars. He is (co)author and/or (co)editor of twenty-five books. His most recognized works include *Righteous Gentiles of the Holocaust*, *Kingdom Ethics*, *The Sacredness of Human Life*, and *Changing Our Mind*. His new book, *After Evangelicalism*, charts a theological and ethical course for postevangelical Christians. Professor Gushee also has published over 150 academic book chapters, journal articles, and reviews.

Amir Hussain is Chair and Professor of Theological Studies at Loyola Marymount University. He teaches courses on Islam and world religions. His specialty is the study of contemporary Muslim societies in North America. He is vice president of the American Academy of Religion, and a fellow of the Los Angeles Institute for the Humanities. His most recent book about Islam is *Muslims and the Making of America*. He is the author or editor of eight other books and over sixty scholarly book chapters or articles.

Jacqueline J. Lewis is a public theologian and the senior minister at the progressive, multicultural Middle Collegiate Church in Manhattan. Rev. Dr. Lewis is the first woman and the first Black person to serve as senior minister in the Collegiate Church of New

York, the oldest continuous Protestant church in North America, founded in 1628. A graduate of Princeton Seminary and Drew University, she is the creator of the MSNBC online show *Just Faith*, and the PBS show, *Chapter and Verse*, in which she led important conversations about culture and current events. She curates an annual national conference focused on activism and imagining a more perfect union, Revolutionary Love, and she is the co-producer of the annual star-studded *Juneteenth Now—Get Us Free* celebration. Rev. Dr. Lewis is the author of four books, including *Fierce Love*. She is a member of the Auburn Senior Fellowship, a group of influential faith leaders who are committed to advancing multifaith movements for justice.

Tat-siong Benny Liew is Class of 1956 Professor in New Testament Studies at the College of the Holy Cross. His publications include *Politics of Parousia; What Is Asian American Biblical Hermeneutics?; Postcolonial Interventions; They Were All Together in One Place?; Reading Ideologies; Psychoanalytical Mediations between Marxist and Postcolonial Readings of the Bible; Present and Future of Biblical Studies; Colonialism and the Bible;* and a *Semeia* volume on "The Bible in Asian America." Liew is also the series editor of T & T Clark's Study Guides to the New Testament, and currently chairs the Council of the Society of Biblical Literature.

Joerg Rieger is Distinguished Professor of Theology, Cal Turner Chancellor's Chair in Wesleyan Studies, and the Founding Director of the Wendland-Cook Program in Religion and Justice at Vanderbilt University. He is author and editor of twenty-four books, including *Jesus vs. Caesar* and *No Religion but Social Religion*. His works have been translated into eight languages.

Rubén Rosario Rodríguez is Professor of Systematic Theology in the Department of Theological Studies at Saint Louis University. His first book, *Racism and God-Talk,* won the 2011 Alpha Sigma Nu Book Award for Theology. His recent publications include *Christian Martyrdom and Political Violence, Dogmatics after Babel,* and the *T&T Clark Handbook of Political Theology.*

Contributors | 267

Joshua Shanes is Associate Professor of Jewish Studies and Director of the Arnold Center for Israel Studies at the College of Charleston. He has published widely on modern Jewish politics, culture, and religion in academic and popular outlets and is currently writing a history of Jewish Orthodoxy from its German origins to the twenty-first century.

Susan Brooks Thistlethwaite is Professor Emerita and President Emerita of Chicago Theological Seminary. An ordained minister of the United Church of Christ since 1974, she is the author or editor of thirteen academic books, including two different translations of the Bible. Recently, she has published three mystery fiction books and a fourth is in production. Thistlethwaite is also a well-known media commentator and has written numerous columns both for the *Washington Post* and the *Huffington Post* as well as the *Chicago Tribune*.

Tink Tinker, a citizen of the Osage Nation (wazhazhe), is Emeritus Professor of American Indian Studies at Iliff School of Theology. As an Indian academic, Tinker is committed to a scholarly endeavor that takes seriously both the liberation of Indian peoples from their historic oppression as colonized communities and the liberation of eurochristian americans, the historic colonizers and oppressors of Indian peoples, whose own history of violence has been largely suppressed. A scholar/activist, Tinker has worked closely with both Four Winds American Indian Council in Denver and the American Indian Movement of Colorado. He has written several books and dozens of chapters and journal articles.

Jim Wallis is a globally respected writer, teacher, preacher, and justice advocate who is also a *New York Times* bestselling author, widely recognized public theologian, renowned speaker, and regular international commentator on ethics and public life. He is the founder of Sojourners and is the author of twelve books, including *Christ in Crisis, American's Original Sin, God's Politics, The Great Awakening,* and *The Call to Conversion*. He served on

President Obama's White House Advisory Council on Faith-based and Neighborhood Partnerships and teaches faith and public life courses at Georgetown University's McCourt School of Public Policy, having previously taught this subject at Harvard.

April M. Woodson is currently a Postdoctoral Fellow in Theology at Saint Louis University in Missouri. Her research interests include postcolonial womanist theo-ethics; Black geographies; and African Americans and public policy. In 2015, she became an ordained Elder in a nondenominational Christian Church.

Aizaiah G. Yong is Assistant Professor of Practical Theology and Pastoral Care at Pacific School of Religion in Berkeley, California. His academic work is at the nexus where critical (mixed) race theory meets spirituality and pastoral care.

Amos Yong is Dean of the School of Mission and Theology and Professor of Theology and Mission at Fuller Theological Seminary in Pasadena, California. He has (co)authored or (co)edited almost sixty scholarly volumes.

Index

Abdul-Jabbar, Kareem, 171
Abdul-Rauf, Mahmoud, 171
abortion
    and Catholic single-issue voting, 201, 202
    and Covid-19 pandemic, 96
    and opposition to Affordable Care Act, 209
Abrams, Stacey
    fight for fair elections, 54, 55, 56
    and Georgia electoral victory, 18
    roots in Black church, 55, 56
Abumayyaleh, Mahmoud, 170, 173
Affordable Care Act, 203, 209
African Americans, Muslim, 170, 171, 172, 173
Alfred P. Murrah Federal Building, attack on, 171
Ali, Muhammad, 171
"All Faiths and None," 72
American anger, 65
"American" Christianity, 23, 24
American exceptionalism, 27, 193
American experiment, white racist ideology of, 27, 28
American Indians
    present colonialist situation, 191, 192
    view of Biden Administration, 184

Americanism, as civil religion, 176, 177
Angelou, Maya, 51
Angry Tias and Abuelas of the Rio Grande Valley, 211, 212
antidemocratic agenda of Trump movement, 63, 64
anti-immigrant nativism, 131
anti-sharia laws, 167
Arbery, Ahmaud, 146
Arctic National Wildlife Refuge, 190
Arendt, Hannah
    on thinking as world-building process, 83
    on trial of Adolf Eichmann, 82, 83
Asian Americans, scapegoating of, 130, 131, 138, 139, 144
Atwater, Lee, and white supremacism, 5, 6, 8, 15
Auburn Seminary, 72
authoritarian figures, and Cuban community, 124

Babbitt, Ashli, and QAnon conspiracy, 101
Baker, Ella, 50, 57
Bannon, Steve, 168
Baptist Joint Committee for Religious Liberty, 72, 73

Barber, Rev. Dr. William J., III, 176
  on American evangelicalism, 28, 29
  and religious values of nationalist religion, 180
Barr, Bill (US attorney general), and death penalty, 208
Bears Ears National Monument, 190
Bellah, Robert, on civil religion, 176, 177
Bensonhurst riots, 158
Bethune, Mary McLeod, 50
Biden, Joe
  inaugural address, 116
  and religious values of nationalist religion, 180
  role of Black women in election of, 58, 59, 59n23, 60, 105
  and 2020 presidential election, 58, 155
Biden administration
  call to reconcile with Trump supporters, 70, 71
  on environmental and systemic racism, 95, 96
  immigration policy, 241, 242
  policies on Land sacred to Native Peoples, 190
  policy on border wall, 246
  policy on mineral extraction, 190, 191
Big Lie, 115, 116, 207, 210, 257
birtherism, 88, 174
Black churches
  and Black Lives Matter movement, 150–52
  and LGBTQ people, 151
  and Martin Luther King Jr., 151
Black female freedom fighters, 50
Black Lives Matter movement, 50, 51, 106, 146, 153, 154, 157
  activism, during Trump administration, 147, 148, 153
  and Black churches, 150–53
  origins and mission, 146, 147
  and traditional civil rights movement, 151, 152
Black Muslims, in civil rights movement, 170, 171
Black women
  collective social and political action of, 48, 49, 57–60; in Georgia, 54, 55, 56
  work to save democracy, 57
Blacks
  and Democratic Party, 5
  disenfranchising of, 257, 258
Blue Lives Matter, and Black death, 49, 50
Boebert, Lauren, and QAnon, 25, 26
Bolton, John, 168
Bonhoeffer, Dietrich, and death of truth, 39
border wall, 246
Bottoms, Keisha Lance, 55, 56, 156
Bowman, Jamaal, 51n7
Brown, LaTosha, 56
Brown, Michael, 160
bubonic plague (black fever), and anti-Asian racism, 135, 136, 137, 139, 140, 142
Bush, Cori, 51n7, 160
Bush, George H. W., and white supremacism, 8
Bush, George W., Electoral College victory of, 21

capitalism
  and postmodern culture, 78, 79
  and racism, 140, 141
Carter, Jimmy
  election of, 20
  white evangelical opposition to, 21

Castro, Fidel, and Miami Cuban community, 126
Catholic bishops, support for Trump administration, 208
Catholic Church
  racial and ethnic division in, 195, 196
  religio-political polarization in, 200, 201
Catholics
  and abortion, 201, 202
  as multi-issue voters, 208, 209, 210
Catholicism in time of Trump, 207, 208
Chaney, James, murder of, 6
Chappelle, Dave, on election of Donald Trump, 166, 167
Chauvin, Officer Derek, 158
Chávez, Hugo, and Miami Cuban community, 126
child-separation policy, of Trump administration, 205, 211, 212, 239, 244
"China virus," 9, 130, 139
Chinatown, Honolulu, 135, 142
Chinatown, San Francisco, 132, 133, 134, 142
Chinese Exclusion Act (1882), 134, 137
Chisholm, Shirley, 50, 57, 59
cholera, and anti-Chinese racism, 132, 133
Christian Coalition, 21
Christian nationalism, 193, 194, 203, 205
Christian unity, and Paul's teaching on body of Christ, 197, 198, 199, 200
Christianity, white, and white supremacy, 63, 64
Christians Against Christian Nationalism, 72
church, as body of Christ, 198, 199
civil religion, 176, 177
climate change, 75, 87, 88
  human responsibility for, 79
  and industrialization, 78, 79
Clinton, Bill, impeachment of, 21
Clinton, Hillary, 47, 166
Coe, Doug, 4
Colbert, Stephen, and religious values of nationalist religion, 180
Collegiate Church of New York, 249
colonialism, and American Indian Peoples, 185, 186
The Color Purple (Alice Walker), 48
colorblindness, as excuse for aligning with dominant white culture, 219
Colvin, Claudette, 57
coming out, 73
Concerned Women for America, 21
Cone, James, on violence against Blacks, 49
Confederate statue removal, 31
Contagion (movie), and anti-Chinese racism, 138, 139, 140, 142
contagious diseases, and anti-Asian racism, 136, 137
Conway, Kellyanne, 33
Cooper, Amy, 100, 101
Cooper, Anna Julia, 50
Cooper, Christian, 101
coronavirus pandemic. *See* Covid-19 pandemic
corporations, preferential treatment in tax cuts, 229, 230
The Covenant, the Sword, and the Arm of the Lord, 171
covenant oaths, and truthfulness, 38
covenants, and covenant declarations, 37, 38

Covid-19 pandemic, 15
  disproportionate effects on communities of color, 87, 91, 92, 93, 96, 108, 111, 160
  and human racism, 96, 97
  influence on American life, 111
  Trump administration approach to, 206, 207
  and wealth inequality, 229
creating space, and redemptive healing, 224, 225
critical race theory, 108, 110
Cruz, Ted, 121
Cuban Adjustment Act (1966), 121, 121n8
Cubans
  as white people, 123, 124
  and white supremacy, 123, 124
Cubans and Americans, similarities, 127, 128
Cullors, Patrisse, and Black Lives Matter movement, 50, 51
Curtis, Charles, agenda for Indian people, 188

Dade County (Miami), Latinxs in, 119
Dakota Access Pipeline, 190
De La Torre, Miguel, on US Christianity, 29
defunding of police, 150
democracy, rejection of, 257
Democrats, view of Latinx community, 119, 120, 124, 125, 128, 129
dialogical offense, 162, 163, 164
Dignitatis Humanae (Vatican II, On Religious Freedom), 202
Dukakis, Michael, 8
Dutch Reformed Church, and slavery, 250

Ebenezer Baptist Church, 13, 156

Eichmann, Otto Adolf, 82, 83
election fraud, claims of, 86, 130, 207, 210, 257, 259, 260
enslavement, biblical justification for, 248
Environmental Protection Agency (EPA), defunding under Trump administration, 78
environmental racism, 87, 88, 91, 92
"Equally Sacred Scorecard," 209, 210
Erdoğan, Recep Tayyip, 168
Estevanico the Moor, 170
ethical humanism, 176
ethical thinking, in postmodern world, 82, 83, 84
ethics, global, 94, 95
ethics of truth, 36, 37
eurochristian colonialist religion, role in colonization and genocide of American Indians, 186, 187
evangelicals. *See* white evangelicals/ evangelicalism
"Exhortation on Holiness" (Pope Francis), 208, 209

Fair Fight, 54
faith, and American Indian Peoples, 185, 186, 187
faith-based organizations, and immigration, 241, 243
"Faithful Citizenship," disregard for pope's teaching in, 208
fake news, 75, 77, 115
false naming, 99
falsehood, systemic, and systemic wrongdoing, 42
Falwell, Jerry
  and the Moral Majority, 7, 21
  on natural disaster and social issues, 96
Family Research Council, 21

Fanon, Frantz, on colonization and revolt, 159, 163, 164
Ferguson (MO) riots, 160
Fifield, Rev. James W., opposition to New Deal, 3, 4
First Letter to the Corinthians (Paul), on divisions in Christian community, 197
Floyd, George, 111, 112, 146, 158, 164, 169, 170, 173, 205
Flynn, Lt. General Michael, anti-Muslim views of, 167, 168
fossil fuel extraction, and Biden administration, 189
Francis, Pope, address to US Congress, 207
Fratelli Tutti (Pope Francis), 201, 210, 212
freedom faith, 52, 57
French, David, on Trumpism, 114

Garner, Eric, 157, 158, 159, 164
Garza, Alicia, and Black Lives Matter movement, 50, 51
gay rights, rollback under Trump administration, 67, 68, 69, 70
genocide, and lying, 40, 41
Georgia Senate election (2021), 13–16, 156, 157, 161
Georgia's Sixth Congressional District, political history of, 14
geotrauma, 157, 160, 162, 163
Gilmore, Georgia, 57
globalist, as anti-Semitic slur, 15
God, in the abstract, 254
God of liberation, 255
Goetz, Bernard, 158
Goldwater, Barry, and southern strategy, 5
Gomez, Archbishop José Horatio, attack on President Biden, 208
Goodman, Andrew, murder of, 6

Gorka, Sebastian, 168
Gospel of Mark, opposition to empire, 250–54
gospel of prosperity, and unite-and-conquer strategy, 234, 235
Graham, Billy, opposition to progressive social programs, 4, 6
Grand Staircase-Escalante National Monument, 190
Green Belt Movement, 81
Green New Deal, 189
Greene, Marjorie Taylor, support for QAnon, 18, 19, 25
Gülen, Fethullah, 168

Haaland, Deb, 187, 188, 189, 192
Hamer, Fannie Lou, 50, 57
Handel, Karen, 14
Harding, Vincent, 256, 258, 259, 261
Harris, Kamala, role in 2020 presidential election, 58, 59, 105
hate crimes, 169
hate groups, and President Trump, 257
Havel, Václav, on truth and political malfeasance, 38
Hawkins, Yusef, 158
Heritage Foundation, 257
Hirsch, Rabbi Samson Raphael, 176
hopelessness, as a praxis, 162
Horton, William, 8
hyperindividualism, and Trump administration, 205, 206, 207

"I can't breathe," 157, 158, 160, 164
imago dei, 109, 113
immigrant deaths, and Prevention Through Deterrence strategy, 245, 246
immigrant workers, stolen wages of, 211
immigrants, Muslim, 172, 173

immigration, Cuban, 122, 123
immigration, US, 85, 86
   policy of Biden administration, 241, 242
   policy of Trump administration, 139, 239–41
Immigration Act (1965), 137
immigration reform, 242, 243
individualism, in pentecostal-charismatic communities, 221
information integrity, in Christian ethics, 44, 45
insurrection, at US Capitol, 24, 32, 33, 34, 45, 86, 113, 115, 130, 159, 160, 163, 166, 171, 177, 193, 194, 205, 210, 215, 216, 234, 257, 260
   as judgment on theological schools and seminaries, 217, 218
   white Christian complicity in, 2, 3
   white Christian nationalist support for, 32, 33, 34
   Republican support for, 9, 10
integral option for life, 201, 201n27, 202, 203
integrating life anew, and redemptive healing, 226
intersectionalism, 110
Islamophobia, and American racism, 93, 94
Israelism, 178

Jericho March, 33, 114
Jesus
   and conservative family values, 235
   as Messiah in Gospel of Mark, 252
Jewish community/Jews
   opposition to Trump, 175
   response to Muslim travel ban, 169
   See also Orthodox Jews

John Paul II, and Jesus as political figure, 251
Johnson, Lyndon, and 1964 Civil Rights Act, 63, 64
Jones, Doug, 56, 58
Jordan, Barbara, 50, 57
Justice for Immigrants (JFI) campaign, 208

Kaepernick, Colin, 143, 171
"Karen" meme, 98
"Karens," in white supremacist culture, 99, 100, 101
Kemp, Gov. Brian, 16, 17, 54
Kennedy, John F., 171
Keystone XL Pipeline, and Biden administration, 189
King, Dr. Martin Luther, Jr.
   on church's defense of status quo, 249
   critique of white Christianity, 28
   and Ebenezer Baptist Church, 13, 156
   opposed by Black churches, 151
Kingdom Ethics (Gushee and Stassen), 36
Ku Klux Klan, agenda, 244
"kung flu," 88, 130, 141

LaHaye, Beverly, and Concerned Women for America, 21
Land Back Movement, 185
language and meaning, 77
Latinxs, Cuban, 122, 123, 128, 129
   view of Democrats as socialist, 126
Latinxs, Cuban and non-Cuban, 128, 129
Latinxs, support for Donald Trump, 118, 119, 126
Law, Rights, and Religion Project (Columbia Law School), 72

legal votes, as white votes, 259
leprosy, and anti-Chinese racism, 134, 135
Lewis, Rep. John, 13, 14
LGBTQ justice advocacy, 73
LGBTQ persons, and Trump's politics of restoration, 67, 68, 69, 70
liberation theology, 99, 100
    approach to right-wing white women, 100, 101, 103, 104, 105, 106, 107
lies, and confusion, 42
Line 3, 190
Loeffler, Sen. Kelly, 13, 14, 15, 16, 18, 56
lost cause, 10

"Make America Great Again"
    as assault on racial diversity, 194
    for white people, 26, 47
Malcolm X, 170, 171
Manahatta, purchase of, 250
Manifest Destiny, 27
mask wearing, and Trump administration, 206
Massingale, Fr. Bryan, on whiteness of US Catholicism, 29, 30
McBath, Lucy, 14
militarism, of Trump administration, 143, 145
military, and contagious diseases, 141, 142
military operations, against US citizens, 143
militias, and law enforcement, 171
Miller, Stephen, 168
    and immigration policy, 239
Milošević, Slobodan, lying of, 41, 42
misogynoir, 48
Monae, Janelle, 55

"The Monkey's Paw" (W. W. Jacobs), 1, 2
Moore, Beth, on Trumpism, 114
Moore, Roy, 56
Moral Majority, opposition to progressive social programs, 7
Murray, Pauli, 50
Muslim community
    and Black Lives Matter movement, 170, 173
    and Trump administration, 167, 168

Nation of Islam, 170
National Association of Manufacturers (NAM), 3, 11
National Defense Authorization Act, 142
National Quarantine Act (1878), 140
nationalism, 177
    in pentecostal-charismatic communities, 221
nationalist religion, liberal, 177, 180
natural law, in Catholic thought, 196n9
neocolonialism, and institutionalized racism, 159
neoliberalism, elements of, 140, 141
NETWORK, Lobby for Catholic Social Justice, 204, 209–11
Never Trumpers, and the choice of truth, 40
New Deal, 236
    white Christian opposition to, 3, 4
New Labor, 211
New Underground Railroad, 240
Nixon, Richard, and white Christian nationalism, 5, 6, 7
noncooperation, 106
nones, vote for Democratic candidates, 64

nostalgia voters, 67
Nunes, Devin, and Presidential Medal of Freedom, 165, 166
Nuns on the Bus tour, 211

Obama, Barack
   and birtherism, 88
   immigration policy, 120, 240
   and postracial society, 147
   and vote of Black women, 58
Obama, Michelle, 58
Ocasio-Cortez, Alexandria, 51n7
Olympic Project for Human Rights, 171
Omar, Ilhan, 51n7
Orthodox Jewish institutions, and insurrection at US Capitol, 180
Orthodox Jews/Judaism
   attraction to American fascism, 181
   ethno-nationalism of, 177, 178, 182, 183
   political views, 177, 178
   support for Trump, 175, 181
   value system, 175, 176, 179
Orwell, George, and death of truth, 39
Ossoff, Jon, election to Senate from Georgia, 13, 14, 15, 16, 56

Palestinians, ethno-nationalist prejudice against, 179, 183
pan-Hispanicness, 128
Pantaleo, Officer Daniel, 157, 158, 159
Paris Climate Agreement, 78
Parks, Rosa, 57
Paul (Saint), and divisions in Christian community, 197
Pence, Mike, 59, 168
pentecostal movement, anti–medical-establishment strain in, 216

Perdue, David, 14, 15, 16, 18, 56
Perez, Tom, on Black women as backbone of Democratic Party, 57
Pew, J. Howard, support for capitalist ideology, 4
"Pizzagate," 30
police reform, 148, 150
political neutrality, 182
politics of encounter, 210
politics of inclusion, 212
pollution inequity, 92, 93
Pompeo, Mike, 168
Poor People's Campaign, 72
poor, as victims of climate change, 80
postmodernism
   and consumption, 78, 79, 84
   and truth, 76–79
presidential oaths, as covenant oath, 38
Pressley, Ayanna, 51n7
Prevention Through Deterrence strategy, 245, 246
"prophecies," about Donald Trump, 216, 217
prophecy, in pentecostal-charismatic communities, 220
prosecutorial discretion, under Obama administration, 240, 241
Proud Boys, 3, 124, 257
public lying, systemic, 37
purple, symbolism of, 47, 48, 49, 59, 60
"Purple Rain" (Prince), 47
purple rain, symbolism of, 49–51

QAnon, 18, 19, 113
   and pedophilia, 101, 102
   political theology of, 26–31
   relation to "Pizzagate," 30
queer social ethic, 73

racialization, through theological formation, 218, 219
racism
  and American Indians, 187
  as America's original sin, 108, 109, 117
  anti-Asian, 131, 132
  in Christian churches, 116, 117
  and the environmental crisis, 93, 94
  as human invention, 93, 94, 95
  as religious issue, 111–17
  systemic, 91
  and Trump administration, 205
Raffensperger, Brad, 16, 17
Reagan, Ronald
  and American exceptionalism, 27
  and Moral Majority, 7
  and states' rights, 6, 7
  and white supremacism, 5, 6
reconciliation, 70, 71, 73, 111, 112
  and truth, 113, 116, 117
redemptive healing
  in pentecostal-charismatic communities, 222
  spirituality of, 222–27
Reed, Ralph, and Christian Coalition, 21
religion
  and political impact of Black women, 58
  and unite-and-conquer strategy, 234, 235, 236
religious leaders, and confrontation, 253
Religious Right, 5, 7, 8, 112
  and Georgia politics, 15, 16
  and liberal nationalist religion, 180
  on natural disaster and social issues, 96
  and political power, 257, 258
  and Republican Party, 21, 22
  and spiritual warfare against Democrats, 71
  and unite and conquer strategies, 235
  as white Christian nationalist party, 22
repentance and redemption, in evangelical and pentecostal-charismatic communities, 218–22
Republican Party/Republicans
  as party of Trump, 16
  and QAnon, 18, 19
  support for Capitol insurrection, 99
  and tax cuts, 228
  and Trumpism, 260
  view of Latinx community, 120, 121, 124
  and white evangelicals, 19, 20, 21
  as white man's party, 11
  as White Power party, 64
resource colonialism, 190, 191
Robertson, Pat, and Christian Coalition, 21
Robinson, Amelia Boynton, 57
Roe v. Wade, 145, 202, 209, 210
Romney, Mitt, and the choice of truth, 40
Roosevelt, Franklin D., and New Deal, 3, 4
Rubio, Marco, 121

sanctuary
  for immigrant families, 239, 240
  religious tradition of, 240
sanctuary cities, 241
Saro-Wiwa, Ken, opposition to Shell Oil Company, 80, 81
Schwerner, Michael, murder of, 6
self-care culture, 225

self-interest, and taxes, 230, 231, 232
sensitive locations, and Obama administration immigration policy, 240, 241
September 11 (2001) terrorist attack, and American Muslims, 173
Sessions, Jeff
 and child-separation policy, 239
 and US immigration policy under Trump, 35
setting intention, and redemptive healing, 224
severe acute respiratory syndrome (SARS), and anti-Asian racism, 137, 138
Shell Oil Company, and climate crisis in Niger Delta, 80, 81
Silent Majority, and election of Trump, 34
Slave Bible, 248, 249
slave rebellion, Turner's, 163
slavery, in New Amsterdam, 249, 250
slaves, Muslim, 170, 172
slow violence, 79, 80, 81, 82, 89
small narratives (*petit l'écrit*), 76, 77, 78, 83, 84
smallpox, and anti-Chinese racism, 133, 134
socialism, and Miami Cuban community, 125, 126, 127
Sojourner Truth, 50, 57, 163
Solzhenitsyn, Alexander, and death of truth, 39
Southern Baptist Convention
 dismissal of critical race theory, 108, 109, 110
 support for whiteness, 110, 111
southern strategy, 5, 7, 15
spectacular racism, 88–91; of Donald Trump, 88, 89, 90
Spiritual Mobilization, 4
the Squad, 51, 51n7

St. John's Episcopal Church, removal of protesters from, 205
Stassen, Glen, on information integrity in Christian ethics, 44, 45
states' rights, 6, 7
Stop AAPI Hate website, 131
story telling, 76
submerged consciousness, of Cuban immigrants, 123
syphilis, and anti-Chinese racism, 134, 135, 142, 143

Tarrio, Enrique (Proud Boys), 124
tax cuts
 economic logic of, 228–30
 financial impact on low income earners, 229
 political logic of, 230, 231
 religious logic of, 229, 230, 231, 232
Tax Cuts and Jobs Act (2017), 206, 228, 229, 236
tax policies, and common good, 236
Taylor, Breonna, 146, 160, 205
Tea Party, and taxation, 231
theological education, response to January 6 insurrection, 217
thinking, as world-building process, 83
Thornwell, James Henley, defense of slavery, 249
Tlaib, Rashida, 51n7
Tometi, Opal, and Black Lives Matter movement, 50, 51
toxic masculinity, in Cuban community, 123, 124
trachoma, and anti-Asian racism, 136
trauma, 155, 160
 intergenerational trauma, 161
 neocolonial trauma, 161, 162

postcolonial trauma theory, 159
and Senate election in Georgia, 155, 156, 157
See also geotrauma
travel bans, Muslim, 168, 169, 205
resistance to, 239
triumphalism, in pentecostal-charismatic communities, 220
Trump, Donald J.
and anti-Chinese/anti-Asian immigration, 139
assault on truth, 36–46, 113
attempt to overturn 2020 election, 16, 17, 18
as autocrat, 68
Catholic (white) support for, 31, 195
hostility to Muslim community, 167, 168. *See also* travel bans, Muslim
as liar and father of lies, 43, 44, 46
racism of, 87
and restoration of white America, 66
scapegoating of Asian Americans, 130, 132, 144
on the Unite the Right rally, 32, 163
as "wartime" president, 141, 143
white evangelical support for, 9, 11, 22, 23, 24, 31, 32, 33, 43, 44, 67, 95, 112, 114, 156, 215, 244
and white nationalism, 9, 113, 116
and white supremacy, 147
Trump administration
agenda, 145
anti-immigrant policy, 239, 240, 241
and Covid-19 pandemic, 148
and Cuban political structure, 127
and racism, 258

Trumpism/Trump movement
antigay stance, 67, 68, 69, 70
as autocratic movement, 61, 62, 63
white Christian nationalist agenda, 63
truth
assault on, under Donald Trump, 36–46, 113
and freedom, in New Testament, 113, 115
and postmodernism, 76–79
in post-Trump era, 75, 76
Tubman, Harriet, 50, 57
Turner, Nat, 163

unclean spirits, 252, 253
unite-and-conquer strategy, and tax policy, 232, 233, 234
Unite the Right rally (Charlottesville, VA), 31, 32, 89, 163
United States, as Christian nation, 26, 27
untruth, as legitimate, 77

Vereide, Abraham, 4
victim mentality, in conservative movement, 101, 102
Volf, Miroslav
on truth of power and power of truth, 39, 40
on tyranny and manipulation of truth, 39
Vote Common Good, 102, 103
voter fraud, and 2020 election, 16, 17, 18, 45
voter suppression, 54, 257, 258, 259
Voting Rights Act, 259

waiting for insight, and redemptive healing, 225, 226

Warnock, Rev. Dr. Raphael
 election to Senate from Georgia, 13, 14, 15, 16, 56, 156
 and religious values of nationalist religion, 180
Waters, Maxine
 divine calling of, 53, 54
 investigation into Trump administration, 52, 53, 54, 59
Wehner, Peter, on personality of Donald Trump, 62
welfare queen, 10
Wells, Ida B., 50, 57
Weyrich, Paul, and the Moral Majority, 7, 257, 258
white Christianity/Christians
 complicity in insurrection at US Capitol, 2, 3
 privileged status of, under Trump, 66, 67
 vote for Republican candidates, 64
white conservative Catholics, as responsible for social divisions, 194, 195
white evangelicals/evangelicalism
 agenda, 111
 hypocrisy of, following 2016 presidential election, 23
 reasons for support of Donald Trump, 215
 support for claims of election fraud, 216
 support for Donald Trump, 9, 11, 22–24, 31–33, 43, 44, 67, 95, 112, 114, 156, 215, 244
 support for Republican candidates, 102
 theology of, 177, 178
 as values voters, 21
 and white Christian nationalism, 244

white men, cultural displacement of, 64, 65, 66
white nationalists, support for Trump, 257
white normativity, lessening of, 10
white supremacists/supremacy, 5–12, 108, 109
 and American Indians, 187
 as the "Bigger Lie," 115, 116
 heteropatriarchal, 104, 105, 106
 incapacity to enter into dialogue with others, 71, 72
 support for Donald Trump, 113, 114
 and Trump administration, 205
 unite-and-conquer strategy, 232, 233, 234
 and voter suppression, 258
white women, support for Republican candidates, 103
Wiesel, Elie, and death of truth, 39
Williams, Nikema, 56
Winfrey, Oprah, 58
Winthrop, John, and America as the City on a Hill, 27
women
 right-wing, characteristics, 99, 100, 101
 in white heteropatriarchal culture, 103
 See also Black women; year of the Black woman
Wuthnow, Robert, on American civil religions, 177, 180

year of the Black woman, 49, 57, 58, 59, 60

Zionism/anti-Zionism, 178, 179, 183